I'D
MISS THE
BOAT

Memoir of A Vietnam Hoa Refugee

Lea Tran

ISBN 978-1-939237-74-3

Published by Suncoast Digital Press, Inc.
Sarasota, Florida, U.S.A.

Cover graphics design contributor: Bill Gorgensen

Editorial contributors, Tim Rauk and Emily Liu

Dedication

This memoir is dedicated to the five most important men in my life:

My father, Tai Ong

My husband, Duc Tran

My son, Alexander Tran

My brothers, Viet Ong and Nam Ong

Dad and Me,
Vietnam

Dad finally got to see the
Liberty Bell

Contents

Preface

"There is no greater agony than bearing an untold story inside you."
— Maya Angelou, *I Know Why the Caged Bird Sings*

There is a misconception that once refugees settle in a new country, problems are solved, but this is false. Where one problem is solved, new ones emerge. It is in the new found silence that the trauma begins to unfold.

From others' points of view, I appear to be moving through life like a duck gliding across a pond, not a feather out of place, only a calm demeanor. From the exterior, I am living the American dream of a successful immigrant. Beneath the surface, though, the duck paddles frantically, and I live the life of an inferior, disconnected, and terrified woman. My lifetime of scars and unhealed wounds remain concealed.

After years of contemplation, I knew this memoir needed to be written. The story wanted to be told and would not be quieted. It is necessary not only for me to honor my parents' sacrifices and my dad's legacy, but also to help my siblings and other refugees heal their invisible wounds.

This is the story of an adolescent girl who grew up in an unstable society and in a family filled with obligations and responsibilities. She was determined to break the generational curse of poverty and familial expectations. This is how I learned to live my own life, the story of the pain that made me, and how I found my identity when I was living a life between worlds.

I learned that fitting into the American mainstream does not guarantee emotional happiness unless I deal with my past, make peace with my identity, and accept who I really am in a multicultural world. We were Hoa, of Chinese descent, born in Vietnam, with no strong roots in either culture and now we are Chinese-American. We were refugees, moving from a country that was never truly ours to a new one that we struggled to adapt to. I also bear the burden of being from the limbo generation, i.e., those immigrants who came to resettle in their early to mid-teen years, too old to be innocent of their past, yet too young to be sufficiently equipped to carve out a new future.

History repeats itself, but I determined that inherited trauma stops with me. It can stop with you. It can stop with anyone willing to look deeper into their roots and understand how their upbringings have shaped them today, and decide for themselves whether they like who they've become because of it, or in spite of it. The inherited expectations and trauma that one generation passes on to the next is something that can be examined, and changed. It is unraveling the resentment I didn't know I held, learning to forgive, and learning to appreciate after many years of pain. The strength of the human spirit cannot be measured, underestimated, or even understood, yet it is a powerful source of inspiration.

I have always been grateful to have the opportunity to experience the freedom and abundance my parents worked so hard to provide. I am humbled to say that this story is a small representation of how adversity can inspire opportunities in life. It is a privilege to share with you my influential teachers, generous families, and moments of profound inspiration; my intention is for you to find strength and inspiration from my story.

No matter how difficult your challenges or how dire your situation seems, you have the power to navigate your own way through. You can build your own boat so you never have to miss one. Thanks to my dad, I did not miss mine!

Lea Tran

Disclaimer: This memoir is totally based on my own recollections, conversations with my parents, siblings, and additional research on the internet. There are mostly real names with few fictitious names used throughout the story.

1

Our Hoa Family Background

The Most Powerful Person in My Universe—Dad

The first thing one noticed about my dad was his teeth. Dad had a beautiful set of pearly white teeth. When he smiled or laughed, his white teeth would bring a kind of radiance to his face. Unfortunately, that laughter was reserved mostly for friends and acquaintances, and only sparingly for his family.

My father, Ong Tai, was born on March 14, 1936, in Guangdong, China. When he was three years old, his parents migrated from China to Vietnam, along with his older brother, Ong, Dac Dinh (9), sister Lan (6), and younger brother, Dac Hoa (1). After moving to Vietnam, Grandma and Grandpa Ong later added two more daughters to the family.

When Dad was ten, his father was accidentally shot by a French guard while carrying a bike to a merchant boat on the dock. Grandpa Ong was a boat merchant who traveled often. The guard mistook the bike for a gun and shot him. Since it was an Indochinese life taken in a foreign land, there was no recourse for the family. In Vietnam, there was no system of justice available for refugees and immigrants who didn't speak the language. So, there was no punishment for the killing. No compensation for the family. The only thing Grandma Ong received was an apology from the guard. "Sorry for the mistake."

Grandmother Ong was left as a young 38-year-old widow with six children to care for, ranging in age from a newborn to 16 years of age. [Grandpa Ong also left behind a Vietnamese mistress who had two young children with him (we called her *Ba noi,* which means grandma in Vietnamese). Dad also accepted and took care of his stepmother in his adult life.]

In order to help the family, the 16-year-old son went to work as a coolie, and the 13-year-old daughter as a maid. Although my father was only in the third grade, he felt obligated to quit school and join his older siblings in the working world in order to help provide for the family and his three younger siblings. At ten years old, he sought out a wealthy distant relative and became his personal lackey. He did everything, from running errands to shining shoes and helping in the kitchen.

As a young boy, my dad had already developed a strong work ethic. His boss admired him for it, and often awarded him with candy money. Even at a young age, my dad would rarely spend money on himself, and instead saved his tips and candy money for his family. He saved so much that when he brought it home for his mom, she didn't believe that he earned it. She accused him of stealing it from his boss and whipped him for it. It was only after she had dragged him to her second cousin that she found out that he had indeed saved every cent from the extra allowances. He became the one his mom relied on most.

After some time, his wealthy boss passed away, and my dad struggled with odd jobs until he saved enough to start a company that dyed fabrics. It was called "Song Nghia" (Double Righteousness). He built the company with his friend, and a seasoned accountant who had previously been the personal assistant for his old boss. Dad oversaw the procuring and delivery of thousands of meters of fabric to the manufacturer, an external hustling position, while his partners took care of the internal finance and operations. Dad was only 18 when he became a partner in this company. They put in an incredible amount of hard work and the company prospered. Dad was doing well.

Because Dad was unable to go to school beyond the third grade, education was a huge priority for him. He didn't want his younger siblings to be called a "blind ox" like he was (disparaging term for an uneducated person) and he worked hard to pay for their tuition. When Dad was 23, his mom died suddenly at the young age of 51. He promised his mom that he would care for his younger siblings for as long as he lived. His older siblings had married and moved away, but his three younger siblings continued to live with him. Dad took on the parental role and the responsibilities of caring for his younger brother and sisters. His younger sister, 18-year-old Auntie Diep (whom I called *Yeeco*, which means second aunt), got a job working in a factory weaving fabrics. Auntie Keean (*Soico*, which means little aunt), on the other hand, was 15 and refused to go to high school. She had contracted polio in her early childhood, and it had left her disabled and unmotivated to continue with her education. His younger brother, Dac Hoa (*Soijek* means little uncle) had the highest education in the family at sixth grade, had gotten married, and he and his wife lived with Dad and his sisters.

Dad at Song Nghia

No Higher Calling—Mom

My mom, Phung Trinh, is the youngest daughter of four children. She was born in the summer of 1940 in the Go Quao District, Kien Giang Province, at the tip of South Vietnam. Her parents had migrated there in the 1930s from China, where her father (my Grandpa) had been an accomplished accountant, and where her oldest brother Thach Sanh ("Jade Born") was born.

The family story is that once in Vietnam, Grandpa Trinh preferred chasing women to chasing numbers on the abacus. At one point, Grandma Trinh was even tempted to find a second wife for her husband, hoping to keep him from flirting with everyone in town. Even so, he and Grandma had three more children: another son, Thien Sanh (meaning "Heaven Born"), a daughter, Tu Nhien ("Natural"), and finally, my mom, who was nicknamed Tu Do ("Freedom"). Ironically, Mom was anything but free.

Up until third grade, she was forced to wear boy's clothing, apparently because it was more convenient for her parents. Kids would tease her about her appearance, and neither the boys nor the girls wanted to sit next to her. She hated school because of this, and it wasn't until her mom let her grow her hair out and wear the girl's uniform that she started making friends.

Not long after my mom was born, Grandpa contracted polio. The disease left him disabled, and Grandma Trinh became the breadwinner of the family. She was the load-bearing wall that supported the family in many ways. As a businesswoman, Grandma Trinh was crafty and reputable. Well-liked and fair in her dealings, she treated her customers with integrity, and modesty. Through her knack for trade and her determination, Grandma was able to make connections to import fine goods that no one else in her area had for sale. And *everyone* had something for sale.

Though no economic trend felt stable, Grandma managed to keep the family going, always having several ventures aloft at the same time. She had a business trading fabric for rice from farmers, and then selling the rice to people in the city. She also had a storefront at home in her open living room that was organized and well-stocked with imported perfumes and silks.

At that time in Vietnam, there was little distinction between a store and a residence. Rather than having separate commercial and residential districts, families turned part of their houses into a place for trade. Many times, the shop area far exceeded the family's living space. Having a family business was how people got by, and part of the social structure. People left their front doors wide-open for others to stop in and make purchases. Any area of the house which faced the street was usually turned into space for trading. While some were quite humble, such as a small front-porch table spread with fruits and vegetables, others were more intricate with shelves and counters.

One of the more elaborate as well as riskier ways Grandma Trinh made money was by organizing a community-based rotating savings and credit scheme called "Choi Hui." This is a complex money-lending system where participants are able to borrow money from the other members of the group. Even before the communist times, very few people used or trusted the banks with their money, and as a result, this kind of financial trading system was popular. As the organizer, Grandma was in charge of recruiting and vetting all participating members. She would only invite people from the community that she trusted.

Every month, all the participants would bring the equivalent of $100, which would be put into "the pot." Each person would then bid the amount they were willing to pay in order to be the first to get the pot. Their bid essentially represented the amount of interest the bidder would be willing to pay to get the money immediately. If the highest bid was $10, then all the other participants would give that person $90; so the high bidder would get $90 from each participant (for example, $900 if there are 10 other participants) that they could then use immediately. In this example, the lenders each got $10 as their fee. The next month, every person again brings $100, and again the highest bid gets the money, minus the size of their bid. This time however, the "dead member" who received the first "pot" the month before, is obligated to pay $100 and cannot bid again. This continues until everyone has received "the pot." The size of the bids tended to go down each month as fewer people were able to bid on that month's pot. This continued every month until the last member would get paid $100 by the other members.

Grandma Trinh was also responsible for collecting all the money and awarding the pot to the highest bidder. In return, she would receive $100 each month for being the host. Sometimes, Grandma would be hosting several groups a month and she would have her children (and later, her grandchildren/my cousins) collect debts from the "dead" members. Since they already had their money, they were less likely to show up to the monthly meeting. When the debtors refused to pay, or worse, ran off, Grandma was responsible for covering all debts because she was the organizer. It was certainly a risky game. Even though Grandma only invited her trusted circle of friends and acquaintances, when money was involved, trustworthiness was not always predictable.

When the business was brisk, Grandma Trinh hired a nanny to take care of Mom. When the business went bankrupt, Mom was sent to live with a distant relative for a while. No matter how the business was doing, Grandma rarely had time for her children, so they had to learn to take care of themselves. As the youngest in the family, my mom often felt forgotten and unimportant.

With her oldest brother having been sent to China for unclear reasons, and her older brother being in the service, Mom spent most of her time at home with her older sister, Nhien, who liked to boss her around. From working and helping her mom with their business endeavors, she developed survival skills that would help her in difficult times. But she never had the luxury of developing long-term goals for her life, or an identity outside of her family. She resented the fact that she never had a childhood picture, and swore that her children would have plenty.

While business was soaring high like a kite in the wind, all of that changed one night when a group of men broke into Grandma's shop. They grabbed and blind-folded Grandma and stole all the imported goods: silk fabrics from France, perfumes, and jewelry. They threatened to shoot Grandma Trinh in the head if anyone screamed. They kidnapped Mom's older brother, but released him the next day. Mom was ten years old and hid, shaking, under the table. All she could see was the notorious rubber sandals that were worn by the Viet Cong, the guerilla force that supported the northern communist party.

After this devastating incident, Grandma Trinh decided it wasn't safe to stay there any longer. They packed up and moved from one small town to the next, as they would also have to do when future businesses failed. From Bac Lieu to Rach Gia, then to Go Quao…life was hard. The family became so poor that Mom only had two sets of clothes: the one she was wearing, and one hanging on the clothesline. There were times Grandma had to split a hard-boiled egg with her entire family. Many of their meals were simply rice and salt—and sometimes, there wasn't even any rice.

When recounting her early memories with her family, my mom has told me, "Ba chim, bay noi, muoi tam cai linh dinh," meaning, "Three sunk, seven float, and there are 18 drifters." This is an idiom which means that there is so much uncertainty that no one can predict the circumstances of their destiny.

When my mom reached fifth grade, Grandpa told her, "Girls only need to know how to read and write. You don't need any further education." Without any say in the decision, Mom was taken out of school. In order to help the household, she set up a stand and sold fruit to passing pedestrians. As she began to grow, so did her responsibilities and obligations to the family. Mom was expected to cook, clean, and help her parents make money by doing any number of odd jobs.

Because Grandma was so busy with her business ventures, Mom also became a full-time caregiver for her disabled father. To keep himself entertained, Grandpa collected all sorts of exotic animals, which he kept in cages. There was a monkey, a snake, goats, rabbits, and even birds. At twelve years of age, Mom not only had to take care of her father, but all of the animals, as well. As an adult, she never wanted to have another pet again.

With all her obligations, Mom did not have time for hobbies. In fact, she has not shared with me anything about her childhood that doesn't sound grim. For example, Grandpa Trinh was very demanding and hot-tempered. When he was upset, his children had to line up and each take the beating. No one dared to run away even though they knew he couldn't chase after them.

When Mom was about fifteen, one of Grandma's most lucrative ways of making money was trading with the ethnic minority in the rural areas. Mom would paddle upstream for hours in a canoe, helping her mom bring dry goods to the Cambodians in the small villages along the Mekong River. Even though neither Mom nor Grandma knew how to swim, twice a week, they would brave the river to bring fabrics, medicines, and women's accessories to trade for rice, which was used as currency at that time.

On their return, the canoe was often so heavy with rice, they were afraid it would capsize. Mom said the gunnel of the canoe was only a few inches above the waterline. Even though it was scary, Mom had to set aside her fears to help keep her family afloat. She had no choice but to do it.

Drowning was not the only imminent risk along their trade route. Every so often, there would be bombs dropping from the sky and exploding along the riverbanks. Whenever they heard an airplane flying overhead, they would quickly paddle to the bank. They would hide their canoe in the bushes until the sound faded to a safe distance, or after the thunderous roar of exploding bombs had stopped. The planes and the bombs were the U.S. military and French forces, attempting to halt the supply channels to communist North Vietnam.

As early as 1947, President Harry Truman stated that the U.S. policy was to assist any country whose stability was threatened by communism. American military support continued for many years. I shudder to think how harrowing these upriver trips were for my grandmother and mother.

In Vietnam, multiple generations often live in the same house. Mom recalls that when she was growing up, the average household had five or six children. Uncle Thien Sanh was forced to get married early, and his family moved in with my grandparents. By age seventeen, Mom already had four nephews to take care of, living in the same household. In addition to her caretaking duties, she was confined to her home working as a tailor. She was rarely able to leave the house, except when she had sewing lessons or had to run errands for Grandma. She has often said that her sewing machine was her best friend, since she spent so much time with it. She envied her friends for being able to live the normal teenage life that she could not. Sometimes, she would lie and say that the sewing machine was broken and that she needed to sew at her friend's house. That was the only way she could go out.

Mom never had a carefree moment to enjoy her childhood. She didn't know what dreams or goals might be possible for her life because nobody ever asked her what she wanted to be when she grew up. She was molded and taught to take orders from her parents, siblings, and then her husband. She was never taught that she could take responsibility for her own life, instead believing that she must rely on others to make decisions for her. She lived in fear of what other people thought, and craved the attention that she was denied as a child.

As our mom and Dad's wife, she often used self-pitying and guilt to get what she wanted. Duty and obligation were all that she knew, and when she raised us, she expected us to fulfill our traditional role of filial piety.

"Trauma not transformed is trauma transferred." – Ashley Judd

Young Phung Trinh

Grandparents Trinh

A Love Story? Or Just a Story…

Three years after Grandma Ong had died, Dad was on his routine trip to work from Xom Cui to Lo Xieu. His route brought him through a neighborhood where the doors of the houses were left wide open to let the air circulate. As he passed a bend in the street fifteen minutes from work, he often spotted a young girl sitting by the front door of her house at her sewing machine. He definitely noticed her. She was petite with a cute little face and short hair. Sometimes she would be out for a walk, and other times she would be sitting outside the house talking with her friends. He was intrigued but didn't think much of it.

One day, his business partner's father-in-law, Mr. Lam, was telling him about his distant cousin who had recently moved into the city. He showed Dad a picture of his niece, and Dad instantly recognized her as the girl he had seen on his way to work each day.

"I know that girl," my dad said.

Mr. Lam looked at him, confused. "How could you know her? They've only just moved here from Go Quao."

Looking more closely at the picture, my dad was even more convinced that this girl in the photo was the same one he had seen coming to work.

"No, I've definitely seen her before. I pass her on the way to work every day. I know where she lives."

Mr. Lam didn't believe it. "If you can prove that you know where she lives, I'll introduce you to her, and arrange a date."

"Deal."

Dad wrote down her address. It was correct, and Mr. Lam made good on his promise. A week later he arranged for my dad to be introduced to her family. "This young man is an honest, diligent and kind person and would make an excellent son-in-law," Mr. Lam told his cousin (my grandma). "You don't want to miss out on meeting him."

Dad and his friends

*Young Dad,
fashionable as always,
posed with hands on hips*

A Cup of Tea

The reason my grandparents and Mom fled from Go Quao and moved to the city so quickly was because Mom had blossomed into quite the beauty and had caught the eye of the governor of Go Quao. At the same time, the Viet Cong were trying to recruit Grandma to have Mom spy on the governor by dating him. Grandma knew how dangerous it would be for Mom to get involved on either side of the political rope, so they did not even bother to pack. They took the next bus to the city without leaving a trail. They stayed with one of Grandpa's cousins in District 11, outside of Saigon.

"Can I take a walk with Sieu Hue tonight after dinner?" Mom asked Grandma.

"No. We have visitors coming over tonight. You need to stay home to serve tea. Uncle Lam is bringing a guest and I want you to be on your best behavior," Grandma Trinh warned my mom.

Even though she had made plans to meet a friend in the park that afternoon, she obediently canceled her plans. She felt uneasy, sensing this was more than just a casual cup of tea. Mom was nervous, but she knew her place, and agreed to serve. She was told nothing about this being a potential marriage meeting, but her instincts were correct, and this became the first time she would meet her future husband.

A Marriage Arranged—Filial Piety Obligation

Mom's first impression of Dad was that he wasn't her type. She recalls that he was loud, shorter than she preferred, and a bit chubby. He seemed like a stereotypical Chinese man and although he had a bright smile and seemed attentive, she wasn't really interested. On the other hand, her mom found him to be a respectable, charming young man. He seemed very grounded and practical and she instantly liked him.

Mom's intuition (that this was more than a casual cup of tea) turned out to be right. After he left, Mom was told that the young man's name was Eng Tsai (translated in Vietnamese, Ong Tai) and that he was interested in courting her. Grandma told Mom that she and Grandpa had talked it over and they decided that it was best that Mom settled down soon before the Viet Cong found them. Mom did not have any say in the matter. Dad seemed like a good man, had a great reference from Mr. Lam, and they had agreed to accept Dad's marriage proposal.

In the Chinese tradition, no reputable girl could go out with a man unless she had some form of security, like an engagement. So, an engagement plan was made. The next time they met after their initial introduction was to buy the engagement ring. It was only after they were officially engaged that they were allowed to go out alone together. The first time Dad took Mom out on a date was to the jeweler to custom make the gold engagement rings. His name was engraved on her ring and her name on his ring.

Because Mom had only learned to sew basic styles of men and women's clothing, Dad enrolled Mom in a well-known design school so she could learn to draft and sew modern dresses and up-to-date fashionable outfits. Twice a week, he would come over to drive his future bride to sewing lessons. He would arrive in the evening at 6:00 p.m. and bring her back home when the class ended at 8:00 p.m. During these trips, she made sure to keep her purse firmly between them on the motorcycle rides. Occasionally, Dad took her out to get dessert, but made sure they were back home before 9:00. Grandpa Trinh was very strict about the curfew. He would sit by the clock to make sure that his daughter got home exactly by nine, and not a minute later.

Even though their time together was brief, Mom was getting to know Dad little by little. She could see that he had a quick temper. If someone cut in front of them in traffic, Dad fully expressed his anger, and it scared her. He was kind and protective and, while she believed he cared for her, he did not show affection or the softer side of being a gentleman. Dad had grown up as a hustler, living a rough life on the streets. I am not sure why Mom was expecting a soft and gentle person. Many times, I urged Mom to share some good things about Dad during their dating period, but the stories she told me were not good memories. Mom did not want to marry him and just could not find him attractive.

Mom begged Grandma to cancel the engagement. He was chubby, and she did not like chubby men. He had a temper; she didn't know how to control his anger. But most importantly, nobody asked her if she wanted to marry him! They were engaged before she could protest. In that day and age, the women did not have a choice.

"Daughter, it is not easy to find the perfect man; some soft-spoken handsome prince with a fit body. Tai is a family man. He will take good care of you and treat our family well. He will be good for you, and good for our family," Grandma explained. "He has ambition and a kind heart. He may not be well-educated, but he has a sound, logical mind. Mr. Lam admired him for his resiliency, drive and integrity. You can't go wrong with such a grounded person. There might be little flaws in his personality, but that could change when he has children. Love will come once you marry him."

It wasn't hard for Mom's parents to accept the marriage proposal. Mr. Lam assured them that Dad would be a great son-in-law and provide well for their family. Dad was happy to have found a beautiful, skillful, hard-working wife. She was talented, frugal, and obedient, and he needed someone to help manage his siblings and to raise a family with him. She was the perfect candidate.

In many Eastern cultures, we are taught to sacrifice for our families. I have witnessed the obligation to put our families before ourselves become a source of resentment in my family and in others. Decisions are made to benefit the family more than yourself.

Both Mom and Dad had been trained to set aside their individual lives and take care of the needs of their families. Mom helped Grandma Trinh run her business. Dad was taking care of his younger siblings. Now he needed someone to help him manage the household so he could start a family of his own. He was working all day, and his younger brother's wife didn't know how to cook or do much around the house. Dad knew that having the right wife would make life work better for his household.

This was not a marriage resulting from romance, love, or even deep affection. This was a marriage of obligation. A filial piety duty Mom had for her parents and a duty Dad had for his siblings.

"I have two younger sisters. You have to love and take care of my sisters," Dad told her.

"I have my parents. You have to take care of my parents," Mom replied.

So, the contract was made.

Mom and Dad were engaged in April and the wedding was six months later, in October of 1961. Tai Ong was 25 and Phung Trinh was 21 when they married, and Mom moved into Dad's household. Mom inherited two younger sisters and a married younger brother and his wife who were soon expecting their first baby.

For the most part, everyone got along fine. Mom set to work making it her home, her priority being to thoroughly clean the house. Mom was (and still is) a clean freak. Dirtiness bothers her a lot. She scrubbed the black soot from all the pots and pans, organized the kitchen, and cleaned the entire home. While Dad continued to work hard throughout the week, Mom cooked and managed the family. "I was used to taking care of my parents. The only difference now was that I would be taking care of strangers." It used to bother me when Mom said those phrases casually to me when I was young.

Tai Ong

Phung Trinh

A game they played at the wedding

A Successful Business

Because Dad had become a boss so young, he was quite well off by the time he met my mom. Dad's fabric dyeing company, Song Nghia, was flourishing. Business was good and Dad was very generous in financially supporting Grandma Trinh. He gave Mom a weekly allowance and let her make whatever decisions she needed to take care of the family. On the weekends, Dad would bring Mom and his sisters to visit her parents. Some weekends, they would all go out to the movies. Other times, it would just be Mom and him.

Despite not having a choice in the engagement, marriage was liberating for Mom. Being married meant she didn't have to work as hard to support her parents or take care of her father's zoo anymore. (Her nephews took on that role, after she left.) Even with cooking and cleaning for her new household, she had more free time than she had ever had before. But of course, there were also new expectations. Before she was married, her parents didn't talk about children. Now, the pressure was on.

A side note: Mom told me that years later, she found out from Grandma that Dad had been previously engaged to another woman, but he canceled the wedding because the woman was not honest with him. I have also heard from my aunt that Dad was in love with a very pretty girl who was just as determined and stubborn as he was. They were engaged for a little while, but the relationship fell apart because both were so headstrong. This girl backed out of the relationship and left a large wound in my dad's heart until the day he died. Mom said she found a picture of this girl in Dad's wallet which he had kept for years. He was too proud to tell that girl about his love for her and was too proud to try to work out their differences. He would rather love in the shadow of pain than say he was sorry and try to reconcile. He found solace in working and building his business, Song Nghia.

I can't help but wonder if Mom was a rebound relationship for Dad a way to fulfill the obligation imposed on him as a man by the community. Mom was a country girl, pretty, frugal, obedient, skillful, able to manage his household and give him a family of his own. Was getting married back then just another task a man was expected to fulfill? Finding a marriage partner was not the same as finding love or a soulmate. I've heard it can happen, but I wonder how many marriages in that era grew into a love-based relationship.

One of the most important moral tenets of Chinese philosophy is something called "filial piety," a strong loyalty and deference to one's parents and one's ancestors. My mother and father's marriage was based completely on filial piety. Mom only married Dad because her mother begged her to do it for the sake of saving her family. It saddens me that I am the product of my dad's pride and my mom's obligation and not the result of a love they felt for each other.

It was heartbreaking to hear Mom tell me that she hated my father and saw him as a chubby guy with an ill temper. I've tried to make sense out of why she would tell me those things. Maybe she's afraid her children will not embrace their filial piety responsibilities towards her, making sacrifices for her as she did for her parents. It seemed as if the seeds of expectations were being sown in me.

But, in my opinion, the result of Mom and Dad's union was indeed a victory for us, whether they realized it or were able to acknowledge it. They raised five caring, kind and good children. They gave my siblings and me the chance to work diligently to break this cycle of pain that was passed down from their previous generations, and we have.

2

A Growing Family

Here I Am

In 1962, my mom became pregnant. Soijek's wife was also pregnant, and gave birth to their first baby in the spring. They moved out that summer, because there was no way that house could hold their baby girl and another incoming baby.

Everyone knew my dad wanted a son. In Chinese tradition, a son is worth more than a daughter. If you have a son, someday, you will gain a daughter through marriage. If you have a daughter, you will lose her to marriage. That's why it was so important to Mom that Dad would help take care of her parents, since both Mom's brother and sister were unable to help. And that is why it was so important to Dad that they have a son.

In October of 1962, I was born as Eng, Li Cheng (translated in Vietnamese as Ong, Le Thanh. The correct way to say a name in Asian culture is last name first, then middle name followed by first name. Usually middle name and first name are called out together). Mom tells me that she had craved the smell of gasoline while pregnant with me, and that she sniffed the fumes every chance she got. She had no idea how toxic this was, or how it could affect her health or mine. Ten days past my due date, mom was growing increasingly irritated. I'm fortunate that I was not born in the toilet since Mom insisted that she needed to have a bowel movement before heading to the hospital. She had no idea she was fully dilated. There were a couple of close calls for an inexperienced mother.

"A girl?" Mom told me that Dad had said this loudly in the waiting room. "What a disappointment!"

Nevertheless, one look at me and his heart melted.

Even though I was a girl, my dad loved me just the same. I was the first born and only baby in a house with four adults, so I was adored and well-protected. Perhaps too well protected!

The first few years of my life were a learning experience for both Mom and Dad. Like most babies, I kept them up a lot for the first four months, crying all night and sleeping all day. I had a bad case of colic and assorted health problems, such as coughing and repeated ear infections. I often wonder if it had anything to do with Mom's habit of sniffing gasoline. I wasn't the easiest baby to tend to, that was for sure.

Mom has told me many times about how I almost grew up without a father. After a big fight with Dad when I was just an infant, Mom was tempted to run away with me to Ha Tien, a small island in South Vietnam where she had a friend. Luckily, Yeeco, Dad's second youngest sister, hid me, so Mom missed her opportunity to escape. Mom admitted that, subconsciously, she wouldn't have allowed herself to run away and raise a fatherless child. By telling me repeatedly, she had made me feel guilty, like I was the obstacle preventing her from living a free life, from ever being happy.

Like millions of Asian women, Mom was now on a journey of settling and accepting a life of obligation to her parents, her husband, and now to me, her child! Countless previous generations had accepted the same life of obligations. Mom expected me to follow in her footsteps, to serve our family as she had served her own.

After year two and three, pressure was mounting for my mom to have another child. She was under a lot of stress and didn't get pregnant until three years after I was born. During that time, Mom took me back to visit her parents almost every weekend. When I was three, the children in Xom Cui were playing a lot of card games and I was learning fast. Mom raised concerns with Dad about the influence of the neighborhood and Dad agreed that they should move closer to my grandparents. And so, our family, along with my two aunts, moved out from our house in Xom Cui that Dad had inherited from Grandma Ong, to District 11 near Dinh Minh Phung.

After living for so many years in the somewhat neglected house he had inherited, Dad was eager to make a home that was his own. He bought the house right across from Grandma Trinh and had it demolished. He then worked with an architect to design a new, three-story house with room for his future (larger) family. The house's first floor had a very high ceiling, with a large loft, and on top of that was another story with a flat roofed patio for plants, and a big storage room.

Living close to my grandparents was one of my favorite childhood memories. Their house was full of fun and joy. I loved the fact that I could just cross the street to be spoiled by my grandparents and play with my cousins. Grandma Trinh was the only person who could cool down my dad's hot temperament. I greatly admired and respected her. Her calming aura always made me feel safe. She loved my dad like her own flesh. In turn, my dad gave her respect and care as if she were his own mother. Dad admired Grandma's wisdom, and learned through her life experiences. She was not only his mother-in-law, but also became his life and business consultant. Having Grandma nearby, I felt confident that she could mitigate the tense situations between Mom and Dad. She was the referee, the umpire who Dad complained to when he was mad at Mom. Dad respected that Grandma never took sides or covered for her daughter.

It was around the time we were moving into the new house that Mom found out she was pregnant again. She was happy about the move as it meant she would be closer to her mother and wouldn't have to take a taxi to visit on the weekends anymore. She was also happy that her kids wouldn't grow up in a neighborhood where kids were becoming gamblers. We were able to move into the house just in time for my mom to deliver her second baby in December of 1966.

To my dad's dismay, this baby was also a girl. They named her Eng Li Kheng or, translated in Vietnamese, Ong, Le Khanh. With two daughters in a row, dad was worried that mom was unable to produce a male heir for him. He suggested adopting a son, but mom shut him down, and urged him to be patient. "Unless there comes a day when I can no longer bear children, adoption is not an option," she told him.

Mom and me in the old house in Xom Cui

Yeeco and me

Me and Dad's Vespa at the old house

I finally got some hair at 3

Mom, Grandma, Khanh and me

Khanh, Grandma and me

Khanh and me

Khanh and Mom

Me, Mom and Khanh   *Khanh and me*   *Soico and Khanh*

My Schooling Begins

In Vietnam, Chinese communities were intra-ethnic, and spoke many different dialects. In Chinese school, Mandarin was taught as the national language. Every kid would learn it, even if they didn't speak it at home.

At our house, we spoke Teochew. When I was finally old enough to start kindergarten, I spent the first two years at Hue Quoui, which was heavily populated with Cantonese-speaking people. I couldn't understand what anyone was saying. Fortunately for me, Soico understood Cantonese and volunteered to come to school with me and translate.

For the first two years of my education, Soico came with me to school every day. The bus picked us up at our house, and during the school day, Soico would stay outside the school under a tree where she could see me, and I could see her. She was about 18 years old and did not want to continue her high school education. Dad would readily pay for her tuition and whatever else she needed, but she didn't want that. And since she didn't have another job, she happily took on the role of being my personal bodyguard.

I was terrified to go to school without her. She was my protector, and my voice. When a kid stole my pencil, instead of speaking up, I went to my aunt and she intervened. She explained to the teacher what had happened, and even though I knew the name of the kid who stole my pencil, I let her do all my talking. She fought my battles, big or small. During recess, instead of playing with the other kids, I stuck to her like super glue. When she wasn't around, I felt separation anxiety. She was

21

my safety net, and I didn't want to let go. She wielded an enormous amount of power over me, and for those two years, I would do anything she asked. All she had to do was say, "If you don't obey, I won't go to school with you."

At home, I was super happy to be the big sister of Khanh. I had my own real baby doll to play with. She was like an angel. Very compliant, and no colic. She was the perfect baby who brought joy to everyone. Not too long after, Mom found out she was pregnant again. Grandma and Mom were praying hard for God to give her a son. If it were another daughter, Dad was going full force to adopt a male baby.

In the chaotic month of February 1968, Mom's prayers were answered. My brother Eng Toc Oui was born. (This is his Chinese name and what everyone in the family and Chinese community would call him. My brother's Vietnamese "official" name is Ong, Doc Viet).

It was around this time that the Tet (meaning "new year" in Vietnamese) Offensive was taking place. This was a series of coordinated attacks by the Viet Cong (communist-supporting allies) in Southern Vietnam and it was very close to where we lived. The reach was far, and no area seemed to be safe.

In fact, attacks were carried out in more than 100 cities and outposts across South Vietnam, including Hue and Saigon, and the U.S. Embassy was invaded. The Vietnam War had been happening on the periphery of our childhood, but this event hit close to home. These surprise attacks took place during the Lunar New Year, leaving people in panic and confusion. Firecrackers were always part of the celebration, but this year, you couldn't tell if the sound was from firecrackers or gunshots. This resulted in fear, dread and disorder whenever people heard a loud sound.

Even with my vague memory of being five-and-half years old, I still remember how terrifying it was to hear the gunshots so close to our streets. At some point, it became too dangerous to stay at our house, and my parents took all their children and my cousins from Mom's side to stay with my dad's youngest brother. Soijek by that time also had three children of his own and they were all in a similar age range as our family. Soijek lived with his wife's family, so there were a lot of extended aunts and uncles who played with us. Their home was in a safer part of the city, I was told. While the adults were busy making sure we were safe, we were busy having fun in the new house, hiding under the furniture and playing in our carefree way.

I cannot imagine now how the adults managed to keep life as normal as possible while on such an edge of high anxiety. If it hadn't been for Yeeco's quick reaction, we would have all been traumatized children. News came to Soijek that Mom had been hit by a bullet while chatting with a neighbor outside our house. The bullet pierced through Mom's upper arm. If it had been a few inches higher, it would have struck her neck. My brave aunt held Mom's arm and squeezed out the bullet before taking Mom to the hospital.

I remember the thick white gauze wrapped around her arm when she hugged me and my infant brother. It took her months to recover. I can't imagine how terrible my life would be if that bullet had claimed my mom's life. The Tet Offensive really shook up our family. We were so thankful when the situation calmed down.

A Resentful Life of Obligation

1969 was a big year for our family. Dad's company was doing well, and Mom was pregnant with her fourth child. During the summer, my three-year-old sister Khanh became very sick with a high fever. She was diagnosed with meningitis, and within a week, it claimed her life. It was a shock to us all, and the deep sadness followed my family for months.

In the fall, I started first grade at a different school. It was a smaller private Chinese school that was a bit closer to home but I can't remember the name of it. What I do remember is that my aunt was no longer able to come to school with me which meant I had to learn to make friends and speak up for myself. What I mostly remember about this school is that I was very lonely. Everything else was a blur.

Sometime in November, Grandpa Trinh also passed away. It was the second death within a year that brought more grief to our family. But it also lifted a big burden for my grandmother who had been taking care of him and faithfully serving him their entire marriage.

I was devastated to lose the only grandfather I ever had. My memory of Grandpa was totally beautiful. To me, he was a gentle old man with a white beard who had all kinds of candies around his chaise lounge and always indulged me with anything I wanted. (When he moved to the city, he had to get rid of his animals, so he replaced his zoo with many jars of yummy candies). Grandpa never raised his voice to me. He was always pleasant to me but not to my other cousins who lived with him. I always felt that I was his favorite.

The deep sadness of these family losses was lifted a month later when (in December of 1969) Mom gave birth to her third daughter, Eng Kui Hun, or in Vietnamese, Ong, Que Phan. The baby looked exactly like my deceased sister Khanh, and Mom believed Phan was her reincarnation. With Viet and Phan only 21 months apart, Mom was super busy. Both of my aunts (Yeeco and Soico) were now married and had moved out of the house, so the only adults left were Mom, Dad and the maid.

It was quite common in Vietnamese cities for people to have maids. They were generally women from poor, rural areas who had come to the city seeking employment. We had about half a dozen different maids ranging in age from late teens to over 50 in the first decade of my life. Labor was cheap and they rotated in and out through the years that I grew up in Vietnam before the communists took over. Their jobs were a range of domestic tasks: cleaning the house, mopping the floors, shopping for and cooking fresh food from the market daily, hand-washing and line drying the laundry, dropping-off and picking-up Dad's dry cleaning, and any other tasks. The domestic help gave Mom and Grandma a little space. In fact, they partnered to start a small business selling soda pop.

Dad was still getting paychecks from Song Nghia but, because of the draft for the military, Dad spent his time hiding at his brother's house to avoid being drafted. He was not the only one. Some of his cousins also hid in our attic for the same reason. It was common for people to go into hiding during their military draft age. Luckily for us, Dad continued to be paid because he was the partner, co-owner, and co-creator of the fabric dyeing company.

I was seven at the time and old enough to help around the house. My job was to play with my younger siblings and keep them safe, obeying those who were older, including the maids. I started to learn to speak Vietnamese so I could communicate with the maids. Since Mom was often busy, I became a second mom to my young siblings. It was a role I've taken seriously since.

The best place to raise a mentally healthy, confident child is in a peaceful family. We did not enjoy that luxury. Like thousands of other families living in an oppressive culture, everything was fear-based; fear of what society, family, friends, and neighbors were thinking of us; fear of our parent's authority; fear of punishment; fear of expressing our thoughts; fear of being visible and fear of speaking our voice. I saw many examples of how my parents' lived in those fears. Fear of being laughed at by relatives or neighbors, fear of being judged by friends and fear of letting others know they were unhappy.

Dad would come home from his hide-out a few times a week to see us and to check on the family. He hated the thought that Mom had to take care of business and, therefore, could not spend much time with her children. Mom sometimes sought attention in a negative way, infusing Dad's insecurities and jealousy of her associations with other men in the business. Arguing and fighting became all too common, with accusations flying, met with passive aggression.

I remember vividly one incident when I was about seven. Choked up with fear, I ran to Grandma's house to plead with her to come over and stop Dad from hitting Mom. She rushed into our loft bedroom and yanked Dad away from Mom. She scolded him for not being able to control his hot temper.

"Whatever you think she did wrong, you can reprimand her without raising your hand. But if you are so mad, you can hit me instead!" Grandma said.

Dad stormed out of the house to cool down. Grandma started to lecture Mom about something and then left. I stayed in the loft with Mom, holding her and hugging her and crying with her. I felt so powerless. There was nothing else I could do. Mom lay in bed, soaking her pillow with tears. Suddenly she stood up and locked the door. She pointed to a bottle of sleeping pills on the nightstand and looked at me crying.

"You have to take care of your little brother and sister. I am going to take these pills and die. I don't want to be here with your father anymore!"

"Mom, what are you talking about? Please don't take the pills, please, please, Mom! Don't leave us!" I pleaded through my tears.

"Let me die, let me die!" She cried as my little body rushed to stop Mom from taking the pills. I grabbed the bottle and put it in my pocket to hide the pills from Mom.

This was all too common a scene—me kneeling beside Mom, crying with her, and handing her the tissues to wipe her tears. These scenes played over and over, first in the incidents and then in my head as I grew up. As an adult, whenever I see a bottle of pills on the end of a table, I go back to being that powerless, fearful, seven-year-old girl, trying to protect her mother. I know Mom was desperate but it was wrong and it was unfair to impose those fears on her little daughter.

Even after all these years, there are still times I hear Mom's wailing and crying in bed after a physical assault from Dad. I cried with her in secret. I vowed I would never ever marry any man who laid a hand on me.

This was the beginning of many episodes where I witnessed Mom's sarcasm and antagonistic behaviors while Dad could not control his temper with her. It was simply a series of misunderstandings or the result of their stubbornness that instilled the predicament. Whatever the reason was for these fights, as an adult I suppose they would have found a way to work it out if they knew how much pain they had caused us. But both sides were full of pride, no one would admit their fault, and no one was willing to apologize for what they did wrong.

I learned to cope by simply obeying and doing everything without question. Eager to please, I made sure my siblings were in a safe place, and then I would try to become invisible and hide when the situation was tense. The bickering became more frequent, and each time it happened, the knot in my stomach grew a little bigger.

I was sure Mom wanted to end her unhappy life with the husband she did not love. I am grateful for her decision to live, even if it was only out of obligation: obligation to us, her children. I believe my mom has selective memory to block out all the pains in her life. The saddest thing I recognize about my mom is that she lives resenting the past and wishing for the future but never seems to be content with the present. Either with herself, with Dad, with us or with anyone she loves.

A Complicated Man

Despite all this, my father was a man who took extraordinary care of his family's necessities and material needs. His family was always his priority over himself. Dad did not smoke, drink, or indulge himself in any unnecessary luxury, except a few dollars of lottery tickets each week.

Even then he would buy the lottery tickets from the street orphan vendors to help support them. While always frugal and modest when spending for himself, he was consistently generous to Mom and to us. The moment he married my mom, he took care of her parents as if they were his own. Dad adored his mother-in-law as a knowledgeable, confident woman with good rational thinking, more so than his wife.

I believe that, deep-down, Dad was a loving family man. I valued this quality so much that I later married a man with this same commitment to family as priority. However, I also think that the traumas of my dad's early life made him insecure with a need to control and protect the people he loved. Coupling with his temperament, it was a recipe for disaster.

When Dad was in a good mood, he was the man of reason. When his temper flared up, all bets were off. My mom always seemed to know how to push the wrong button to defy him, adding fuel to the fire that caused every argument to end in turbulence. Mom liked to give contradictory statements which drove my dad crazy. As the screaming and yelling escalated, the ultimate outlet for the anger was physical assault. These episodes sometimes repeated themselves several times a month. I sat on the sidelines, helplessly feeding the ulcer in my stomach, agonizing over things I could not control. And it got worse as the years went by.

Dad governed his family in an old-school, traditional, authoritarian style. Fear was a major motivating and disciplinary vehicle. He expected Mom and us to follow orders like little soldiers. Dad had high expectations of me and my brother, his eldest daughter and son.

He was so protective of his children that we were not allowed to sleep over at Grandma's house even though it was only across the street. Dad's original plan was to buy the lot adjacent to her house to build our house, so we would not have the danger of crossing the street. Somehow that plan did not happen, and they bought the lot across the street instead. Dad's fears were proved to be valid after my sister Phan experienced a terrible accident. Phan was crossing the street to go to Grandma's house when she was hit by a motorcycle and dragged for quite a long distance before the motorcycle stopped. It was my Dad's worst fears being realized. She had many stitches and bruises, but after a slow recovery, thank God, she fully recovered. But someone sure got in trouble for not watching Phan. (I can't remember if it was me or Mom—probably both.)

Dad was always afraid that something bad would happen to us when he was not right there to protect us. His fear of losing his loved ones was enormous, probably because he lost his parents at a very young age. I can only speculate as I try to understand who my father was.

I grew up thinking that, being Asian, it is normal to not express physical affection or emotional love to one another. I did not realize how starved I was of warm affection, approval and praise of my father. Dad believed that praise was only appropriate for children under the age of ten, and that when you get older, praise will make you conceited, less humble, and arrogant. Dad believed that if he did not reprimand you for the job you did, that should be satisfaction enough. And most of the time, he felt it was his duty to offer some sort of criticism. His greatest strength was also his biggest flaw, and I want to believe this is more of a cultural trait than an individual characteristic.

Our family and Dad's Vietnamese stepmother in Dalat

Chinese Buddhist Temple School

After second grade, I changed schools yet again. For the next two years, I attended Len Quang Chi, another private school that was held in a Chinese Buddhist Temple. This school was chosen mostly out of convenience because it was close to our home. I hated having to start over yet again but was glad to not be alone this time. My older cousin, Thang Hoa, would be going to school with me. Thang Hoa was like an older brother to me. He was the third son of my mom's brother and lived across the street with my grandmother.

I became Thang Hoa's shadow for two years at this new school. The thing I remember most about this temple school was that every time there was a heavy rain, the classroom would be immersed in several inches of water. More than once we had to sit on top of the tables to finish the class. Other times, the flooding was so bad we were dismissed early from class. Flooding was not unusual during the rainy season in Vietnam. It was part of normal life at home and at school and it didn't stop us from learning.

I loved having my big cousin with me as a protective brother. Every morning, Thang Hoa walked across the street to my house and accompanied me to school. I was always late, but he had an enormous amount of patience. Even though he was only in the sixth grade, I loved listening to his philosophy of life. Those two years of walking to school together created a lifelong bond that continues to this day. (Thang Hoa now lives in Germany with his wife Regina and is the proud father of two grown children. As the chef and owner of a high-end restaurant in Belgium, he represents another successful "boat people" story of refugees creating a new life in Europe.)

By fourth grade I was fluent in Cantonese and getting better at making friends. I learned to appear brave on the surface, but internally, I was still a nervous wreck. Because I had changed schools so often, much of my confidence had been chipped away. Even so, Mom didn't notice how the constant changes affected me. She rarely paid attention to our school progress or our emotional needs the way Western mothers were portrayed. The most important thing to her was that her children were clean, fed, and had pretty clothes to wear. She always had a list of things to keep us busy. Things like being nurturing or showing concern with how she was doing socially and emotionally were never addressed in her own life, so she didn't know that they were missing or important in ours.

To be fair, it wasn't just my mom. Most parents in that society were more concerned with their children's physical needs than with their emotional wellbeing. They rarely thought to ask about whether their kids, or themselves, were happy. There were too many other important things to attend to. Unlike in America, psychological and emotional needs were not an issue of key concern.

Soico, Mom and Pe co (Dad's cousin), back row.
Far left second row, me, with Minh Thu in the back,
Thang Hoa in the front.
Three other cousins are Auntie Nhien's daughters.

My Cousin—Minh Thu

During the Lunar New Year in February of 1972, Mom gave birth to her fifth child: my adorable little sister, Eng, Kui Li, or, Ong, Que Loi in Vietnamese. (She liked her middle name more than her first, I am calling her *Que* here.) It was a year of joy. Que was a happy baby, always smiling, bringing so much happiness to everyone around her.

30

That same year, my uncle Thien Sanh, my mom's brother, also had a new baby girl named Xuan, born three days after Que. Tragically, Xuan's mother died from a sudden illness when Xuan was only six months old. Uncle Thien Sanh was not prepared to care for a new baby along with his other children. So, baby Xuan, her 13-year-old sister, Minh Thu, and two younger brothers all moved to the city and took refuge at Grandma's home. Grandma was really not equipped to take care of them, but because my family was nearby, we all (Dad included) helped raise my uncle's children and deal with this difficult situation. No one considered any other option: our relative had died leaving behind her children, so the family rose to the challenge.

For several years Grandma Trinh would often have three to five grandchildren rotating in and out of her home as needs arose. Some were older than me and others were around my age. The cousin I became closest to was Minh Thu. She is the fifth of eight children, with four older brothers, two younger brothers, and her baby sister, Xuan. At the age of 15, Minh Thu instantly assumed the maternal role for her younger siblings. I admired her strength and treated her like an older sister. We played very well with each other as children and shared many great memories as teenagers. We always thought that she was two years older than me until recently, when her older brother discovered from an old document that she is actually four years older than me. It did not alter the fact that she was a very brave girl whom I continue to admire.

Whenever I faced a challenge, Minh Thu was my invaluable advocate. She helped me fight for things I was afraid to ask for. When I was about 12, a new movie was released that Minh Thu and I were desperate to see. She got permission from Grandma Trinh, but when I asked Mom, she told me she couldn't grant me my request, and that I had to ask Dad. Ask Dad?! That was out of the question! Just the thought of asking Dad paralyzed me with fear.

I begged Minh Thu. "I'll do anything you want if you ask Dad to let me go."

"Why don't you ask him yourself? What are you afraid of?"

"You don't understand. If I ask, he will reject the idea immediately. I will likely get punished for even asking." That might not be true but it was always the scenario in my head.

"I don't think that will happen…but if you buy me some candy, I will ask him for you."

So that was how it was typically done. If I wanted something from Dad, I didn't dare ask him directly. But if I asked someone else to intercede for me, I might succeed. It was so wrong, but that was what I believed. I'm ashamed that I never had the courage to even try to get to know who my father really was during my tween and teen years.

Minh Thu was able to use her charm with Dad and get him to agree to let me go to the movie with her. However, there was one condition: We had to come right back home immediately after the movie. When we got to the movie theater, its matinee show was sold out. My body trembled as my cousin decided that we were not going to waste the 25-minute bike ride and we should stay and see the next show, which started at 7:00 p.m. I told her that I would be in trouble for coming home late, but she insisted that she could explain to my dad. "Besides," she reasoned with me, "this will likely be your only chance. Your dad may never let you see the movie if we don't stay."

I bought into her logic. I reassured myself that she would be the one I could blame for this decision. Unlike today, with everyone owning a cell phone, there was no way of letting Dad know why we were not going to be home at the time we were expected. I didn't know that Dad had been waiting outside for several hours.

My heart almost jumped out of my chest as I saw Dad standing at the corner of the street as our bike got closer. My body shook with dread and I almost passed out, thinking of the punishments that come with the screaming and the scolding. The only reason I didn't actually faint with fear was that my dear Minh Thu was there to offer a contrite and sound explanation on our behalf. Once again, Minh Thu was my shield. How I envied her bravery and how she could talk to my father. It turned out the anticipation of punishment, as usual, was more traumatic than the discipline.

In general, I never understood why Dad felt it necessary to discipline me so strictly. I was never defiant or daring to misbehave. But as I have grown older (much older), I have also come to realize that he did it out of love and out of concern for my safety and protection. He deeply loved us all. He just had a very poor way of showing it.

Me and Minh Thu
(1973)

Lifelong Friends, Australia
(2012)

Sydney Harbor Bridge Climb (2012)

Paris (2018)

The Power of Hối Lộ

For the most part, our family had been able to avoid direct contact with the war. Unfortunately, in 1972, that inevitable day came that the war was at our doorstep. Dad was busted for using a fake ID to avoid the draft. The sentence was jail time in Thu Duc Prison.

Mom went to work conjuring up the necessary bribes to arrange for Dad to be in a safe place. Bribery was a given part of how everything worked in that culture at that time. Its nickname was hối lộ, which essentially means money is paid to speed things along in a particular direction ("hoi" means *to speed up*, and "lo" means *road*). Through my mom's determination and the power of her payoffs, Mom arranged with our district government representative to have Dad placed in a non-combat zone. Dad would not be sent to the front.

It took multiple layers of bribes, but finally Dad was in uniform as a jeep driver for a colonel in a nearby station. Dad only had to show up every Monday in uniform and drive the colonel around to various meetings. He never saw a single paycheck for his service and he even had to pay additional bribes to the colonel to keep his position, but he was fine with that. We were lucky to be able to trade money for Dad's safety in our war-torn country. Hối lộ could buy almost anything back then.

Although it may not sound honorable to avoid service in the army, many people did not feel that the war was justified, especially the Chinese minority. It wasn't our war to fight. And besides, we weren't ready to give up our lives for a country that never made us feel that we belonged.

At 36, Dad still couldn't speak Vietnamese. It was in jail that dad finally developed some skills, but unfortunately, he learned to swear in Vietnamese better than he could converse. Things at home got worse after Dad was released from jail. He got upset easily, exploding more frequently at home and now he cursed in both Chinese and Vietnamese.

He was very suspicious of Mom, convinced that she was flirting with clients and government officials. But often it was the little things that set him off. If Mom complained that the children were misbehaving or being disobedient, Dad's anger would explode toward us. Viet was the most frequent target of Dad's fury, but it was also often directed at me, since Viet was my responsibility. Either way, I suffered from massive anxiety. I felt a deep compassion for Mom and for my brother whenever witnessing their severe physical punishments. No human being should have to endure this kind of physical aggressiveness, let alone from your husband or father.

For years, I would go to sleep every night lying on my stomach, trying to suppress the pain. But nothing seemed to bring relief. It was getting so bad that Mom took me to a gastrointestinal doctor. I was told that I had an inflammation in my stomach and symptoms of a gastric ulcer. Back then, no one talked about stress or psychological issues as being the cause of ulcers. I had been medicated on and off all my life to tame the ongoing inflammation of my stomach and intestinal pain. Nothing helped relieve the discomfort. It has accompanied me throughout my life and intensifies whenever I feel lost in a stressful place or situation.

Catholic School

When I was ready to enter the fifth grade in my school, my brother Viet was ready for kindergarten. Dad decided Viet should go to Thanh Gioan ("St John"), a private Catholic French school taught by Vietnamese nuns and that I should go to the privately owned Cantonese-Chinese Catholic school next to it called *Thanh Tam* ("Sacred Heart"). He felt my brother could benefit from a better education and strict discipline, and that a Catholic school would give him both. I was to change schools yet again, so I could watch out for my brother. Sending us to the same area for school certainly made transportation easier, and again, I was apprehensive about the new environment.

Obviously, I didn't dare to question Dad's decision. It was distressing but I was also excited. It was a step up from the Buddhist Temple school. The Catholic school was in Cho Cu ("old market"), located in a more prominent Cantonese-speaking part of the Chinese community. I was now quite comfortable speaking Cantonese and told myself that this would be a positive move for my future education. It was nice not having to deal with flood waters in the classroom every time it rained hard. And since I had no say in the matter anyway, I looked on this change as a chance to explore another religion. Most of the students there were children of entrepreneurs who owned big businesses in a well-off Chinese sector of Saigon.

In Cholon ("new market") and Cho Cu, the dense Chinese community in Saigon, it was not unusual for people to switch from one Chinese dialect to the other, then to Vietnamese and sometimes even to French. I loved the multilingual diversity. I enjoyed the freedom I felt to be myself during my fifth and sixth grade years at the Catholic school. I joined the choir and was happy going to school early almost every day. Dad's cousins or the maid would drive, or I took the public transportation of Xe Lam, a motorized tricycle that could fit up to eight or ten people.

Xe Lam

I am grateful for these memories, as it was one of the only times in my childhood when I did not feel my burdens and limitations far outweighed my sense of excitement and opportunity. This change of school afforded me the ability to travel to further parts of town. The frosting on the cake was that Mom let my older cousin, Minh-Ngoc, accompany me to the same school. Minh-Ngoc was Mom's sister's daughter who had come to live with my grandma across the street. I quickly realized what an upgrade this school was, better quality education and teachers. No more Buddha chanting; instead, I was taught the Bible in class and found it so much more interesting.

I was old enough now to understand the importance of making friends beyond the first two rows around me in class. I felt more grown up and I was building some confidence. By this time, there were only a few Teochew kids in this part of town. The most frequent dialect was Cantonese. Some of the teachers were from Taiwan so we spoke to them in Mandarin. Standard reading was also in Mandarin. Vietnamese was treated as foreign language in Chinese schools, as was French. We were taught both Vietnamese and French along with Chinese. Since French was still new to me, Dad hired a private tutor who came to our house once a week for French lessons for my brother and two of my cousins, Soijek's kids. The French teacher later passed her position on to her fiancé and then to her sister-in-law. Despite the ever-increasing economic and political turmoil, my parents continued to fund private French lessons for us until we left Vietnam in 1979.

A New Religion

This switch from a Buddhist Temple school to a Christian Catholic school was quite strange to me. My image of God before I attended Thanh Tam School was the happy overweight Buddha. Now I was taught that a white, bearded man named Jesus was the real God. The concept that I needed to save myself by doing good deeds meant hoping to be reincarnated to a better form of being in the next life was out the window. The new prayers were to the loving and merciful God who offered us salvation by redeeming us from our sins. It was a relief now that I didn't have to worry that if I behaved badly, I would be reincarnated as a dog to guard houses or a pig to be eaten. It was reassuring to know that I had the option to be saved.

I noticed that Christians are more passionate about spreading the Good News than Buddhists are about their teachings. Buddhists are more self-focused, seeking nirvana through individualized efforts. I now had a small circle of friends and was starting to be a little more adventurous. Most of my new friends were Cantonese and Catholic.

I first encountered Christ in this school, in a Cantonese translation of the Bible. Even though I didn't quite get it, I followed along. My religious background was rituals and vastly influenced by the Chinese philosophers, Confucius and Laotzu. That was the moral and cultural belief that my Dad lived by. Those were the virtues and teachings that governed his life and his understanding of family.

At Thanh Tam, I had a wonderful homeroom teacher named Mr. Zhau. He offered extra math tutoring classes in his tiny house at the back of school. I did not realize at the time how poor these teachers were. Most of them had to do tutoring outside of class to supplement their meager salaries. One thing I learned from Mr. and Mrs. Zhau had nothing to do with math. I was standing in their kitchen and was confused by two tall glasses of water with lids sitting on top of the cupboard. Mr. Zhau saw my confused face and said, "If you drink a big glass of boiled water every morning after you get up, your gut will be cleansed, and you will never have to worry about constipation!" He smiled and pointed to the glasses. "These glasses are for me and my wife." Funny how that simple visual with that short conversation stuck in my mind. It was the first time I had been taught about good health practices. I started drinking a large glass of water first thing every morning, hoping that would resolve my stomach issues. It didn't help.

I was curious and loved to learn new things at school and then go home to play with my cousins, Minh Thu or my auntie Nhien's daughters, Minh Ngoc and Minh Ha, or whomever was staying with my grandmother at the time. The rainy season in Vietnam was a lot of fun for us kids. Sometimes we folded origami paper boats and let them sail with the flood water on the street. Other times during the afternoon downpour, we would run up to the rooftop and dance in the rain. The maid would let us play and soak in the rain for ten to fifteen minutes before calling us into the house for our real showers. When we were all cleaned up, we would draw paper dolls on cardboard and design and make fancy paper clothes for them. It was a simple, fun time I remember having with all my cousins. At a young age, I became passionate about sketching fashions, designs, and creating art. Eventually this was expressed in my adult career.

In the sixth grade, I had my first slumber party at a classmate's house. Thankfully, her dad was also my dad's friend and he guaranteed Dad that he would watch out for me and drive me home the next day. Because I was so afraid to ask, I often missed out on an overnight slumber party. Or I would beg Mom, Grandma, or one of my cousins to speak up for me. It was a ridiculous fear, but it was something I faced every day.

A remarkable field trip to the beach concluded my sixth-grade graduation. I was sad that I had to part with the friends I had made the last two years. Most of my friends advanced together to a school that was close by, but I was again put into a new private school. It had recently been built in nearby Dinh Minh Phung. This was the fifth school I attended in the short seven years of my educational career. Five schools in seven years. This had a profound impact on me and I'm sure it was one of the contributing factors to my lack of self-confidence.

Looking back, every school I attended contributed to my life experience. My two years at the Catholic Thanh Tam Elementary School gave me a great opportunity to explore new concepts, make new discoveries, even while tasked with keeping an eye on my little brother, Viet. It was my responsibility to meet him after school for our ride home. Once I got into big trouble when Viet decided to take a cyclo (three-wheel bicycle taxi) home by himself. I was a little late picking him up and Viet somehow squeezed through the front gate without being noticed. He hailed a cyclo and gave the driver our home address.

"Can you take me to 43 Duong Thai Phien?"

The driver told him, "Forty dong for the trip."

Viet hadn't quite learned the concept of bargaining. "How about 50 dong? That's what we always pay."

The driver didn't hesitate to say yes, and Viet promised him that Mom would pay him when he got home.

My legs went limp when I came to the gate and Viet was nowhere to be found. By the time Viet arrived at home, everyone at the school was out looking for him. Dad stormed into the school. The gatekeeper who was supposed to be guarding the front gate, Mrs. Nhung, was terrified that she might lose her job. She begged Dad to forgive her so she wouldn't get fired by the nuns for her oversight. After this incident, both Viet and I got a good whipping from Dad. I remember thinking that at least, by being Dad's outlet for his anger, I had saved Mrs. Nhung's job.

Me, Minh Thu and Grandma in the back row, with
Viet, Phan and two cousins from Uncle Thien Sanh

A Complicated Relationship

Dad always desperately wanted a son, and as the first-born male child, there were very high expectations placed on Viet, my five-and-half year old younger brother. And because I was the oldest child, the responsibility to look after my baby brother and keep him safe often fell on me. Dad knew his first son was special, but he wasn't ready to deal with his rebellious spirit. Dad wanted an ordinary son who would be obedient, take criticism constructively, and live up to his expectations. What Dad got in Viet was exactly the opposite.

Even when I was very young, I remember Dad saying to Mom that Viet will grow up to either be the president of a corporation or a gang leader. He knew my brother was smart, curious, fearless, and always daring to test his limits.

From the time he was very little, Viet loved trying anything and everything, no matter how dangerous. He was bold and audacious, showing no fear despite Dad's punitive efforts to suppress and tame his defiant behavior. Dad felt it was his responsibility to break Viet's daring, disobedient spirit, as he worried constantly that something might happen to his beloved only son. Dad's attempt at strong disciplinary control only seemed to incite Viet to test the limits and rebel even more. So, despite his favored position, or maybe because of his favored position, Viet endured the worst physical aggression and psychological damage at the hand of our father. Looking back today, I feel grateful and relieved that Viet survived his childhood and was able to move on in life as a very compassionate, loving person.

Both Viet and I were competing for attention from Dad. He did it in a very assertive manner, while I was the exact opposite. I tried to be compliant, showing complete deference to anything I thought Dad wanted. I would not dare to challenge him. Viet was the risk-taker. The more I watched how my brother was being punished, the more frightened I became for Viet and for myself.

While I grew up with low self-esteem, Viet grew up full of confidence. (I don't know if he would agree with my assessment, but that's how I feel about him.) He loved to prove that he could get away with anything. From the nun teachers at school, to the maids, to Mom and even to Dad, he stole just to get caught. Getting caught didn't seem to faze him, he would just try again. Heavy lashings and punishment only seemed to encourage him to try harder to perfect his skills. A challenge he must overcome. It

40

appeared as though both of us craved love and attention, but looked for it in completely different ways.

Dad's favorite phrase to say was, "You are good at being a thief, but I am better at catching the thief!" He was determined to always stay ahead of the "game" and constantly looked for something to punish us for. Mom and I were supposed to keep the house in order, so if one of my younger siblings got hurt from an accident, it would be my fault or Mom's fault for letting it happen. When Viet was injured from being a daredevil, Mom or I would be in trouble. Viet had more scars on his face and body than I could count. I still remember getting whipped when Viet (as a toddler) decided he would climb to the top of the table and jump to the floor. He scraped his knee and got a deep cut at the tip of his left eyebrow. The bleeding was profuse, but it did nothing to dampen his desire to test how much further he could go.

I believe tough love, punitive discipline, and corporal punishment will cause physical and psychological damage. Sometimes there were legitimate needs for discipline, but too often it was motivated only by anger, and Viet became the scapegoat when Dad responded to Mom's complaints. Viet liked to test the boundaries, and Mom did not hesitate to tell Dad. The moment Dad stepped in the door after a hard day at work, the atmosphere in the home changed.

One day Dad came home from work and Mom reported some mischief that Viet had gotten into that day. Without hesitation, Dad took the duster rod (his most notorious choice for administering a whipping) and hit my brother, *while he was sleeping!* I was horrified! I was shaking uncontrollably with fear as I witnessed my brother waking up in terror with no idea what was happening.

These instances of harsh domestic discipline happened several times a month, sometimes several times a week. Daily, we were subjected to screaming, cursing, and belittling insults. Watching my mom and my brother on the front line of these attacks made me feel frightened and helpless. I cried in fear, slept in fear, woke up in fear. In the presence of my dad, I walked on eggshells, trying to avoid anything that might cause the volcano to erupt.

As I got older, every episode added to my anxiety and the pains in my stomach grew. According to his health history, Dad had ulcers and stomach bleeding that became more severe when he was stressed. Perhaps those ulcers were also a result of his past traumas. Dad was now passing that trait on to me. My parents always assumed that my stomach problems were genetically inherited from Dad. They didn't recognize that the tumultuous environment was the source of stress. Even when Dad was having a happy loud conversation, to my ears it sounded like Dad was screaming and it put me on edge.

Was our family different? I suspect that the constant social and political disturbance in Vietnam at this time made it difficult for all parents to be aware of the psychological or emotional issues and consequences of raising a family in a fear-based atmosphere. Most people were just doing their best to survive another day.

Another Family Business

While Dad still managed his fabric dying business, Mom and Grandma were also very entrepreneurial. They started another business that gave several family members an employment opportunity. Thang Gia, the eldest son of Uncle Thien Sanh, came to live with Grandma with a few of his younger siblings. They joined forces to help Mom and Grandma run an estate sale auction business. Some of Dad's nephews (his older brother's sons) and cousins also joined in this venture.

The business plan was simple. When a building that had been used by Americans was evacuated, people would go to the auction and bid on all the interior items that were left behind. Whatever remained in the building was covered by their bid: tables, chairs, mattresses, beds, shelves, kitchen sink, toilets; anything that could be detached, we would buy. One such property was a hospital. Another one, an electrical warehouse. They would then sell the items individually. It was a lucrative and trendy business. The term "đồ lạt son, meaning iron junkie, was commonly used to describe that business.

Before long, a lot of people on my street started to run the same kind of business, driving up the bidding. Soon, my neighborhood looked like one giant American yard sale. Some of the bargain items were not resold, but used by our family. Our home had the most up-to-date furniture: spring-mattresses from the military, a stainless-steel desk from the hospital, a toilet bowl was installed to replace squatting over a hole, and a stainless-steel sink and gas oven were installed in the kitchen.

It was a collaborative effort between Grandma, her eldest grandson, my parents, and so many family members that I lost count. It was profitable.

We had a maid in each house, and when it was mealtime, we ate together as a big family. The real Chinese style.

Tragedy, Change, and a Huge Family Loss

A year before the North Vietnamese communists invaded the South in 1974, tragedy struck our family. The matriarch of our family, Grandma Trinh, suffered a massive stroke while bending over, washing her very long hair. She died on the way to the hospital. It was a huge loss for the whole family. Grandma was the glue, the hub, the main load-bearing wall in a house which I feared now might collapse. She helped raise the five children in our family, the eight kids from my uncle's family, and the children of Auntie Nhien who lived with her on and off over the years.

Everyone felt a deep sense of loss. I lost my most reliable source of protection. Grandma was the only one I could count on to buffer Dad's temper. Mom lost her greatest advocate and protector. At 32, Mom had always relied on her mom's guidance and direction, and now she would have to struggle on her own to keep peace in the family. Dad was also deeply grief-stricken. Grandma Trinh was the soft-spoken mother he never had, and she had been a great advisor and business partner. Dad respected and valued her.

Grandma was well-liked and highly respected by everyone in the community. The funeral ceremony lasted seven days. The casket was placed in the middle of the house and we all wore white as we kneeled around the casket. Hundreds of people came to pay their last respects, burn incense, and pray for her. Monks chanted every day, well into the night until the burial. A big shrine was created by covering a table with a white cloth and displaying lanterns and Chinese symbols of mourning along with daily offerings of food. Incense were burned non-stop for 49 days.

It was the most somber environment I had ever experienced. Life suddenly stopped. Even two-year-old Que, cute and adorable as always, could not cheer us up. Uncle Thien Sanh, who had just lost his wife months before now, came up from the countryside to attend his mother's funeral. He was a mess, numbing his pain with alcohol and offering Mom and Dad no help with the funeral arrangements. There were a total of 20 grandchildren who kneeled by the casket: eight from Uncle Thien Sanh, eight from Aunt Tu Nhien and four from my mom. It was a rare and sad reunion of the entire family.

I was fortunate to have had Grandma in my life for 12 years. I experienced her love in a way that none of my other siblings did. Even after she died, I prayed to her whenever there was a catastrophe, fighting or quarreling in the family, especially involving Mom or my brother. Grandma was my patron saint. It seemed to work every time. Whenever anger or abuse erupted in the house and a distraction would calm things down, I believed it to be divine intervention from my beloved grandmother. I found comfort and peace in that thought.

They say disasters always strike in threes. For us, this seemed to be true. First was the death of my aunt, Uncle Thien Sanh's wife. Then, Grandma died. And within months, Uncle Thien Sanh also died from depression and from excessive drinking, leaving three children behind. Their second son, 19-year-old Thang Dinh, and his brother Thang Truong, lived in their house in Go Quao. The eldest son, Thang Gia, started to manage Grandma's house and supervise his five younger siblings. My parents ultimately became the Trinh children's guardians, helping Thang Gia take care of his siblings.

When Uncle Thien Sanh died, Minh Thu and Xuan, the two girls, moved up to the city with their brothers. Thang Hoa and Thang Loc also moved up. Five of the eight children were then staying in Grandma's house. They were part of our family across the street, under my parents' guidance.

So much had happened that year. It was a big adjustment for everyone on both sides of our family. There were so many people grieving loss in their lives that my parents did not have time for their personal fights. There continued to be minor episodes, but I believe my prayers to Grandma were working, as conflicts seemed to diffuse more quickly.

Memorial Day at the cemetery in Vietnam

One More School Transition

As I started the seventh grade, I was faced with yet another school transition to Dong Tam ("United Heart"), but this one turned out to be relatively easy and positive. I had become a pro in changing schools. At Dong Tam, the education system was modeled after Taiwan's. This school had a good mix of Cantonese, Hokkien, Teochew, Hainam, Hakka and other Chinese dialect-speaking children. The most popular dialects were Cantonese and Teochew.

Dong Tam was about a 20-minute walk from my house. It was built by a group of wealthy Chinese businessmen in the community. As a private school, it had strict regulations and mandatory uniforms—white shirt, blue skirts for girls, and blue pants for boys. A clean and tidy haircut was expected. The school hired many Chinese teachers from Taiwan. Vietnamese, French, and English were considered foreign languages. I had become less fearful this time. I looked forward to making new friends and was optimistic about communicating since I finally had mastered several dialects.

Language was no longer an issue, but now I was more concerned about my physical appearance. Since there is no alphabetizing system in Chinese, the seating arrangements were based on height, not by name. Because I was shorter than most kids, I think that caused me to feel insignificant, vulnerable and unsure. However, the advantage of sitting in the front row was there were no distractions. I got to pay close attention to the teacher who was the only thing in front of me. The disadvantage was that I didn't know what was happening with the students who sat behind me. School was a mixed experience.

I loved an environment where I could learn new things. I strived to be a good student who never rocked the boat as I witnessed the unfair treatment of some teachers who favored the obedient female students over the more active male students. Another strong emphasis about being compliant and obedient, I really took that to heart.

I had made some meaningful friendships that lasted for years and I was having a productive year learning the wonderful world of math and science. That is, until the communist north took over the democratic south on April 30, 1975.

3

Vietnam Post War (1975–1979)

Goodbye Saigon – Hello Ho Chi Minh City

On April 30 of 1975, the communist army from North Vietnam marched into Saigon with tanks and guns as people lining the streets cheered. They were happy that the takeover was swift without a lot of damage or casualties. There was virtually no gunfire or death in the city and the streets were littered with military uniforms from former South Vietnam servicemen. No one wanted to be associated with the old regime.

Books, pictures, and documents that were linked to the South Vietnamese government were burned or destroyed. While the people were thankful that the takeover had been decisive and without blood in the streets, there was a hidden underlying terror in the hearts of those who knew how communists ruled in the North. Most of us were oblivious to what the future would bring.

Dad was among the people out on the street cheering for the new regime. He had high hopes that the country would not follow the communist path, but instead would grow into a peaceful socialist country. He was optimistic that things would soon get back to normal and he refused an offer from his colonel to get out of Vietnam at the last minute on a private jet.

His family, his house, his little kingdom built from his own sweat and tears—why would he want to abandon everything and take the risk of an unknown future in a foreign land? To impulsively leave Vietnam was a ridiculous suggestion!

Dad had invested everything building a life in Vietnam from scratch. He was a partner of a successful company which gave him a stable stream of income. Song Nghia, the fabric dyeing company, was prospering. His ambitions for his family were foremost on his mind, and he fully expected that what had worked for him in the past (namely, a very strong work ethic) would continue working for him in the days to come.

But the cheers of the people soon died down and, as the dust settled, everyone began to whisper in fear. What will this new unknown regime be like? Will everyone get a clean slate, or will those associated with the former regime be punished, imprisoned, or executed? The speculations fueled inner terror which was concealed at all costs.

The first year, the South was governed by the Provisional Revolutionary Government whose leaders set out to integrate the country. Northern cadres flooded the city to oversee the transition. The primary goal seemed to be "cleaning house". They wanted to make sure that all former democratic soldiers, military personnel, and their intellectual staff were purged from the government and sent to re-education camps. Because dad served in the former South Vietnamese army, he was sent to the re-education camp, but only for a few weeks. He was granted amnesty for what was labeled "minor crimes." Luckily, he had never fought in combat against the North nor been an officer in the army. He had only been a colonel's driver.

The formal reunification of the North and South did not take place until a year later. By June 1976, Saigon was renamed Ho Chi Minh City. In private, the name was mocked and hated, but of course no one expressed resistance in public. People had no idea who was working as government agents. There were eyes and ears everywhere. Your neighbor, friend, or even a family member could be spying for the government. Saying the wrong thing to the wrong person could lead to you vanishing into thin air.

Trust No One

Following the invasion, the most sudden and disturbing change was that some people who had always been thought of as regular citizens instantly became high-ranking neighborhood commanders.

Mrs. Muoi was our neighbor across the street, living next-door to Grandma. She was a Vietnamese lady who married a tall Chinese man. I don't know how they were able to communicate with each other, as Mr. Muoi could barely speak Vietnamese and his wife spoke no Chinese. I sometimes overheard him speak to his son in broken Vietnamese. "May la mat troi moi mot, tao la mat troi lang." Translation: "You are the sun just rising and I am the setting sun." This was followed by some mumbling in Chinese I didn't understand. His son, who was in his late teens, ignored and laughed at his father as each talked in their own different language. It was a rather peculiar family dynamic. Then, overnight, Mrs. Muoi became the most powerful person on the block. It turned out she had been with the Viet Cong underground for many years, hiding in plain sight, and no one suspected a thing. Fortunately (to say the least), we had never said anything against the communist government in front of her.

Three doors down from our house, there was a Hainam Chinese family who had a son in the military. One morning, he was seized and the whole family disappeared without a trace. Yellow tape hung over the door as a reminder of what happens to those who dare to ask questions.

The transition to socialism did not take long to cripple the economy. The government took control of the free market. Food was regulated and distributed to each district through neighborhood leaders. Weekly food ration coupons were given for vegetables and bread, monthly coupons for rice, and a lottery for meats such as pork. The lines were long, and the process lengthy. Often the food was gone before it reached the middle of the line.

Sometimes, I would be sent to stand in line for hours to get our family some pig organs—stomach, kidneys, ears, or tongue were all considered a luxury. Dad was an expert in preparing animal organs. He could take any unwanted organ parts and turn them into a gourmet Chinese delicacy that we loved. Even though we had money to buy extra protein in the under-ground market, we still had to stand in line and give the appearance that we were giving up our former capitalist lifestyle. No one wanted to be noticed and put on the government's watch list.

At home, our lifestyle dramatically changed. Mom's auction business of buying and selling furniture from American estates and hospitals collapsed and shrank to just selling the remnants of left-over inventory. My household of relatives (Dad's cousins and nephews) coming and going freely, suddenly became a much quieter place. Dad was still working for his company, Mom continued to manage the domestic front when she wasn't busy conjuring small deals in black market trading.

It was dangerous to show any sign of wealth or affluence. If it didn't look like you were struggling, you were suspect. We let go of the maids to not draw attention to our household and I started picking up many of the domestic chores in the family. Gone were those days of a carefree childhood.

School: A Tool for Propaganda

At the time, I was just entering junior high. I was very interested in algebra and science, especially chemistry, but the school curriculum was changing. The main language of education in Chinese school was now Vietnamese. Things progressed quickly and aggressively to a totally new system. All Chinese books from Taiwan were destroyed. The superintendent and teachers of the old regime were let go and replaced with the loyalist communist teachers.

In the Hoa (Chinese minority) community, Chinese was no longer the main language. We were required to sing revolutionary songs and learn the ideology of Uncle Ho and the communist party. We were constantly reminded how corrupt capitalism was, and that the influence from foreigners, especially Americans, was horrible for society. History lessons were the opposite of what we had learned our whole life. Math and science were no longer considered important. We just sang, sang, sang our way to ignorance and advanced our education by becoming stupid. Propaganda was embedded in all the lessons, indoctrinating us to love Uncle Ho and the Party more than our parents.

School hours were shortened from a full day to half a day. There were two shifts of students, morning and afternoon. Every week on Wednesday, the girls would wear (Áo *bà ba*) Vietnamese traditional blouse and black satin pants to school which represented community labor. This was something I did not hate, but resented. I never felt comfortable wearing the Vietnamese traditional outfit.

My classmates and I were divided into small groups. For the first half of the day we would have classes. For the other half we were sent out into the streets to pick up trash or tend to one of the gardens in the city. The communists enrolled students into the Red Scarf Youth Pioneers Club, called "Thieu Nien Tien Phong." We were taught that our loyalty should be strictly to Uncle Ho and the Party. We were instructed to be the government's eyes and ears—we should spy on our parents and report them if they were secretly doing things or saying things against the government.

WHAT? Report my own parents? I was appalled by the suggestion! I was devastated by what school was becoming. I went home and told my mom how disappointed I was that school was no longer teaching interesting subjects, that now it had become an instrument for government propaganda and brainwashing. We agreed that I needed to stay in school to maintain the appearance of normalcy, but I was beginning to understand how dangerous this situation was becoming.

Family Duty and New Responsibilities

In the spring of 1976, Dad was ecstatic that Mom bore their sixth child, a second son. This perfect little baby boy demonstrated a host of good characteristics from the moment he was born. Dad named him Nam. He had been blessed with the gift of two sons, naming them Viet and Nam, as one way to embrace his adopted country.

With a new baby in the household and no extra help from maids or my aunts, my responsibilities at home mounted. School was becoming less important and interesting. The government was unpredictable, people lived in fear of the unknown, and survival became a primary concern for our family. No one had any idea of what would be happening from one day to the next. I still went to school, but I had no aspirations that my education was preparing me for something worthwhile. Classmates began dropping out. Some moved to the countryside, but many were looking for a way to flee the country. Every family seemed to have a plot, a secret plan that would allow them to start a new life in a dreamy foreign land. They were careful to maintain a façade of normalcy, but worked hard to accumulate skills that would allow them to start a new life someplace else.

Even though I was only going to school half the day, I was still busy from sunrise to sunset. If I wasn't in school, I was helping with the chores at home. My responsibilities included daily food shopping with Mom or my Minh Thu, cleaning and chopping vegetables, cooking rice, preparing food, and then washing all the dishes from the day's three fresh-cooked meals. In the evening, after dinner when the dishes were done, my job was to bathe my three younger siblings. This took an enormous amount of time since they were always running around. Pinning them down was like trying to put frogs on a dish. After what seemed like hours of chasing after them to get them to cooperate, I bathed them, mopped the tile floors upstairs and sprayed DDT mosquito repellent in the rooms a few hours before bedtime. I didn't have a lot of time to spend on homework (mostly Party ideology).

Electricity became scarce. Electric power was cut off two or three times a week in the evening in different districts in the city. So, I had to try to finish my chores before the house went dark. My poor little sister Phan was afraid of the dark and didn't want to go to bed by herself. She would fall asleep on the staircase waiting for me to finish my chores so I could go to bed with her. I was 14 years old, but felt like 25. Phan was about seven years old and was my closest buddy, following me wherever I went.

By this time, Vietnam was a united country under a communist government, but citizens living in the South faced far more restrictions than those in the North. And those who were part of the minority Chinese immigrant community faced increasing hostility and discrimination. This oppression was intensified as the Vietnamese government went to war with Cambodia to the west and China to the north. The Chinese diaspora who lived in Vietnam were under constant suspicion. The Vietnamese government worried that everyone from the Chinese community in Vietnam could be spies from China. Since the Chinese minority in Vietnam controlled a large sector of the trade economy, the government's goal was to sweep out the capitalists and strip them of their power in order to extinguish all potential threats.

While I was preoccupied with my busy little world of chores, tasks, and endless errands for my mom, my dad was beginning to put together a plan for our family to escape. It was obvious that the country was going downhill and that we were rolling down with it. My dad and his company struggled to stay afloat while trying to comply with government demands. They knew time was running out and soon the company would be taken over and nationalized by the government. Capitalism and private entrepreneurship were fast disappearing and would soon become a distant memory. Dad and his partners were discreetly liquidating the assets of Song Nghia, converting them to gold and American dollars while they still could. Thankfully my dad had this foresight. Many business owners simply lost everything when they acted too late.

By late 1977, the relationship between China and Vietnam was abysmal. The ethnic Chinese became scapegoats in Vietnam. "According to Goscha, seventy percent of the capitalists who were targeted in the post-war period were Chinese." [https://asiapacificcurriculum.ca/learning-module/vietnam-after-war]

The Vietnamese government did not hesitate to flex their muscle and harass capitalists who they suspected to be disloyal. Within a few short years under the new communist regime, the economy in the South had spiraled downward. People who had never imagined the possibility were struggling just to feed their families.

Since school was no longer an interest, I channeled my passions into building life skills, as did many of my classmates. In addition to the chores at home which included being Mom's personal messenger and errand-runner, I enrolled in a series of domestic classes after school where I learned things like sewing, embroidering, knitting, and cooking. These were lessons that could be applied to real life and felt so much more worthwhile than singing Ho's praises all day at school. I found joy in creating new dishes. I learned to turn remnant fabrics into fashion clothes for my siblings, myself, and for many of my friends and cousins. My relatives knew how to take advantage of my free labor, and I benefited by having a lot of guinea pigs for practicing my new crafts.

During my life skills training, one of my proudest masterpieces was the embroidery tiger on a 60x80 cm canvas. I signed up for this class to create an heirloom piece to bring with us where ever we may escape. Mom was told that embroidery art that size would be worth at least five hundred to a thousand dollars in the United States. It took me a long month to hand guide the machine stitches to make the embroidery tiger. Most experienced embroiderers would take lessons for just that one purpose. As an overachiever, I finished one then proceeded to try out a smaller one by myself at home. The set of pictures survived the boat and refugee camp journey. It was one of my prized possessions, along with the set of Chinese/English dictionaries. I finally framed them up after 15 years of them sitting in the closet. They mean something to me because in Chinese Zodiac, I am also a tiger. I was supposed to be brave, but truly inside, I was just a kitty cat.

Set of tiger embroideries that I made

Cousin Thang Gia's wedding (1978)

A Plan Takes Shape

I credit my dad for always having a vision and a plan, even in the direst situations. Dad continued to let us take private French lessons. French was now the only academic subject I was spending time on, but I was still very busy throughout the day. My time at home was filled with chores, plus I was always giving someone a haircut, designing a new outfit, or trying a new recipe.

On a typical day, I rode my minibike everywhere to run errands for Mom. I knew every nook and cranny in Cholon and Ho Chi Minh City. I must have ridden thousands of kilometers on that minibike. I loved the feeling of freedom and independence, of getting out of the house and venturing myself in how to trade goods on the black market. The underground market was the only place we could get many of the things we had been accustomed to getting before the communist government takeover.

Once or twice a month, Mom had me trafficking antibiotics and other medicines from the local pharmacy. The pharmacist was Mom's friend and had access to imported items that mom could resell to people who needed them. Like my grandmother, my mom was a creative and clever businesswoman. And she knew that a young petite girl like me would draw less suspicion. So, at 15, I unknowingly became her most reliable "gold and medicine smuggler," carrying out her transactions.

Every so often, Northern cadets would stop by my house unannounced. It was very scary as they interrogated my little sisters and brothers, asking, "Little girl, little boy, did you have pork for dinner last night?" or, "Are your parents planning to go on a long trip?" Those were some of the most common questions.

Luckily, my younger brothers and sisters didn't speak Vietnamese, and I acted innocent. "What on earth are you talking about? The only meat we've had is from the government lottery. We have nothing at home now but lard." I told them, "I don't know what you mean. The only trip my parents ever talk about is to the New Economic Zones up in the highland." It was all too common for children, especially in Chinese families, to be terrorized like this.

In 1978, Dad and Mom decided that I should be taken out of school. First, there was no real educational value, only communist propaganda. Secondly, our family was thinking of fleeing the country, and if I were enrolled in school, my absence would immediately be noticed. Better to be absent from school completely. So, we started the rumor that our family was planning to move to the countryside to do farming. Thirdly, with the birth of my youngest brother Ong, Quoc Nam, the last child in the family, Mom really needed me at home, and I would use the year away from school to learn the domestic skills. We thought often about the most important survival skills the family might need if we left for an unknown land.

Effects on the Family in War-torn Vietnam

Children growing up in my culture in the 1970's experienced a harsh family life. They were raised to not expect to have any say in any part of their lives. The accepted way of raising a child was to be quick to scold and to use negative feedback as a motivational tool. I don't know how much of this came from living in a chaotic, war-torn country, and how much was the traditional Asian way of life, but children were not encouraged to take risks. (The irony here was I was incurring plenty of risk doing trafficking and not knowing about it.) They were taught to simply obey: Mom and Dad always know what's best. Teachers and doctors are always right. Children are to listen, obey, and never question someone in authority. Psychological and physical punishment was constantly at the ready, doled out by adults, some more harsh than others.

It was thought that threats, suppression, and punishment built character. For example, if a child would not eat dinner, they would be told, "If you don't finish your dinner, I am going to tell the police to arrest you!" It's a phrase I learned from my mom and aunts, and as the oldest child, I repeated the same tactic to threaten my brothers and sisters to get things done. Children would comply out of fear, not because they felt loved and respected by their parents and wanted to please them. And if those threats didn't work, the ultimate threat was, "I'm going to tell your father." We knew that meant we would be severely punished. We were trained to accept insults as words of inspiration. The purpose of tearing us down was to keep us humble so we would build ourselves up. It was a very contradicting method that suggested that praise would make us arrogant, overconfident, and egotistical.

I carried a hidden resentment throughout my life because my confidence was never built up but was continuously stripped to the bare bones. I witnessed the punishment of members in the family and so I did everything I could to be the good, dutiful, and responsible child. I was not a natural born risk-taker or a particularly brave person, but I was always very responsible, so I lived with continuous and excessive fear. I would worry about anything, everything, and everyone, and all that anxiety became a perpetual knot in my stomach. I had, and still have, heart palpitations just before bedtime and first thing in the morning. In America, I learned that those are symptoms of PTSD (Post Traumatic Stress Disorder).

We were all doing our best to survive an increasingly impossible situation that was eating us up with fear, both from the outside as the government became more and more oppressive, as well as within our anxious family. And things were only going to get worse.

Anti-Capitalist Campaign Toward Citizens in Ho Chi Minh City

In the spring of 1978, the government launched an anti-capitalist campaign that targeted the middle-class citizens of Ho Chi Minh City and was especially horrific for the Hoa Chinese minority. People's homes were ransacked, private property confiscated and "donated to the people," meaning taken by the government. Private businesses were nationalized and operated under government rules. Big Brother's government watched our every move. Because we had lived under a free-market system before, we were excruciatingly aware of our stolen lives.

One day, three secret cadres showed up at our house and camped there for five days. My parents' business was seized and the possessions in our home were inventoried. The government could come and confiscate them anytime they wished. It was a toxic environment with citizens being robbed by their own government. There were secret police and spies embedded in every neighborhood. Regular people you thought you knew were watching your every move closely.

I learned very quickly not to trust anyone or say anything. The only way to survive was to lay as low as possible, keeping under the radar. People found many ways to outsmart the government. Some would bury valuables in their backyard or build secret compartments in the wall. Many were forced to relocate to the New Economic Zones in the remote highland areas against their will. Their houses often were sealed overnight, and they disappeared without a trace. Several of our neighbors vanished that way and Mom was afraid we were next. We were trapped inside a community of terrorists!

No one wanted to use Vietnamese dong. Jewelry, gold, and the American dollar were the currency of the underground economy. A few years after unification, in an effort to purge out the rich and create economic equality, the government initiated a currency exchange. Every household was only allowed to exchange 100,000 of the old currency to obtain 200 dong of the new currency. Rich people immediately started scrambling to find poor relatives who could help them exchange their excess old currency money and in return would receive a commission.

Mom could see all this coming and began using me to distribute our money and gold to our trusted family and relatives. She wanted to keep as little as possible in the safe in our home. Many times, I strapped a wad of money around my waist and biked to the home of Yeeco, Soico and many of Dad's poor cousins to have them exchange the extra money we had for a commission. Mom also wrapped gold and jewelry in a dirty cloth bag, and I delivered these in small amounts to hide in my aunts' homes. As a 15-year-old girl, I was doing dangerous, risky things that send a chill up my spine as I think about them today. Had I been caught, I don't know what the punishments would have been. They would have shown me no mercy. I was only a young girl, but I would have been thrown in jail and forced to betray my parents. War makes children mature very quickly, and parents desperately look for ways to protect the family at all costs.

For several weeks, as the sun was setting at the end of the day, I would put Viet and Phan on the back of my minibike and bring them to Yeeco's apartment. it was about a 40 minute bike ride, to stay overnight. My parents were concerned that if they were arrested in the dead of night, at least three of us would be safe under my aunt's protection. Fear was our constant companion, as we never knew what would come next.

During the daytime, everyone acted as normal as possible. But we all knew that just under the surface, there was a major earthquake waiting to shake up our lives. One wrong move and the result would be a catastrophic. The morale of the country was at an all-time low. Ethnic Chinese were being suppressed by a vigorous Vietnamization program that was being directed at the younger Chinese generation. We were blatantly discriminated against and were treated as second-class citizens. More like zero-class citizens.

Everyone Had One Question: How to Escape

Almost overnight, it seemed as if everyone was brewing a plan for how to realize the dream of escaping the regime. The movement became everyone's obsession. Some crossed the borders by land to Cambodia or Laos to Thailand, while most saw fleeing by boat to the open sea as the best way to Malaysia, Hong Kong or the Philippines. Along with tens of thousands of other people, my family started developing ideas on how to escape Vietnam. A massive underground network connected people with money to people who could organize a boat needed for the escape.

Secret conversations were taking place throughout the community. My favorite cousin, Minh Thu, eloped with her fiancé. Together, after just two weeks of planning, they escaped on a risky, dangerous boat with 300 other people.

I was anxious and also started dreaming about going back to school in a free country. I didn't know where or how, but the dream of wearing a school uniform and learning real subjects pushed me to do whatever it took to help my family escape from this hopeless place. Every day, we looked for news about friends who had escaped. Some made it to Malaysian refugee camps. Tragically, sometimes the news was of a boat that sank in the ocean.

Many families were broken apart because there were not enough resources to buy passage for the entire family. Many of my parents' friends had just enough money to send only their elder children to board one of these dilapidated boats for the dangerous journey. They desperately hoped that their children would somehow arrive safely in a Malaysian refugee camp and would someday be able to unify the family in the future. But they were also painfully aware that they may never see their children again.

Mom had a plan where Viet and I would leave with her pharmacist friend's family. We would have ended up in Japan and God knows where that path would have lead as we separated from our family. Luckily, Dad put his foot down and insisted that he had saved enough money so we could go together. He was adamant that we would all live or die together on our journey. The crisis had become so severe in Vietnam that even the bad news of sinking boats did not discourage our plan to escape. We were all excited and encouraged when we received the good news that cousin Minh Thu's boat had arrived safely in Malaysia and that she was staying at the Bidong refugee camp. We put our focus far more on this word of hope rather than on the fear of death.

Dad found a group of four mutual friends who were willing to invest funds to build a boat. He became the project manager and would oversee every piece of wood and every nail that was used to make a boat secure enough for at least 400 people. Dad had never built a boat in his life, but he was a quick and thorough learner. His friends knew that his keen observation, practical mindset, and attention to detail would provide them with a sturdy boat.

Boat Construction Begins

In the spring of 1978, the government intensified their purging of capitalists and morale was continuing to fall. Many people lost their life savings or were put in jail because their boat-escape plan had failed. Either they trusted the wrong people, or they paid money only to find out there was no real boat, or they got caught from an informer. Sometimes people were stopped at the port because they did not sufficiently bribe the local officials. And other times their boats were halted before they reached the international waters. There was especially severe jail time for people who had formerly been soldiers or military personnel. I know people who attempted to escape a dozen times, got caught and put in jail a dozen times, and still looked for a way to escape. (My brother-in-law, Toan Tran, was one of those brave people. He now lives in Holland.)

Our family was an average middle-class family when Saigon was taken over by North Vietnam. My parents had planned very carefully how best to hide the gold needed to buy us passage to freedom. There was no room for mistakes. The gold we saved was only enough to pay for Mom and the five children. Because Dad was overseeing the project of building the boat, he didn't have to pay for himself, but it was still a hefty 40 taels of gold to pay for the boat trip. (A standard unit of measuring 24K gold in Vietnam, one tael = 37.5g of the precious metal.)

In planning for the trip, the boat owners and Dad settled on the port in Rach Gia, a city in Kien Giang Province (my Mom's birthplace). Located on the eastern coast of the Gulf of Thailand, 250 kilometers southwest of Ho Chi Minh City, Rach Gia was a well-known city on the southwest tip of South Vietnam and would be the port from which the boat would depart. Coordinating this semi-legal exodus from Vietnam required a tremendous amount of Dad's energy. He was constantly traveling to Rach Gia, but because he had to have a permit to travel there and was only allowed one permit a month, he had to be extremely careful. The government was always watching people's movements and where they were going.

In addition to monitoring where you were going, they insisted on knowing why. In an effort to deflect suspicion from our plan, my parents bought a fruit orchard in Thu Duc in the New Economic Zone, to show the government that we were not evil capitalists and were willing to convert to becoming farmers. But the piece of land that my dad bought was not able to be cultivated, so we abandoned the land and told the government that we would like to sell our house and move to Kien Giang to do rice farming and fishing.

Corruption was at its finest in Vietnam. Like in many poor countries, corruption was how the country's officials governed. Knowing who to bribe made it easy for Dad to get permits to travel back and forth to Kien Giang to manage the building project. In fact, arranging for the necessary bribes with the necessary officials was essential if we ever wanted to leave the port when construction of the boat was completed. Thank God the government back then had zero technology. No phones or computers to check on things. Every town, every county, had its own head officer with whom to negotiate a bribe.

On the surface, we carried on the normal day-to-day activities of struggling like the rest of the country. I really disliked Monday and Thursday nights when the power was cut off to save energy for the government. I had to hand-wash the family's clothes by candlelight using a washboard on the kitchen floor. I could barely see the garments and I got into trouble when the color of one piece of clothing spread to the other. I would soak the clothes in a big round aluminum tub with soap overnight and then early in the morning, before my daily food shopping in the market, I would wash, rinse and hang the clothes out to dry on our third-floor balcony. It didn't happen often, but occasionally the wind would rip the clothes off the clothesline and sweep them down to the street below.

During that period, Dad was only home between trips to Rach Gia and was experiencing many frustrations and stress as he constantly faced challenges for the boat project. The target date was set for spring to avoid the stormy season at sea in the Gulf of Thailand. Dad was understandably consumed with his project, easily irritated, and we were careful not to get into trouble when Dad was home.

One morning, I heard my name being called out very loudly. Dad could not locate his new expensive blue shirt and was in a rage.

"Where did you put my blue shirt after it was washed?"

I could see that the storm was going to only get worse. Nervously I said, "I don't know, I haven't seen it."

Without even finishing the sentence, I felt a slap on my face and received an angry reprimand for being so careless as to lose his expensive shirt from the wash. I blamed myself for not looking carefully at what I washed in the dark. How could I not have seen the brand-new shirt? It really bothered me. I walked up and down the street to see if maybe the shirt had flown down to one of the neighbor's homes or might be on the road somewhere. Nothing turned up!

I had been so careful not to get into trouble for the last few years as a teenager. It had been a long time since I had been physically punished. But punishment always left psychological pain that hurt me far more than the physical pain. I was puzzled that I couldn't remember the brand-new, light blue shirt being in the wash.

Two weeks later, I saw dad wearing a light blue shirt. The lump in my throat prevented me from mustering the courage to ask Dad if that was the shirt he had been looking for. I went to Mom and asked if that was the same shirt. Mom casually said, "Oh yeah, your dad left his shirt at his friend's house and he just found it." That was it? I was punished for his carelessness, and nothing, not a word was ever said to me of his own mistake.

In a culture where the parent is always right, an apology is seen as weakness and it is thought that the child will think less of a parent who apologizes. I was not angry at my dad for wrongly accusing me. I just wish he would have acknowledged that he was sorry for slapping me. Looking back, I believe that I have forgiven him. But I could never forget. The anger, the resentment, and the fear had such a lasting impact on my confidence. We never talked about it. For me, it was a lifelong scar. For him, it was like it never happened.

The Ong family, Vietnam (1978)

A Nearly Missed Opportunity to Escape

Day by day we were moving closer to our planned departure. Oh, to find out we almost lost all of our life savings to a family guest! A final straw of luck saved the day.

Mom's cousin, Uncle Thoan, a quiet man from the countryside, came to visit us for a few days. Dad was away building the boat, I was busy taking sewing lessons, and Mom was arranging to sell our house to get ready for our "farming relocation." That afternoon, Mom was away at a meeting with her friend. Uncle Thoan seemed eager to get everyone out of the house. He gave me money for the cyclo transportation and movie tickets and told me to take my brothers and sisters to a movie. He said he had someplace to go and would come back after dinner, but that he wanted us to be gone when he got back. He then left the house. *Something was not right*, I thought. He had spoken to me more in that one conversation than he had the last few days combined, and he seemed nervous.

I had a weird feeling about it, but wasn't sure what to make of it. One of my blouses was missing and I hadn't seen it since the day before. I don't know what prompted me to go up to the attic to look for the missing blouse, but in the attic, I saw an old suitcase in the corner, half open. Out of curiosity, I glanced inside and was shocked to see my blouse and other clothes all being used to wrap the gold bars, neatly stacked in the suitcase. My heart dropped. My hands were shaking as I tried to put everything back. I ran downstairs so quickly that I almost tripped on the steps. I ran across the street to my grandma's house and told one of my cousins to guard our house and not let anyone in or out of the house. I then ran straight to find Mom and told her what I had found.

Mom and I raced back to the house. She immediately checked the empty paint bucket under the staircase by the kitchen where the gold had been hidden and should be. There was nothing in the bucket except black coal. Apparently, Uncle Thoan had been sneaking around the house and had found the gold inside the can of paint.

When he came back that evening, Mom confronted him and kicked him out of the house. Thank God he was such an inexperienced thief. He was so ashamed. He had always been such a nice guy and he told Mom he was at the end of his rope. He figured we must have a lot more money than what he had found. Mom simply explained, "You were planning to take my family's livelihood! I want you out of this house and never return again!"

I'm not sure if Mom had ever told Dad the story! It was the closest call we ever had to a major theft, and had he succeeded, we couldn't have reported it to the police. Poverty can lure even the most honest of people to do contemptible things. Mom would never have speculated that her kind and honest cousin would betray her trust.

Our family did the best we could to cope with the stress that war, political turmoil, and economic uncertainty can cause. These were traumas we experienced and traumas that we inherited from our ancestors. And when there is no recovery time in between traumas, they just keep transferring from one generation to the next. As we prepared to attempt leaving Vietnam, my hope was that our family would be able to rise above our circumstances to create a better life and leave the bitter life behind. Starting with my dad's remarkable determination, we somehow were able to keep our spirits up by concentrating on this opportunity to advance our future in the free Western world.

By the end of April, our family officially moved to the New Economic Zone in Kien Giang, according to the government's document. We temporarily stayed with Mom's friend Y Lung until the boat was ready. May 3, 1979 was the fateful day.

24K Tael of gold

4

Seven Days' Boat Journey

The Departure

"This is a safeguard," my mother said. "In case our family is separated, and you need to survive on your own."

A month prior to our escape, Mom had sewn an embroidered patch on my shirt and tucked an American hundred-dollar bill under it. This was one of many clever ways she devised in order to better our family's chances as we abandoned everything we knew to take a risk so enormous that none of us, not even my father, could fully appreciate its recklessness at the time.

The morning of the departure on May 3, 1979, is remembered as terribly uncomfortable, from both nervousness and the relentless, hot and heavy air. The temperature approached 100° F and the humid tropics were especially steamy, since early May marked the beginning of the monsoon season. I put on the specially embroidered shirt and two more over it. Mom warned me to keep them on in case our luggage got tossed overboard. I was roasting but silently obeyed.

She slipped a 24K gold ring on my finger and fastened a gold necklace around my neck. "Sell these if necessary," she whispered.

Perhaps the most important thing I learned from my mother was how to be a skillful survivor. In my family, Dad was the king who ruled the domain, the provider and the ultimate lawmaker. Mom was the general who managed the domestic front, but also, she worked hard to add to the family income.

I became Mom's second in command. I shared everything with her, as she counted on me more every day. As the oldest child, I was told my responsibility was to protect my brothers and sisters if anything happened to my parents. Plain and simple, I was instructed to trust no others.

At the dock, Dad stood side by side with a local deputy who wore the khaki uniform and hard hat. He held a whistle in his mouth, and a list of names in his hands. Dad was checking each family as the uniformed man called out each family's name. Most of these people were Chinese descendants, some were Vietnamese with fake Chinese documents. Many understood this could be a death sentence to the sea, yet nothing could hold us back from seeking freedom.

There was a huge wave of people—men, elders, women and children. Bags in hands, they all clustered by the water's edge. The sight of all these people frightened me. Since Dad was the project manager of the boat, the boat owners and their family secured a seat for him and his first-born son, my 11-year-old brother Viet, in the cabin. My dad also snuck his adult nephew Cao (the son of his older sister) to the cockpit to help the crew. My mom and the children were to board with the rest of the crowd. Mom was holding my baby brother Nam, who was about to turn three and was squirmy from the heat. I held a hand of each of my sisters; Phan was nine, and Que was six.

I was trembling as we waited in line. I perspired profusely, listening for our names to be called. In front of us were my neighbor's family and his in-law's family. His sister (My Linh) did not register, but still tagged along hoping she could get on board. Her face was covered with a scarf, and she held her brother's baby, plowing through when their family name was called. My heart was pounding for her and I let out a big sigh of relief when she got through the gate, heading straight to the lower deck. As she passed by where I stood, we had a brief exchange of glances.

"Ong family!" the officer barked.

Dad looked at him and pointed to a bunch of us. In this moment, my eyes widened. Our family had doubled in size. We were registered as a family of seven. Looking around, I saw my mom, four of us kids, five other cousins (three from Auntie Nhien and two from Soijek) all moving in close, trying to board with us. Q, a friend I met a few months prior and who had come to see me off, was now also among us, masquerading as part of our family.

There was panic in Dad's eyes, though he tried to sound confident. "Here they are, quickly, let's get through!" The uniformed man raised his eyebrow at Dad, then looked back at all of us, squeezing together, unable to look him in the eye. He motioned sharply for us to move. Dad had taught me in the past year that everything could be bought, including a check-in officer. From the look on his face, the officer was thinking that he hadn't charged Dad enough, but he still let us all through. We had passed the first hurdle of our journey.

On the boat, there were about a dozen crew members scattered around to give instructions to the mass. I was surrounded by mostly strangers. Out of the hundred passengers, I knew about 15 people. They were neighbors, friends and cousins, though I lost sight of the cousins after we boarded. Most of these people, including my family, had never been on a boat trip before. Even so, throughout the boat there was a hushed quiet. No one dared to speak (too loudly). We had all been warned of the dangers of being captured and thrown in jail, and there were coast guards nearby who did not get a cut from the bribery. The longer we stayed in the port, the higher the risk was. Since all agreements were made under the table, we could only hope there wouldn't be another group of local officers showing up and disrupting the departure.

During this time, there were many semi-legal departures like ours, allowed by design to purge us from the country. Boats were fleeing Vietnam steadily since early 1978. The government allowed hundreds of thousands of ethnic Chinese to buy their way out of the country, traveling either through minefields, dense forests, or through perilous waves of the sea. The departures by sea were arranged through boat organizers who had the ability to fund capital to build the boats. They also sold fare to their fellow citizens and provided bribes to the corrupt local officials. The agreements to build the boats and rent the docks were planned almost a year in advance. It was extremely expensive to board these boats—each adult would pay about twelve to sixteen of 24K gold taels, which equated to $2-3 thousand American dollars per person at the time. Children under

14 were charged half-fare. In order to save eight taels of gold on me, my parents used my younger, deceased sister's birth certificate.

Though it was expensive, this was the price of a chance for a life outside of Vietnam. Some know intellectually that freedom is priceless; my family and I learned this deeply through personal experience.

The Harrowing Boat Journey

Our escape boat was larger than many, but it was still packed. It was around eight by twenty-eight meters long, with over 500 passengers onboard. Divided into sections, the cockpit/main cabin at the bow was large enough to fit about 60 people. It was filled with the captain, navigators, organizers, and boat owners and their families. Outside the cabin was the main deck where my mom, my little sisters, brother, and a wave of other small children, their moms and elders were settled. There was a guard rail around the boat, but no roof cover. We were resigned to experiencing whatever the elements threw at us, scorching sun and heavy rains included. Families were clustered together, sitting on the bare wooden floor with their bags in front of them. They only had each other's backs to lean on.

As I was walking to sit with my mom and my siblings, a loud shout stopped me in my tracks. "Young girl, you go down to the lower deck. All healthy young men and women belong in the lower deck! The upper deck is for children, their moms and the elders only!"

Mom put her hand on my shoulder and assured me, "You'll be alright. I am here if you need me." Reluctantly, I parted with my family. As I climbed downstairs, immediately I choked as the sea-breeze air changed to that of saturated diesel fumes. Below, the sound of the motorboat engine was deafening. The lower deck was dark and dreary, and lacked ventilation. There were only a few small fans to move the air around, and this did nothing for the throng of us who were packed in like human sardines. People were breathing down each other's necks. I felt suffocated and claustrophobic.

"Little girl, sit here. Quickly!" Another voice called out. Quietly, I squeezed into a small space between two strangers. They both looked older and bigger than me. As I sat down, my eyes scanned the room, looking for familiar faces. It was hard to see in the dim light, but no one looked familiar.

I heard an announcement: "Attention! Will the young lady named My Linh get off the boat! You are not registered! We cannot let the boat depart until you get off."

Oh no! It was our neighbor who had snuck in earlier. Somehow, they found out she wasn't on the registry, and no one with power would vouch for her now. Not even my dad.

Did someone tell? In that moment, everyone's head turned towards her. There she was, scarf still covering her head, looking around, pretending it wasn't her. A lady nearby screamed, her voice filled with urgency and panic, "You're My Linh, aren't you!? Please GET OFF! You don't want to ruin it for everyone. We cannot go to jail because of you!"

Everyone's eyes were on the poor girl now. Her scarf had dropped, and her face was flushed as her hands gripped her elbows as she tried not to cry. Even her brother called out to her, telling her to get off. Poor My Linh! I could feel her humiliation. I guess this boat was just not meant for her. (Years later, I learned that she made it to America after all. She was sponsored by her brother and came to California by plane.)

Seeing her, I thought of the fear that my cousins and my friend Q must have been feeling, since their names also were not on the registry. Lucky for them, they were under my dad's wing. I was proud at the thought that Dad would be saving another seven lives if we ever made it out of Vietnam.

A few minutes later, I felt a jolt and lurch. The boat was moving! There was a collective sigh of relief. It must have been 5 o'clock in the evening by then. The boat was escorted by a small government boat toward the open sea, leaving behind the small town of Kien Giang.

Farewell Vietnam!

Several hours went by, and it felt like eternity. Being separated from the rest of my family and sitting among strangers in the dark was very scary. We were all alone with our thoughts. I wondered how they were doing on the upper deck.

A crew member poked his head into the lower deck entrance and announced, "Dinner time! (Bánh tét) Sticky rice patties will be passed around to everyone. Make sure you put the banana leaf wrappers in a bag when you are done with the sticky rice. There are water containers behind you, by the wall. Drink sparingly. You will have to make all the food and water last for at least seven days!" Then he lowered his voice and shook his head. "Hopefully, that's all we'll need."

Listening to the announcement, I thought about how real this started to feel. It was very difficult to orchestrate such a massive underground boat escape like ours, as there were many moving parts. From finance to operation, to inside connections with the government, and to finding well-paying passengers—everything was done secretly by word of mouth.

It took about ten months to build the boat and Dad knew every nook and cranny. Dad and the boat owners named the boat KG-0108. "KG" was short for *Kien Giang*, where the boat was registered. It was a town known for fishing and rice farming. The numbers were arbitrarily arranged, but they picked the lucky numbers 1 and 8. It was very important that the sum of the numbers added up to 9, symbolizing luck and longevity. I had faith that our boat would succeed and would take us to a place of hope—even though the boat was over max capacity.

The sticky rice patties were passed around. I took a few bites of mine and a sip of water to wash it down. Even though I didn't have much of an appetite, I knew I would need strength for whatever lay ahead. After my meager meal, I poured some water to wash my sticky fingers on a piece of napkin. This place was a sweaty, smelly dungeon at the bottom of a stuffy boat. Even if the conditions were barbaric, I did not have to be. This was essential. Besides, we were told we had enough water to last for ten days, and I wasn't the only one washing my hands.

The scant light in the lower deck was getting dimmer as the night settled in. People were tired in the oppressive heat and were dozing off to the rhythm of the engine. I tried not to lean on the people next to me. There was a girl on my left, and a guy on my right. Both appeared to be older than me. I tried not to make eye contact with anyone, mostly spending my time staring down at the floor.

I was able to doze off sometime in the wee hours. I was dreaming of sleeping in my bed, yearning to get up to turn on the fan when I felt a hand on my chest. My eyes shot open. I straightened myself, thinking I had leaned on the guy next to me, but when I looked over, he appeared to be sleeping. I didn't want to go back to sleep. I was terrified, but I was also tired and drowsy from the sea motions. I felt the hand on me every time I closed my eyes. Everywhere I looked, people seemed to be sleeping.

I couldn't figure out where the touch was coming from. By then, it was totally dark. Not wanting to be alone with someone's wandering hands, I decided it was probably safe to go up and look for Mom. If anyone found me, or tried to give me a hard time, I could just pretend I needed to go to the bathroom on the stern of the boat.

Stepping over and around people as best I could, I slowly made my way in the dark to the steps. As soon as my head reached the open air, a cool breeze hit my face. Ahh! The fresh air felt so nice. I could breathe again! I stood up for a moment to stretch after hours of being cooped for so long and closed my eyes to readjust.

For the first time in my life, I could see the night sky with a million stars twinkling in it. Beautiful. We were wrapped up in the vastness of the universe. Our boat was just a tiny speck in grand almighty. We were insignificant. I thought of the dangers, the gloomy death looming in the oceans, and beyond. There were five hundred and two souls on this tiny wooden boat. We may be insignificant, but this was the journey of a lifetime, and this boat was everything to us. There was not a single complaint. Maybe it was because of exhaustion, but even the little kids knew this was life or death.

I remembered my dad telling us about his parents. They too fled their country to avoid communism and famine. Prior to World War II, they had escaped by boat from China to Vietnam, when Dad was only a three-year-old. My youngest brother was about three as we embarked on our own journey and my dad was about the same age as his dad. I was astounded at how history seemed to repeat itself.

I took a deep breath, looked up in the sky again. Was this really happening? The weight of the journey was slowly sinking in. We left the only world we had ever known, the only home I had ever had, for an uncertain future. If something happened to this boat, my entire childhood, my parents' entire lives, the family they built, and hundreds of other people on this boat could disappear in an instant. If we became stranded in this vast and endless ocean, would anyone know? Would anyone care? Who would rescue us? What does our future hold? Thousands of questions ran through my head, and I was glad I wasn't an adult. My parents were both here, somewhere on this boat. They would figure it out for us. Dad had done everything in his power to ensure this boat would be protected, and I believed luck would be on our side.

Returning from my thoughts, I continued searching for my mom and my siblings in the dark. Outside the cabin, on the bow of the boat, I saw their familiar faces. My mom was holding both my sisters in her arms, and on her lap was my little brother. All were sleeping peacefully. Tears started welling up. I was safe. At last, I had found my family. I was home. I walked carefully over the other women and children, trying not to step on anyone or wake them. It was a rush of relief when I finally reached my loved ones. Quietly, I found a spot and sat down next to Mom and hugged her. Mom opened her eyes and gave me a gentle smile. It was only then that I let the merciful sea rock me to sleep in the safe presence of my mom.

The First Few Days at Sea

In the Vietnamese Communist society, there was no real news. The only "news" we had was propaganda for the state, usually broadcast through radio and television. It wasn't enough to severely limit our access to news; it was strictly forbidden by the government. Listening to any news from the outside world was an offense to the government, and anyone who listened would be jailed if caught. Still, this didn't stop people from trying. The information was far too valuable and important not to be listened to.

For months, every night whenever Dad was home from travelling for the boat project, he would go alone up to the third-floor bedroom and quietly tune in to BBC on a little radio to listen to the refugee conditions and updates. The news said that humanitarian ships were out there looking to help refugees, that all we had to do was make it out to sea, past the coast guards. My parents had strategized and schemed for months about how to hide our possessions from the communist officials. It occurred to me that we were now away from Vietnam, that we had actually escaped and were all okay. It seemed our preparations had paid off. We were safe. There was comfort in that, even if the rest of the ride was not very comfortable. There were no more guards to sneak past, no one to report us to the authorities. Hope was high that we would be saved, if only we could find an international ship to rescue us.

In the course of a day, we had sailed several hundred miles into the Gulf of Thailand, entering international waters. Under the morning sun, people came alive. They took turns standing up and stretching after spending the night curled up in fear. There were so many people trying to stretch and lean on one side of the boat that the boat became unstable. You could hear the shouts, "Sit down! The boat is tilting! People sit down!" It'd be tragic if we'd made it this far and our journey ended with being capsized!

To pass the time, we made small talk with a nearby family. There was an elderly lady, along with her daughter and two small grandchildren. In talking with them, we were surprised to learn that they were Vietnamese citizens who had fake Chinese documents, rather than being people of Chinese descent living in Vietnam. Their fake documents allowed them to register to be on the boat. Even though they were welcome to stay in their country, they too wanted to leave. Such oppression was not good for anyone. While we were talking, I noticed the head of their household wasn't around. Maybe he was somewhere else on the boat, like how our family was separated.

Later into the day, news arrived that we had our first casualty. Sometime during the night, an older woman had fallen ill and then died. From the corner of my eye, I could see her family holding her body, crying. Death was different on the boat. On land, there might have been a Buddhist celebration. There would have been monks to guard the casket, children and adults crying, everyone dressed in the mourning color of white. It was traditional to mourn for 49 days, wearing something white for that time and then changing to black when the 49 days passed, to show there had been a death in the family. On our boat, there was no ceremony. There were no monks, there were no rituals to honor her life—the only option they had was to say their final goodbyes and toss her into the ocean. We had all been experiencing the heat, the crowd, and the rocking of the sea, but it was sobering to face the reality that not all would survive.

Even though there were dreary stretches, there were exciting moments too. For a while, a group of dolphins swam alongside us. I had never seen them so close before. We were far away from land now, and their presence in this seemingly endless ocean was more than welcome. They leapt through the waters, swimming along beside us. It felt like a sign of hope after such a dismal afternoon.

Sometime in the early evening, the sound of a newborn's cries flooded the boat. It was almost poetic—just like how the woman had died, our old life had ended, and with the birth of this baby, our new one was beginning. My family was Buddhist and we were taught to believe in reincarnation. Was it possible the old lady had been reborn as this precious baby? The tiny little girl had a new world and life ahead. What would her future hold? Where would she call her home? If someone asked where she was born, would she say, "The international waters in the Gulf of Thailand?" For me, I knew what I was leaving behind, but for this young baby, would she ever know where she was from?

The sun was setting on our first full day out at sea. Aside from some passing news and a few conversations, the energy level was down to minimum. Somehow, I managed to stay with my family for the rest of the day. I was thankful no one shooed me back to the lower deck.

Dad poked his head outside the cabin occasionally to check on us. A small amount of oatmeal rations had been distributed in the early evening, and we were told to be careful, and not to waste anything. We didn't know how long the trip would last. Even with the food, people only ate and drank a little. Motion sickness started to affect us all. Most were more sick than hungry, and no one wanted to step on people to go to the back of the boat for the bathroom. I was somewhat lethargic, so were my sisters and brother. Mom was the only one who was alert. Ever resourceful, she had been sucking on dried ginseng roots that she brought along. She knew the caffeine would provide her enough energy for at least a few days on board.

We were heading south into the entrance of the South China Sea. The ocean was still relatively calm as was usual in early May. Every so often, we got a strong gust of wind, but for the most part, it was very calm. It was sunny most days, which meant lots of heat, but thankfully, there had not been any downpours. Mom took out a light blanket and made a tent to cover us. It had only been a day or two, but people were getting restless. Clusters of people in the same faith started chanting prayers, hoping and praying that someone in a big ship somewhere would see us and rescue us. One man hung a big piece of cloth with S.O.S. written in red paint high on a pole.

On the morning of the third day, a lady sitting at the far end of the bow of the boat spotted a large ship in the distance. She screamed so loudly that she woke up half the boat up. We were excited. Could this be our chance? Our boat sped toward it. We were sure that big ships were lined up just waiting to rescue us, and with a boat of that size, this had to be one of them! But as we neared, it became clear that we were chasing after a fishing boat. The boat was twice the size of ours, but only had fishermen onboard. When our boats bumped together, there was a loud thump, and in that instance, we knew, these were not our saviors. They may not even be fishermen. Instead of kindness and concern, we felt a strange hostility when our boats met.

A second later, half a dozen men jumped into our boat with guns and knives in their hands. They were barbaric. Some were shirtless with tattoos on their bodies while others wore torn T-shirts. Almost all of them had bandanas on their heads, eager to show their power. Before a word was exchanged, one of the men walked right up to a woman and snatched her gold necklace. We were wide-eyed in shock. These were no ordinary fishermen. These were pirates!

They waved their weapons and a man who looked to be in charge shouted. Even though he spoke in Thai, the message was clear. "Everyone sits, or we will shoot!"

A blanket of fear and panic spread throughout the boat. People were frantic. Children and women were screaming and crying. The pirates walked among us, quickly taking anything that looked valuable, and anything else that was left in plain sight. There were so many of us that they had to call for more men to help scour the boat. By the end, they had so much gold and jewelry in their buckets, it looked like a hostile church collection.

The raid lasted several hours, and they left as quickly as they came. Since they were targeting unarmed refugees, the robbery was nearly effortless. It was easy to prey on the weak and vulnerable, and more rewarding than fishing. I don't think they felt bad for a second looting people's lifelong savings. Though we had been prepared to hide our valuables from the government, nothing had prepared us for this.

Piracy targeting refugees in these waters was not noticed by Dad on his BBC listening. It wasn't a thought that crossed my parents' minds when we were preparing for the journey. I later learned that these pirates were mostly opportunistic fishermen who took advantage of passing ships, and that our boat was not the only one to be plundered. As more and more refugees took the sea as their escape route into the Gulf of Thailand, the situation became more lucrative for these fishermen pirates and more severe for the refugees. This became such a problem that it was given international attention by the early 80's. Piracy was an international crime, and the fishermen who robbed us were rushing because they were afraid of being caught by the international ships.

When it was over, people had time to catch their breath and consider their fate. Sure, we were robbed but everyone was unharmed. Half of the water and food were destroyed, but we still had enough for at least a few more days. We were glad it was over, and never imagined it could happen again.

Later that same afternoon, still licking our wounds, we saw another ship approaching. Our second assault. Unlike the first group, they approached us. We didn't make the same mistake of thinking they would rescue us, but they were faster to pursue than we were to escape. Just like the previous group, they too stormed our boat, but people had grown wiser. We hid what was left of our jewelry in secret compartments on the boat or in inconspicuous places on our bodies. Nothing was left in plain sight. There were fewer pirates on this boat, and they had to look harder to find valuables. They also spoke in Thai, and though none of us could understand their shouting, their tone was the same. Their words were malicious, loud and rushed.

During the search, an older pirate who appeared to be the leader instructed the younger ones to empty out suspicious water and dried food containers to look for hidden jewelry. Though most of it passed in a blur, there were two moments that I vividly remember.

In our bag of belongings, there were a few pure gold spoons and forks plated in silver. Mom had commissioned a jeweler to make them before we left, thinking it was a great way to camouflage the real gold utensils with the fakes to hide them from the local officers. As clever as my mom was, these pirates were experienced. They tested the silverware pieces by bending them. The head pirate broke into a foul grin when the silverware gave easily in his grip. "Jackpot!"

While rummaging through the bags, they also noticed the small, red plastic potty pot. On the boat, whenever anyone had to "use the bathroom," they would sit on the edge of the boat and release it into the ocean. For my little brother Nam, too young for that, my mom had brought a small potty pot for him. She would put a bag over it for him to poop in. After the last round of pirates, Mom buried a few gold rings in the potty using Nam's poop to hide the jewelry. They took the spoon and picked around the stool and saw the gold rings peeking through. Another win for them! The pirates seemed to enjoy scavenger hunting by the way they looked at us, had a big grin and then laughed out loud when they got a great find.

They were so busy searching the bags and containers that they didn't search me. The gold ring and necklace on my body were safe. We were huddled together, letting them take whatever they found. We just hoped that we could salvage whatever food was left after they had ransacked us.

I heard Dad and a few men whispering back and forth in Chinese, "We have so many more men than they do. Should we fight back?"

"I think we could take them, but what if people in their boat call for backup?"

"They have guns and we have children and women! It's too risky a move. What if they get angry and shoot our children or women?"

"Maybe it's not worth it. Just let them take what they want."

Though we only saw the middle-aged leader holding a gun, the rest were holding various types of knives. The owners of our boat decided we wouldn't do anything to aggravate them, thinking it would be better to let them take what they wanted than to have them shooting the boat or harming our people.

The fishing boat pulled out before the sunlight disappeared. As soon as the boat was out of sight, people scrambled to see if the pirates missed anything. They tried to salvage whatever food or drink they found on the floor. Mom passed her last small jar of water and let us take turns wetting our lips. A dried plum was passed to my sisters and me. The thought that the pirates had cleaned out people's life savings was not as painful as watching them ravaging our food supplies.

Everyone was exhausted. Between the search, the sun, the sea motion, and the fear of being harmed, the need to be on high alert was constant. There was no rest. For the past two days, we had not been able to keep down anything in our stomachs due to motion sickness. We were weak, hungry, and the foul stench of vomit in the boat made me feel more nauseous. I covered my mouth to hold down the bile that was pushing up and feeling like acid in my throat.

The heat, the blistering sun and the wind added more pain to the injuries. We cared little about gold that we couldn't eat. Jewelry and money at the time was meaningless. We were just grateful that the pirates did not harm us. We thanked God there was no violent storm, that the sea was only doing its slow tango with the waves. Darkness once again gave us some temporary peaceful, quiet time to huddle with our loved ones. The millions of magnificent bright stars once again soothed our spirits. In spite of everything that occurred, under the starry sky, we prayed and hoped.

The Unforgettable Memories

In my dream, Mom was peeling an orange. I held my hand out to receive a juicy orange slice, only to open my eyes and find there was no orange at all—only wet, stale air. My youngest sister, Que, who was a happy child with a bright smile most days, cried herself to sleep. For the last few days, she had been cranky and agitated, kicking everyone who sat next to her. We knew the trip would be hard, but no one ever imagined the conditions to be this dire. Seeing my younger sister suffer made me realize how truly far we were from home. When we set out for the new world, no one ever thought there would be this many tears shed along the way.

Sitting a few meters away, there were several women moaning and groaning about the trip. They were begging the men in the cabin to return to Vietnam, even if this meant imprisonment. They would rather die on the land we'd escaped from than rot on this boat. Thankfully, they were in the minority. The men decided we would persist and move on, despite the dangers and everything that had happened.

Four days in, and we were still not any closer to land or any other boats than we were before. During this time, Mom was as steady as a rock. While it was hot during the day, she was hand-fanning all of us non-stop, one after the other. Had she gotten any sleep at all? Whenever I was awake, I noticed she was also awake. She had to stay alert to care for all of us. Mom also had been helping by scraping (*gua sha*) people around her to help relieve their headaches and motion sickness, and she had been chewing on dried ginseng. It must have worked amazingly, since she managed to stay awake through it all. Or was it simply her mother's instinct?

We were able to have one day of peace before we heard the loud horn in the distance. I squinted my eyes to try and see beyond the sunlight. No! Not again! Coming closer, there were two bigger boats approaching ours from either side. Soon enough, there was the clunking sound of the boats bumping against ours. I prayed. *Please don't let it be more pirates.* Maybe these were international ships coming to rescue us? I closed my eyes, hoping that this time it would be different, even though the situation was becoming all too familiar. In the middle of the ocean, our boat had been sandwiched. We were trapped.

After being under siege twice already, there wasn't that much left to steal. The other groups had taken most of our jewelry and food, but that didn't stop this third wave of pirates from spilling out of the boats into ours. They too, like the pirates before, pointed guns to our faces, and screamed. As if to distinguish themselves, they began rounding people up. I stooped down and quickly slipped the gold ring off my finger and put it under my tongue, hoping that would be a more secure place for it. My gold necklace was still buried safely under the many layers of my shirts. They missed it in the first two rounds, maybe they would miss it again. Amidst the chaos, I found myself with several others my age from the lower deck. Together, we were forced to transfer onto their pirate ship, leaving our families behind.

We were separated. Mom, Phan, Que and little Nam were cornered in our boat with the other young children and the elder women. In my periphery I saw Dad and my brother, Viet, and my cousin, Cao, walk from the cabin as they were forced to climb into the other ship on the right. Just like that, my world was shattering. At this moment, my family had been divided in three directions, on three different boats. My heart was beating so fast, there was a sharp pain in my chest. It was the same feeling I experienced when my parents fought, and when Dad lost his temper with Mom or with us. This time, however, the intensity was much worse. My stomach tightened up in a knot. What if they took me to a remote island, and I never saw my family again? What if they rape me? Or kill me? What will happen to my brothers and sisters? Though I tried to keep it under control, I was hyperventilating and starting to get dizzy.

On my boat, there were about a hundred of us. We were all women, girls—the easy targets. They lined us up to be individually searched. I was trembling by the guardrail of the boat, leaning on it when I heard a loud scream from a woman in the far end of the boat. She was being strip-searched from head to toe. I choked with fear, holding tight to the guardrail, looking down at the ocean. It was only four feet away. *If they lay a finger on me, I will jump.* I would rather die than let them humiliate me like that.

During the rampage, a boy who looked to be 12 years old walked toward me with a screwdriver in his hand. I was amazed. He was about my height, but I knew he was young because his voice hadn't changed yet. It struck me as so incongruent, his child voice and his menacing facial expression. Even though he was so young, he was highly aggressive. He shouted something in Thai that I did not understand, and after growing impatient, he slapped me, motioning for me to open my mouth. At first, I thought of swallowing the ring, but I was afraid I would choke. I opened my mouth and he took the ring, then angrily, he slapped me again.

He also found my gold necklace and yanked it from my neck. I froze in fear. I was paralyzed, and relieved as he walked away. I mentally apologized to my mom. "Sorry, Mom. Two out of the three things you gave me are now gone." The only valuable thing left on me was a hundred-dollar bill sewn under the patch on my shirt. My jaw was clenched from the fear, but I was grateful he didn't make me take off my clothes.

It seemed that these pirates were all part of the same family. From kids to adults, they were all out to loot us. To my surprise, there was one kind, older pirate who walked around with a container of water, who would randomly let us drink from it. He must have been the grandfather. When he came to me, I took a big sip and thanked him with my eyes. He looked at me as if he understood our pain, as if he wanted to make up for the horrible things his children had done to us.

By some miracle, Dad was spared from the pirates. They searched everyone that was on the other boat with him, but no one laid a hand on Dad. He was untouched. It was peculiar that they somehow missed him, and my Dad strongly believed that the amulet paper in his shirt pocket that he obtained from a Buddhist temple had protected him from the searches. However, all the gold that Mom disguised outside our bodies had been taken, except the diamonds embedded inside her molars and the gold leaves in my dad's leather belt. The gold hooks sewn in our pants and the American dollars under the embroidery patches in our shirts were still intact. Thank God for Mom's ingenious preparations. We still had a few valuable possessions to survive on in the refugee camp, if we ever got there.

When the search was over, they let us go back to our boat. It was in complete disarray from the ransack. All our bags had been dumped out and rummaged through. After this third attack, there was barely anything left to eat or drink. As horrible as it was that our boat was repeatedly raided by pirates, our story was nothing compared to the stories we later learned from others in the refugee camps. There were other boats whose women were raped repeatedly by the pirates in front of their husbands. When the husbands did fight back, they were killed in front of their wives. We learned of the tragic story about Mrs. Huang, the neighbor who had lived across the street from our house next to Grandma. Of her three daughters, two of them were raped, and one fell over the boat and drowned. Other refugees told stories of how their boat drifted to an uninhabited island where disease caused them to lose their hair and teeth. Before those survivors could be rescued, their starvation led them to become cannibals. News was often just horrifying.

We later heard that my cousin, Thang Gia, and his wife, Thang Hoa and four younger siblings from Uncle Thien Sanh also fled the country a few months after us. Their small boat was only carrying 27 people. They floated aimlessly, surviving pirates and big waves, coming close to death several times for 30 days in the vast sea. Thang Gia's wife, who was eight months pregnant, almost lost the baby as she suffered from hunger. Fortunately, they were rescued by a Belgium merchant boat. After staying at a refugee camp in Singapore, they were able to become citizens of Belgium.

But not everyone was that lucky. My dad's partner, Mr. Lam, sent the older six of his 12 children to escape with a reputable family friend, only to learn that the boat sank, and all 312 people drowned and died. Before we heard that their ship sank, one of his older sons, Phuoc, who was close to my dad, appeared in my dad's dream to show him that he was submerged under the sea. It was a horrid dream that made my dad cry. A chill ran down my spine when his death was confirmed after Dad's dream. For Mr. Lam, all his hopes and dreams were plunged into the deep sea along with his six children. He was so furious with God that he kicked the Buddha shrine over and over and almost went insane.

Thousands of similar tragic untold stories like these were lost to the sea. We considered ourselves lucky. We were so grateful that the pirates did not shoot the men nor kidnap the women. There was ruthless pillaging and brutality, but they did not kill anyone, or toss anyone overboard.

When we were all reunited back on our boat after hours of rummaging, I was so joyful to be back with my family that I cried. I vowed not to take my parents for granted and I hugged my little siblings so tightly, I almost crushed them. They, too, were happy to see me. That afternoon, we encountered one more fisherman ship, but after pulling closer, they could see we had already been badly battered, and decided that we weren't worth it. We were tired, weak and desperate. Some women were begging them for water, and these men were nice enough to give some people diluted congee, a porridge broth made from rice. We devoured what little they gave before they took off.

Rejection from Malaysia

On the fifth day, we felt the boat had gone far enough to the south through the Gulf of Thailand and we correctly guessed that we had made it to the South China Sea. There was real hope on the horizon as we could see a silhouette that looked to be land. We were elated at the sight. With little fuel remaining, our boat charged toward the mountain we believed to be Malaysia.

As we approached the beach of the remote island, a Malaysian naval patrol boat came out to meet us. There were no other people in sight, just the desolate beach and the endless expanse of forest behind it. The guards signaled to anchor our boat at a distance. We were all anxious and excited as we waited to be accepted to the Malaysians' refugee camp. Several young people who were good swimmers took the wait as an opportunity to jump into the ocean to cool off. I wished I was strong enough to take a dip in the water, but I was too weak and too scared to be in that deep water. In the distance, I heard my Dad's voice. "What do you mean, we can't come in?"

He was conversing with an English-speaking interpreter, trying to negotiate with the Malaysian Coast Guards. When that didn't work, he tried begging and bribing. There was shouting from the guard and pleading from the interpreter. The interpreter then turned to my dad with wide eyes. "The refugee camp is on another island, but it's overcrowded! They said we have to go back!"

"Go back where? To the ocean to die?" my dad asked.

"I don't know! I am just repeating what they said!"

"Did they ask about money?" Dad was used to being able to buy his way out, trained well from a corrupted society. He was eager to look for a solution, and even though we were raided four times, Dad knew he still could gather from people enough hidden gold, jewelry, or American dollars if we needed to as a last resort.

"No. They don't want money. They just want us to leave. We are not welcome." The man shook his head, bitter disappointment in his voice.

The boat owners and my dad contemplated wrecking the boat so they would have no choice but to accept us, but the risks outweighed the benefits. We had over 500 traumatized people on board, and we were miles from shore. If we wrecked the boat and they still chose not to accept us, then we would truly have no place to go. Not to mention everyone on board was feeling tired and weak, and half of them were children, women, or elders. We were miles from the shore, and we couldn't just jump into the water and swim to the beach.

A few hours had passed, and there hadn't been much change with our situation. We were still in the ocean, miles from the shore, hoping to be accepted, and the Malaysian navy was still refusing. They were growing impatient that we had not moved on. They wanted to be rid of us.

By the afternoon, the navy boat approached us and told us to pull up the anchor. I couldn't hear the conversation, but it was obvious that the captain of the navy ship was very upset. He was pointing his finger and screaming loudly in Malaysian. His face was stern, and he said something to another guard nearby, then walked away. The Malaysian guards came back and tied a giant rope from their boat to ours. We were ecstatic, thinking they had changed their minds. We had made it! Our wait was over, and we were going to be accepted after all. The bliss quickly turned bitter when we realized their true intentions.

Their boat started moving faster and faster, but instead of pulling us to shore, they were pulling us out to sea. We were flying like a jet ski, bouncing on the waves as if we were weightless. People were screaming, afraid that they would fall out, or that we would capsize and drown, even though we had made it this far. This went on for hours, the rope taught, and the Malaysian boat speeding towards the horizon. Water splashed everywhere, everyone was soaked, and the wind cut strongly into our faces. Fear overtook the incredulity.

"We have to do something!" the men shouted. "We're going to die if we don't cut the rope!" It seemed our death was imminent. We could die if we stayed attached, but we could also die if we cut ourselves loose and set ourselves adrift in the middle of the ocean. The fear of death was our constant companion as we struggled with what to do next. Our hearts were pounding. But then it was like someone put on the brakes. I have no idea what happened or how the rope was detached, but one moment we were speeding and the next we were not. The men in our boat did it. We didn't capsize! We were all intact! Suddenly, we were free again. We had survived the Malaysian soldiers' attempted slaughter. What did they have against refugees? They didn't hesitate before towing 500 people out to the open sea at high speed. They were trying to kill us. That act was inhumane and brutally heartless. Where else could we go?

At that moment, we felt truly desperate. We had been violated again and again by fishermen-turned-pirates, and now we'd been coldly rejected by the people we thought would save us. People on the boat were huddled together, sobbing. We had no food, no water, and no strength. The boat engine kicked on again with a low rumble. Fuel was running low. How could this have happened? How could we go so far, only to be tossed back out to sea? If there was a God, I couldn't feel him. Why had He allowed such cruelty to happen to these innocent people who were forced to flee their countries? I turned to my mom who had been so strong and brave for so long. "Mom, are we going to die on this boat?"

Tears welled up in her eyes and she pulled her arms out from holding Nam and gave me a hug. After days of hunger and sleeplessness, the ginseng supply was gone, and Mom was on the verge of passing out. She revived a little when Dad found her some liquid. I don't know where he got the broth from, but he only had a little bit for Mom and for Nam. He knew she needed the strength to care for his flock. Viet was with Dad and I hoped he still had scraps of food left in the cabin to share with his son. I laid on the boat floor with Phan and Que, drifting in and out of consciousness. Little Nam, who had collapsed into sleep, lay limp against Mom's chest. He was tormented from sea sickness, dehydration, and starvation.

My lips and throat parched, my relentless thirst compelled me to act, to try something, anything. In a zombie-state, I grabbed a mug, crawled over people and slowly inched toward the edge of the boat. I laid flat on my chest on the boat and lowered my arm over the edge, reaching to scoop some sea water. In my mind, even the saltwater could stop the scorching thirst. Phan and Que crawled after me. At the edge, they waited for me to give them what was in that mug. I added some sugar that Mom brought along with us to the sea water. Thinking that would help reduce the saltiness. I gave them a sip and took one myself. We all gagged from the incredible, undrinkable liquid. It was impossible to swallow the saline sea water, no matter how little the sip was and no matter how thirsty we were. Frustrated, I splashed the rest of the water to cool our faces instead and to wet both of our blistering lips. The irony was cruel: we were surrounded by an enormous amount of water that we could not drink.

The conditions of the rest of the boat and its people were dismal. The stench was sickening. People were crying, moaning, and praying. Others were complaining that we should have risked jumping off the boat. One woman lost it and shouted that she and her family should not have left, that it would have been better to be oppressed under the barbaric communists than die without a grave in the deep ocean. She wasn't alone in her opinion. There were other people who were silent, and God knows what kind of regrets or thoughts they had in their heads. The commotion died down after a while, as the last shred of light disappeared beyond the horizon. The boat was once more drifting aimlessly into the night. Whatever our fate was, it was in God's hands now. We were orphans of the world, with no voice, no country, no rights.

At the time, I thought they were heartless and cruel for pushing our boat back to sea. I did not understand that Malaysia couldn't be totally blamed for rejecting us. The truth was, the mass exodus of Vietnamese "boat people" had flooded their country and other neighboring areas like Malaysia, Indonesia, Thailand, Hong Kong, the Philippines, and Singapore. By 1978 and '79, the number of refugees had escalated dramatically, and the influx of people had created disastrous problems for their countries.

Southeast Asian countries were left to deal with the problem on their own. And many of them felt they had no obligation to help those refugees who kept showing up. There was little help from the U.N. and no clear help from any country to grant the refugees asylum or temporary refuge settlements. The overwhelming demand for help led to frustration and finally such a furious response that began the boat push-backs. It was the only strong message to warn other boats, even if it meant refugees perishing at sea as the result.

It was our sixth day on the boat when we woke up under a quiet overcast sky. The waves were a little stronger but not too scary. Thankfully, the typhoon season that was about to start had been delayed somehow. We were hoping for some light rain to quench our thirst but also hoped there wouldn't be a strong wind, or a huge downpour. We didn't want to be soaked.

By now, people were used to the rocking movements of the boat. It was calming, quiet, and peaceful. Today, something was different. It was too quiet. It was then we realized that there was no sound from the engine. We still had some fuel left but the exhausted engine had given up on us. Could it be any worse? Maybe it was for the best, since we had no compass to guide us and the sun was in hiding. What good was it to keep moving with no sense of destination? We were stranded somewhere in the vast South China Sea, with nowhere to go and our hope waning.

Our fears of the angry sea and rogue storms surging were assuaged as the day carried on. That day, there was a light breeze and a light drizzle of rain. I told my sisters to open their mouths and get water from the sky. Mom was busy finding clean containers to collect the rain drops. It didn't pour, only sprinkled, but it was enough to get us through for a little longer. Suddenly revived, I could hear people mumbling chants of Buddhist prayers. Another small group of families prayed quietly with their rosaries. The sound of Our Father and Hail Mary coupled with the chanting, along with the rocking rhythm of the boat, calmed everyone and it felt like the rain had washed away our fears and left us with peace.

Though we had no one person in charge and no one really knew what to do, we had the sense that we were all in this together and that there was an underlying group will to survive. Without radio connection to the outside world, no one would know what became of us should we perish at sea. With the engine now broken, the ocean could easily become the burial place for 502 souls, including a tiny baby who was just born a few days before. Time stood still as nightfall covered the sky. We clung to each other and in our drowsiness, we prayed that a miracle would happen, or that our deaths would be quick and easy. Whatever our fate, we had no choice but to accept it.

Saved by Grace

The next morning, we were greeted with the most beautiful sight. Our prayers must have reached God's ears. In the middle of the ocean, we were met with a giant floating device. An offshore oil rig! We had found our lifeline. It felt like a dream, a God-sent miracle. Just as we had seen them, they had also spotted us. They sent a few men in a small boat out to meet us and to check on our condition. For once, we were greeted with kindness. These were no pirates out to steal everything we had. We begged them to rescue us, take us back to whatever country they belonged to. They shared their concern and said they could only help us fix the engine and provide us with some food and water.

Sure enough, a few big hoses were passed over to our boat and glorious streams of water started flowing through them. We took turns drinking and filling up whatever containers we could find in the boat. I almost drowned myself with great gulps of the water straight from the hose. After so many days of dehydration, it was amazing to see everyone revived and alive again.

Saltine crackers never tasted so delicious. A few hours later, when our thirst was quenched and our stomachs filled, they gave us a compass and pointed us to the nearest refugee camp in Indonesia. Words could not describe the liveliness of the people in the boat. Indonesia, a place that I'd never heard of, had become my new fantasy. In my head, it was an island paradise with lush greenery and kind people who would welcome us destitute refugees. We were uplifted and hope was restored.

We headed toward one of the nearby Anambas Islands of Indonesia. The Anambas Islands are a small archipelago clustered in the South China Sea east of the Malay Peninsula and north-east of Singapore. Letung is one of those many islands.

On the evening of May 9, 1979, nearly a week after our departure, we docked in front of Letung, waiting impatiently and anxiously for the local Indonesian government to accept us onto their island. Hours and hours passed by. Dad had to keep asking people to chip in from what was left of their hidden gold and jewelry to bribe the local officers. Remembering the previous treatment from the Malaysians, the organizers decided that we would do whatever it took not to be towed or thrown out to the sea, even if we had to offer our boat completely for them to take us in. Unbeknownst to us, Dad had been controlling a small leaking hole at the hull of the boat. There was no need to add panic to the dire situation, but if need be, we could always make that hole bigger. Desperation and determination would decide everything.

The local authority of Letung was far more reasonable than the Malaysian officers. Although they didn't show many friendly gestures, they weren't shouting or pointing hostile fingers to the ocean. It was a huge relief.

Onboard, everyone was anxiously waiting to be accepted by the Indonesian government. We all knew that how hard those officers worked depended on the size of the bribery. Hope was higher than ever before that we would be saved. Dad stopped by and told us to gather our stuff and strength, to prepare to get off the boat. He said that final negotiations were happening, and he would make an announcement to everyone as soon as he heard the news. No one could contain their excitement. They took turns standing up to stretch and gaze out at the lights of the houses on Letung Island as the sky changed to dusk.

Soon enough, word spread from the organizers and from Dad that we had permission to dock at the pier and that we should form an orderly line to get off the boat. We were thrilled with relief. We had finally made it! As exciting as it was to be free, the actual process of getting off the boat was hectic and tiresome. It took almost as long to get off the boat as it did to get on a week prior. The difference was that we had fewer belongings, the mood was a lot less somber, and the people were less orderly now. It was chaos as people were trying to find their loved ones and reclaim their possessions. The boat was in complete disarray from the pirate raids and everything else we had been through.

After a week, Dad and Viet were finally reunited with us from the cabin. No matter how weak we were, all of us carried something in their hands except little Nam. Mom held Nam as I lined up my siblings, Viet, Phan and Que. We were anxious as we waited to get off the boat and into a new world of mystery. Though each day had been an adventure, no one had any idea of what tomorrow would bring. Not even Dad, our family's brave leader.

After sharing my dad with the entire boat for seven days, I was glad he was back by our side. His job concluded when the boat was safely docked at the pier of Letung. After one whole year of plotting the escape, he had done it. Dad had been a part of every step and scheme, from getting funding to building the boat, to then paying for the use of the port from local authorities in the rural town of Rach Gia. In this massive plan, Dad had his hand in every aspect, including the logistics of supplies for everyone like food and water. He personally worked with every authority necessary as well as the boat captain. Dad was a general in this battle, an unsung hero who delivered the promise to the people in this boat. I was so proud of Dad, and even more so when he kept his humility. He never boasted about how much he had done to bring this high-risk journey to its successful end. We were so thankful, and so relieved when our feet could finally touch the ground after seven days at sea.

It was finally starting to feel real to us. We were safe! We were out of Vietnam and into a world of the unknown. By some miracle, all seven of us, plus six cousins and two friends, were intact. Somewhere off the boat, a baby was starting a brand-new life, without any physical attachment to the Vietnam soil. While her parents were struggling to sustain her needs to survive, another family was tormented with guilt that they had not been able to have a proper mourning for the loss of a grandma. Given this harrowing voyage, it is remarkable that the older woman was the only victim to die. Despite the many torturous events, we felt very fortunate. That chapter was over, and we were optimistic about what may lie ahead. We would soon learn the real meaning of going into *uncharted territory*.

5

Letung Island

The First Island

After a week of enduring extreme challenges, one after another since we escaped from Vietnam in our small boat, we took our first wobbly steps onto dry land at the little town of Letung on an island in Indonesia.

It had taken several hours to finally get permission to leave the boat. It was late. We had been sitting, cramped together for so long that it took a while for our stiff and weakened bodies to comply with our fervent desire to leave the boat that had been both our savior and our worst nightmare. As we stood up to leave, we stumbled, holding on to each other. Some were too weak to walk straight, and some of the elderly had to be carried off the boat by the men. It took a surprisingly long time for all 500 of us to disembark. People shuffled together, fumbling with their stuff on the gangplank heading towards the narrow cement street connected to the pier. Gradually, our sea of humanity spilled into the town of Letung. We congregated together awaiting orders.

Letung was a small fishing village on one of the Anambas Islands in the Riau Archipelago between Malaysia, Singapore, and Indonesia. A single, long pier led to a cement road lined with small shops, residential houses, and grocery stores. The road was wide for walking, but there were no cars or motorized vehicles. We followed the road inland towards the foot of the mountains to the market square, a large plaza with a sandy floor where trading took place.

In the distance, small wooden houses appeared on the foothills and along the beach. The village was totally silent, except for the soothing rhythm of the waves. I felt like we had traveled back in time to a simpler place, untouched by modern civilization. Many of the houses in Letung were built on stilts alongside the beach, but on a rise in the distance was a large yellow mansion that belonged to the governor of the island.

An almost full moon surrounded by millions of twinkling stars shone brightly to add to the serenity of this peaceful village. If I were a tourist, this would be a great sanctuary for a vacation away from the hustle and bustle of the world. Except for the soft light of oil lamps, the village was sheltered in darkness.

Modern-day Letung village

The town had been awakened by our arrival and some curious residents came out to greet us. Among these Indonesian villagers was a man named Rahmad. He had been listening to us talking and approached Dad, greeting him in Chinese. We were astonished and overjoyed to meet another Chinese person on this little island. We felt like we had discovered a long lost relative. Sharing a common language and heritage made us instantly trust him. We were surprised to find that he was of Chinese descent because his skin was quite dark. His dad was half-Chinese and his Chinese mom spoke Hokkien, a Chinese dialect from Fujian which was very close to our Tewcheo dialect. (I later surmised he was half-Iraqi.)

He extended a warm welcome to us and we were eager to meet his family. We quickly discovered that his Chinese was limited, but we could see the friendliness in his eyes and body language and didn't mind trying to interpret his gestures.

Like many overseas Chinese entrepreneurs, Rahmad's family owned a grocery store located on the main street connected to the Letung pier. He invited our family and several other families to stay on the deck of his home facing the ocean. We greatly appreciated this offer and formed a small parade to follow him to his house.

Our family, cousins, and friends stayed on the open deck behind the kitchen. We plopped our bags down and used them as pillows. Then, we covered ourselves with a few of the military blankets we had brought along and made ourselves comfortable. I looked up at the same giant, dark sky filled with twinkling stars that accompanied us for the past six nights, but tonight it was completely different! The heavens felt close and comforting instead of reflecting a vast and dangerous ocean. We had reached a safe haven on this tiny island, no longer subject to the unpredictable temperament of the sea and the cruelty of pirates.

I was as mesmerized by the beauty of the Milky Way galaxy as I had been a week earlier when I came up from the lower deck of the boat and saw it for the first time. Being a city girl, I had never before witnessed the infinite midnight blue sky with its twinkling stars and band of soft "milky" light. I suddenly became nostalgic and sad, knowing that I was no longer a citizen of my place of birth. The home where my family and I had *belonged* was no longer a part of my life. The old Vietnam where Phan and I slept together in the second-floor loft was no more. In my mind I pictured the third-floor balcony where I hung clothes out to dry and would look down and observe the activities on the street below. The alleys we cut through to save time and the house I grew up in would only live in my memories now. It was disturbing.

Yet I felt hopeful. My reminiscing gave way to a huge sense of relief that we had made it here alive! The bright stars were the faith we clung to on those dark nights. Right now, the whispering sound of the waves softly crashing to the shore and their tranquil rhythm relaxed me. I couldn't believe we had successfully crossed the ocean. Tonight, we again lay on a hardwood floor, as we had on our boat, but now we would all have a peaceful night of rest. I let go of my worries and imagined a bright future of freedom, our family's dream come true.

First Employment

The residents on this island clearly had more compassion for us than had their Malaysian neighbors. Of course, there were some corrupt officials who demanded gold, but the local folks simply appeared to be curious about the new arrivals. Most of them had never been to Vietnam and they were just as inquisitive about us as we were about them. The population in Letung was probably no more than a few hundred households and a handful of them were of Chinese descent. When our boat reached their beach, I think we doubled the island's population. We heard that several other boats had come before us and their passengers were relocated to the remote islands of Kuku and Air Raya. They were expecting to see more "boat people" arriving from Vietnam before the monsoon season.

By the summer of 1979, the Anambas Islands received an influx of over 35,000 people. Refugees were not supposed to mix with local islanders, so the Indonesian government distributed them to five nearby remote islands. Fresh water was available from streams and some refugees dug wells. Local resources, such as palm leaves and wood from the jungle, were used for building huts and cooking.

Of the five islands, Kuku and Air Raya were about an hour away from Letung by boat. The Indonesian government put 12,000 refugees on each island. I heard that there were more people on the other three islands, but reliable information was hard to get. Before this refugee crisis, these remote islands were uninhabited. They were beautiful but undeveloped, and only accessible by boat. The people from our boat were supposed to be relocated to Air Raya camp in the next few days, unless you had money. Anyone who could afford to rent rooms from the Letung villagers, or work in exchange for room and board, could stay.

My dad decided to look for a place to rent to avoid the Air Raya camp. He had heard that flies, insects, and unclean water caused many there to get sick with malaria and diarrhea. It was a harsh environment and Dad was determined to do whatever he could to keep his family safe.

Dad spoke with Rahmad and his mother to see if they would be willing to help. In Chinese tradition, we never called an adult by their name—everyone was aunt, uncle, great aunt, great uncle, or other familial title—so out of respect, we called Rahmad's mother "Grandma". She was adorable and she spoke Hokkien with us. Grandpa was less enthusiastic about connecting with us, only nodding occasionally. He was quite frail. Rahmad's wife was quiet and his daughter, Heang, was a cheerful teenager. They seemed eager to help. Rahmad introduced Dad to his Indonesian neighbor who was willing to rent us their front porch which would be available soon.

This influx of refugees had created an economic boom on the island. New grocery stores and shops prospered, and it was a profitable period for the residents. Rahmad needed a helper to sell dry goods at his grocery store to serve both Chinese and Vietnamese customers. I was a perfect fit for this job as I spoke several Chinese dialects as well as Vietnamese. The deal was that I would work at his grocery store in exchange for three meals each day and temporary housing for my family on the back deck of Rahmad's house until we could move to the new rental place.

They put me to work right away. It was difficult because I was still recovering from our ordeal on the boat and my legs were still adjusting to walking on solid ground. I was weak and hadn't had a bowel movement for almost two weeks. Breakfast from Grandma was congee (a plain rice pudding) and salty white turnips. Lunch was more water, congee, and some dried fish—but because I was so hungry, everything tasted delicious. Even the curry potato leaf soup at dinner was scrumptious. I had never eaten potato leaves in my life. Back in Vietnam, I was known as the picky queen. I only liked meat and avoided most anything that was green. Salty turnips and potato leaves would never have made it to my bowl. But here, I chowed down like it was the best meal I had ever eaten in my life. Everything tasted like a feast.

I was surprised that Dad allowed me to work in exchange for housing, something he would never have permitted in Vietnam. Dad took pride in being the provider who took care of his family. But the tides had changed. We were no longer in Vietnam and he was just as helpless as the rest of us.

My job was sales, tending to the Chinese and Vietnamese refugee customers. I would weigh the sugar, rice, and beans, and help them find what they were looking for. Heang, the daughter of Rahmad, took care of the local Indonesian customers. One early morning, a local Indonesian man came in to buy rice. He spoke loudly to Heang and said he wanted to talk to the grandmother. Grandma came out and they spoke in Malay for a while. I could see the irritation on the man's face as he began to talk louder. After he paid and walked out with his sack of rice, I asked Grandma what that was all about. She told me not to worry. "Oh, he's just upset because everything on the island used to be cheaper before the refugees arrived. Resources are getting depleted and everything is a bit scarce."

"Have the prices changed that dramatically?" I asked.

Grandma explained, "Because demand now is so high, we can't obtain as much as usual from Pinang [a nearby bigger island]. Therefore, we are forced to increase the prices on our goods."

I could understand why some of the villagers were frustrated. We refugees were causing an economic imbalance on this tiny island, disrupting their tranquil, peaceful paradise. While some local businesses prospered, many of the working residents were frustrated by this chaotic disturbance in their lives and strain on their resources caused by us intruders.

Adopting a New Identity

While I was busy adjusting to my position as a clerk in the shop, Dad's new role was also dramatically different. He used to refer to himself as a "blind ox," a term he used for an illiterate person. He struggled when he had to file documents or read announcements. In Vietnam, he had to rely on his friends to help register our boat and report the names of his family to the local government. But here, since he was the head of the household, our paperwork relied on him alone. In Vietnam he had found it much easier—he could always get things done with a little bribe. Now, it's a different world, and no one knew what the procedures were. There wasn't a United Nations representative or any official organization in Letung to help refugees. People were on their own and many were scrambling to figure out what their next step should be.

It was understandably chaotic. Many refugees could not provide the full necessary documentation of birth certificates, marriage licenses, or proper identification to prove who they were. Many had lost their belongings at sea or had them destroyed by pirates. Some people took advantage of this situation and altered their age. It was quite common for young adults to decrease their age and middle-aged people to increase their age. People wanted to qualify for aid as quickly as possible when they reached a host country. It was thought that those of working age would be pushed immediately into the workforce and there would be less chance to get aid to help them get started.

Around this time was when I had to give up my identity. Dad decided I would no longer be me—I would be my sister, the one who was deceased and had a date of birth four years after mine. Dad decided that everyone in our family would stick to our real age, except me. My parents had already used Le Khanh's birth certificate to purchase a child's fare for my boat passage, so Dad continued to claim that I was four years younger than my real age. Instead of being 16, now I was a 12-year-old child.

I had some apprehension about what this would mean for me when I could finally settle into a new country, hopefully the United States. I imagined my younger age would have its pluses and minuses. I could see the advantage of gaining four additional years of education and told myself that I could now make up for the four years I lost to the communists (who prioritized indoctrination, not education). But I had no idea how this might affect me socially. What would it feel like to be the age of a high school senior, pretending to fit in with 8th graders? It was a dilemma. In the end, I accepted the trade-off as an opportunity to advance my education, and though Dad had made up his mind without consulting me, I was okay with his decision. I begged to at least keep my real birthday and just change the year. And so, it was done.

After Dad submitted all the necessary documents and registrations, all we could do was wait for the documents to be processed. No one knew how long that would take. In the mean time, Dad adopted a daily routine. He checked every day with the authorities to see what news they might have, and scoped out where to get aid. He sought information from refugees from other islands and learned what the gossip was about conditions in Vietnam. He looked for friends among the newcomers and sent telegrams and letters to relatives in Vietnam to update them on our status. There were so many unknown factors and every day brought us some new discovery.

In Vietnam, Dad's job had been to provide for the family, and provide he did! In our new situation, Dad was no longer making money, but he continued to be our steadfast provider. He brought back canned food rations from the UN Refugee Agency (UNHCR United Nations High Commissioner for Refugees) whenever the organization made an appearance. It felt weird for all of us to count on handouts, but this new reality quickly became our new normal. The United Nations and the Red Cross were our best friends and saviors.

One morning I noticed a single boiled egg at the breakfast table. Everyone in Rahmad's family told me, "Don't touch the egg. It's a special protein for Grandpa." I realized at that moment that in Vietnam, we had enjoyed a far more abundant life than this family did, yet they had opened their home to us and welcomed us even though they didn't have much to share. To this day, whenever I see a boiled egg, I am reminded of that family's kindness.

New Living Situation

At the shop, Rahmad hired an 18-year-old Chinese refugee boy named Quoc for heavy labor. Quoc was Cantonese and had left his family behind in Vietnam to escape on a small boat. He had arrived in Letung a month before our family. The other people in Quoc's boat were assigned to Kuku Island which was nicknamed "Dao Ruoi," meaning "flies island" for obvious reasons. Quoc stayed in Letung to work, exchanging his labor for housing while waiting for acceptance to be resettled. In our spare time, Quoc and I had to fold paper into a funnel shape for wrapping sugar, rice, or other dry goods. Heang, Rahmad's teenage daughter, would be around and sang her Indonesian songs for us. I had the feeling that she liked Quoc, but little did I know, Quoc had a crush on me. I was oblivious to this until he told my friend, Q, weeks later.

Before I had time to respond, Quoc received news that he was sponsored by Germany, which accepted all children under 20 years of age as orphans. It all happened so quickly that he never had a chance to say goodbye to me. At the dock, he scribbled a quick letter and had a friend deliver it to me, saying he would write to me soon. I was sad, but at the same time, a little relieved. It's probably for the best to not get tangled up in a relationship in such a chaotic environment, I told myself.

After Quoc left, I missed having a co-worker with whom I could communicate, but I started picking up a few Indonesian words and learning about their culture. I have always loved learning new languages. The first phrase I learned was "Terima kasih." It means "Thank you." I said "Terima kasih" many times, all day long to customers. I found it a little unusual when they greeted me, "Sudah mandi?" That means, "Shower yet?" What an odd way to greet people! But maybe not so odd when you consider our Chinese greeting, "Chīle ma?" means, "Have you eaten yet?" I guess where we Chinese were concerned with hunger, Indonesians were concerned about cleanliness.

My most commonly used phrase when I didn't know what to say was "Saya tidak tahu," which means, "I don't know." I liked my job and would have learned a lot more had I been allowed to continue working at the grocery store, but my parents withdrew me from working as soon as we moved to a new rental place.

My cousins from Dad's brother (Quan and Tri) had found work with an Indonesian family in exchange for their room and board. So instead of 12 people, we were now ten at the time of our move. The Indonesian family we arranged to rent from had cleared out their front porch to accommodate our family of seven, plus my three cousins, the children of my mom's sister (MinhHa, Chi, and Kien).

The porch was maybe about 14 feet by 12 feet with a front entrance, a door to the house, and well-ventilated windows. We stacked our bags of belongings against the wall and then used those bags as pillows at night. Side by side, all ten of us were crammed together in this one room, but we were thankful that we had a dry, clean linoleum floor to lay on. The Indonesian landlady was nice, but firm. We were not allowed to go into any area off our porch except the back deck. This was where the kitchen and the outhouse were. They were Muslim so we were not allowed to cook or even eat any pork products while living there. That was easy since we couldn't get pork anyway. Communication with them was done mostly through signs and body language and we were able to accomplish the essentials.

New Start-up Business

It is common in my culture to believe that adversity creates opportunity. Our new deck apartment looked out on the street connected to the pier, so it was always busy with people arriving from Kuku and Air Raya by boat to buy food and other supplies at the marketplace. Our landlord had a foot pedal sewing machine and Mom saw an opportunity for us to put our sewing skills to work, pass the time, and earn some extra income for our family. Both Mom and I were skillful tailors, so Mom did a quick survey of the needs and opportunities and decided to start taking on clients.

When people walked by the front porch, they would stop and chat, and Mom would ask them if we could make some new clothes for them. Mom rented the sewing machine from our landlady. I would draft and design fashionable clothes and Mom, the expert seamstress, would sew them. Many refugees needed new clothes. And so, a new start-up mother/daughter business was begun in Letung.

Our little porch instantly became a storefront tailoring business. The sewing machine was against one wall, while the other three walls were stacked with our family's luggage. The linoleum floor became my working space where I drafted patterns and cut fabric for countless clients. There was no furniture in the room. The floor also served as our dining room, living room, workroom, and bedroom. Nevertheless, we appreciated that we had fresh water, and in Letung, we didn't have to live in a straw hut battling nuisance flies and deadly mosquitoes.

Many of our clients were refugee women who were able to afford to rent and live in Letung with local residents. We continued to hear how bad the situation was in Kuku and Air Raya camps, where sickness due to crowded conditions and lack of sanitation was all too common.

Every day, Mom and I asked our clients for news they might have heard from the other islands and camps. We laughed and cried with them as they shared their stories, all the while pondering our own destiny. Mrs. Linh was one person who came to us with many stories from her day trips to Letung to stock up on her basic needs. There were tragic accounts of people who fell off the boats being transported from island to island.

We learned that there was not much help coming from the Indonesian government nor from the outside world. These islands were so remote that it took a long time for the world to take notice. There were stories of children and elderly people who died due to lack of medicines and malnutrition in this harsh environment. There were also many stories of people dying of malaria and polluted water. Every time we heard a hopeful story of someone being accepted for resettlement, there was another sad story that came with it.

It felt good to team up with Mom to provide extra income for our family's living and food expenses. My cousin, Minh Ha (Auntie Nhien's daughter), took over my position as the caretaker for my young sisters and brothers. She tended to the kitchen duty for our three meals. Breakfasts were mostly congee and some dried, salty turnips. Lunch and dinner were simple rice, boiled cabbage, and canned sardines. There were a few times Dad was tempted to buy some dried Chinese sausage from the market to get some protein, but we did not dare to risk being kicked off our deck apartment, since the sausage contained pork and the contract expressly forbade us from eating pork. Since our religion was Buddhist/Confucius, Dad did not eat beef, so the sardines became a staple. The occasional fresh fish from the local market was a real treat. We knew we were lucky to be better off than many of the other refugees.

Flashback

Working together with Mom gave me an opportunity to reminisce about the time in Vietnam when I first learned to sew. In the summer of 1978, Dad made me quit school so I used that year to learn as much as I could about sewing and embroidering. I thought about Mr. Cheong, a renowned Cantonese sewing teacher, who taught me about fashion clothing. For six months my cousin, Minh Thu, our neighbor, My Linh, and I rode our bikes three times a week to Mr. Cheong's to learn how to draft patterns and make fashionable clothing using the pictures in the old catalogues from Hong Kong for ideas.

Most of Vietnam used the metric system, but we learned the British system that measured in inches and yards. I was the youngest in the class, but it came very naturally to me. I had always loved watching what my mom sewed and remembered picking up remnants of the fabrics that Mom tossed away and creating fashionable clothes for my dolls when I was seven. I also had lots of practice making clothes for my younger siblings, for my cousins, friends, and anyone who wanted me to sew for them. During our fifth month at the academy, the teacher approached me and asked me to become his aide. He said that I had a gift and he needed my help.

Me? The youngest girl in the entire class? I was flattered and excited. For my work, I was given free tuition. I was proud to have ladies two or three times my age enthusiastically compliment and thank me for helping them. "Little sis, come explain this." "Little sis, how do you draft that?" It was such a great feeling—and quite new for me. Self-confidence and self-worth were not familiar sensations. When the class ended, Mr. Cheong announced that he was going to the New Economic Zone (and we all knew what that meant). Those months as his aide ran through my mind as I sewed in our Letung make-shift tailor shop. I wondered if he ever made it out of Vietnam or might he have been one of those who perished on some boat out in the sea.

Making Impact

My years of sewing and drafting patterns was paying off big time at the refugee camp. There was a great demand for new apparel for women who had lost their clothing at sea. Everyone wanted to look good for the interviews for a new life. Nice clothes made people feel more hopeful and confident. I was so happy to sketch and measure and play once again with pretty fabrics.

The trending fashion was simple pajama pants with matching blouses in many different styles. They could serve both as pajamas as well as a daily outfit. The women would bring in fabric from an Indonesian store and I would sketch several styles for them, or they would tell me what they wanted. I then took measurements and cut the outfits for Mom to sew. Everything was customized to their needs. The familiar process of making clothing decisions and putting on new, well-fitting and attractive outfits helped to normalize the refugee life, both for my mom and me and our clients.

I was proud that, for the first time in my 16 years, I was making a direct impact on sustaining our family's well-being. I learned from Mom the art of networking and how to build relationships with clients. I interacted with women of all ages and I loved how I was able to make them feel beautiful and confident in their appearance. Mom and I both have cheerful personalities and our clients felt comfortable talking and sharing their stories, struggles, and their hopes and dreams with us.

One day a young girl named Lieng came into our shop. She wanted me to design some provocative, sexy outfits to make life at the camp a little less dull. (When I say *sexy*, it is not the same meaning that sexy has in America. It could simply be a blouse with a back that was low-cut.) Lieng was poised and confident about what she wanted. As I was measuring her, she complained: "I am 19. I can do whatever I want. I don't have to obey her. Just because she is my mom, she thinks she can make me do anything she wants?"

I sensed growing anger as she continued.

"Make me something fun and sexy. It's so hot and I want to show as much of the skin of my back as I can."

"Aren't you afraid your mom's going to be mad?" I asked.

"She can be mad all she wants. I couldn't care less!" She shrugged defiantly.

I was shocked at her response and could not believe her boldness. I designed and cut three varying styles of strapless and backless outfits, and Mom sewed them for Lieng. She gave me a big hug and thanked me for making her feel sexy and pretty with these new outfits.

A few days later, Lieng stormed back into our shop with new fabrics. "I want to reorder the same outfits that you made for me last week." I was confused and asked her why she wanted to have the same exact outfits made again.

"My mom took a pair of scissors and cut up all my beautiful outfits. I'll show her who will win this fight! I am not going to give in that easily. If she keeps destroying, I will keep remaking!"

Wow! What a rebel! I would never have dreamed of responding like that. With Dad's temper and Mom's nagging guilt trips, I could not fathom disobeying, let alone rebelling. The thoughts of testing my parents' threshold had never crossed my mind. Secretly, I admired her for her courage in standing up to her mom. I saw her as very brave, indeed.

Another frequent client was Mrs. Nguyen, with her three beautiful teenage daughters. She was a high-status military wife with lots of money from the old Vietnam regime. They wanted to look classy and fashionable even as they lived in such an impoverished refugee camp. After all, hope was on the horizon. Everyone wanted to look their best as they looked forward to moving to a new country. Mrs. Nguyen flaunted her three beautiful daughters as her assets to local authorities and any potential sponsoring country. They needed a new wardrobe and we were pretty much the only Vietnamese gig in town. We were cranking out five to eight outfits a day to address the demands of the community.

Suddenly, I became the cash cow of my family. All day long, my job was to draft patterns and cut out outfits for Mom to sew. We received 1,000 to 1,500 Indonesian rupiah for the labor for each outfit. Given the exchange rate at the time, this would be $1.50 to $2.50 in American dollars. Mom could not keep up with the sewing, so we had to hire a seamstress named Nghiem to help. The rent for our deck apartment was $100 US dollars a month, and the sewing machine cost $50 a month to rent. Our little business brought in a few hundred dollars a month which was enough to pay for rent for the house and the sewing machine, pay our helper, and buy extra food to supplement the canned food from the United Nations. And still we had some left over at the end of each month.

We worked from sunrise to sunset seven days a week, and I was happy to be doing what I loved. The days zipped by so quickly that I forgot what the sun looked like outside that front porch. I was treated like a goose that laid golden eggs during those months, making up for the fortune lost to the pirates. We knew we would need to save every penny we could for the unknown future in the new land, wherever that might be.

Being Pampered

Ever since I was a little girl of five or six, I had chronic stomach pain and ulcer-like symptoms. I was accustomed to this nervous distress and went to bed every night with a sour, nagging stomach ache. I would rarely wake up in the morning feeling refreshed. This continued to happen frequently in Indonesia.

One day, a high fever coupled with an especially bad stomach episode caused me to pass out. I had been working non-stop and was stressed out from all the deadlines. I guess my body just decided to call for a strike. Mom was very concerned but not as anxious as Mrs. Pham, a client who had an 18-year-old daughter with a beautiful voice. Mom used to ask her to sing for us when she was around. They needed new clothes in a hurry for possible interviews with the Australians.

Mrs. Pham came by daily with yummy food and apples to make sure I recovered quickly. She also brought me Chinese ointment for my headaches and rubbed my stomach. I was pampered like a princess. It felt good to know I was making an impact on the lives of people by simply making them feel pretty. Me, a no-name 16-year-old became well-known by word of mouth in that little edge of our impoverished world. I was gratified that I could contribute to people's happiness even in the most desperate of circumstances.

Crossed Cultures

We were fortunate to live on the main strip of Letung where all the traffic from the dock led to the market square. The busy road gave us the opportunity to see and hear many things. Periodically, I saw a young Indonesian man who couldn't have been more than 20. He would walk up and down the strip in the evening when the weather was cool, playing his guitar and singing Vietnamese songs. I was amazed at how he could play the music with such beautiful expression and sing like a native without understanding a word he sang.

I can still hear his voice in my ears. "Khong bao gio, khong bao gio giua mua he tuet roi…" ("Never, never snow would fall in midsummer…") I was very impressed. I asked him how he learned to sing Vietnamese so well. Okay, I must stop here and explain the conversation: Imagine how the duck talks to the chicken. That's how we talked. Even though he sang like a Vietnamese native, he couldn't speak any Vietnamese at all. Our whole conversation was communicated with gestures and body language. I thought I understood what he was saying through his gestures and I assumed he understood me as well. It was fun that we both were trying. I could see he was very curious about our culture. He told me that he learned to sing by listening to the cassettes being played by someone who lived down the street. He liked the tunes and he enjoyed the language. I found him, his musical talent and methods fascinating.

For such a brief connection, I have many vivid memories, and not just of his beautiful voice. I'll never forget the day I learned an important lesson from him. Mom had just peeled an apple for Nam, a very luxurious snack, and it was only for my youngest brother. I picked up a slice of apple and offered it to my singer friend. He looked at me and cringed, then shook his head. *Could apples be a forbidden fruit for Muslims, like pork?* I had no idea why he had recoiled. He was able to explain to me that Indonesians always eat with their right hands, and they don't use utensils. Food is only handled with the right hand, but I had offered the apple from my left hand. In their culture, the left hand, because there was little or no toilet paper, was used to clean their bottoms. So, you should never offer food to someone with your left hand. *Oh, my God!* I was so embarrassed. I told him it was okay, that our left hands were never used that way. He still refused and we both laughed. I don't know if this tradition was true in the big cities of modern Indonesia, but that was what I learned about our small village of Letung at that time.

The End of Letung

It had been three months and there was still no sign of sponsorship for our family from any country. We lived day by day in the hope that something would happen soon. I was quite isolated from the outside world as I worked in my sewing shop all day every day. One day, I was startled by a loud noise on the street. I looked out from our porch to see people being chased by Indonesian guards as they were being beaten with sticks. There was no warning that this was coming. Dad rushed into the house and informed us that we had to pack up and move to Air Raya Island, immediately! How on earth could these things happen so quickly? We were panicked.

Only much later did we learn the reason for this sudden upheaval. The local government wanted all refugees concentrated on two islands, Kuku and Air Raya, rather than have them scattered throughout the

Anambas islands. This was for their own protection. The impending monsoon season in Indonesia would bring rain, high waves, and rough seas that would make it impossible to transport food and medicine to the multiple islands occupied by refugees. All refugees had to move to the two most populated islands (Air Raya and Kuku), including those of us who lived in Letung.

People did not know the reason for the move, so they resisted. We were witnessing the final attempt to get the refugees to obey the order. Violent whippings and beatings were being employed to impose compliance. The screaming was loud, and I was scared. We didn't have many belongings, so we could leave quickly, but what about our clients' garments? Dad said, "They will know where to find us in Air Raya. We need to move before they attack us!"

No refugees could stay in Letung. Not even bribery would work this time. Several boats were ready at the dock to evacuate all refugees to Air Raya or Kuku, and Letung would be returned to its original, quiet tranquility. A limited number of boat trips would still be available to return to buy supplies, but no one could stay.

They evacuated everyone quickly. Within hours, our little temporary rental porch vanished from sight as a boat took us for a choppy hour-long ride to a remote island and the Air Raya refugee camp. The date was August 18, 1979, exactly 100 days since we got off our boat after fleeing Vietnam. Here we were, back on a boat again.

I was afraid this might be a trick. Things were happening so quickly. They might just be dumping us into the ocean. The last few hundred refugees who clung to what little civilization Letung had offered us were forced to say goodbye to faucet water and electricity. My siblings were too young to understand, but I knew well that harsh days lay ahead for us on the crowded island of Air Raya.

"…for every refugee that reaches land, another refugee drowns." This was how one news report described our plight. Canadian TV (CBC) made a special visit to Air Raya refugee camp on Anambas Island, Indonedia. Broadcast date: September 11, 1979. Narrator: Harry Elton. Source: CBC Digital Archives.This video clip gives you a blip of what Letung and Air Raya were like (as I well remember). https://www.youtube.com/watch?v=Bro_Qxlr5AY

6

Air Raya Island

Air Raya

The boat dropped us off on the beach at Air Raya. Our first order of business was to find a place for our family to call home for the duration of our stay. There was absolutely no place near the beach. Those spots were taken by the refugees who had arrived three months ago, forcing us to look further inland for a suitable place to build our shelter. This unpopulated, once dense forest island now looked almost bare, except for the tall palm trees.

Tens of thousands of refugees had cleared the trees and bushes of their branches and leaves to build straw huts and roofing, and to provide fuel for cooking. The resources of the jungles were being thinned out by the ever-growing needs of more and more refugees. It cost Dad a hundred American dollars to hire some men to help him build a hut with a thatched roof and cross-branched walls. It was big enough for our family of seven, my cousin Cao, and a few of Dad's single friends who needed a roof over their hammocks.

By this time, all five of my under-aged cousins had already left, having been accepted by Germany as orphans. My parents were disappointed that my cousins did not claim them as their guardians but certainly couldn't blame them for grabbing an opportunity to leave the dire situation on the island.

Since our hut was far away enough from the beach, we were able to dig a well beside our house which provided necessary water for cooking and washing. It was a luxury, not having to hike to the streams in the woods for fresh water.

Mom set up the seamstress shop again after we settled in the new hut. I don't remember how we lugged the rental sewing machine from Letung to Air Raya, but the sewing continued for at least another month to provide extra income. I was once again being sheltered in our hut from the outside world to do some of the sewing work. Dad was a very protective father and I was not allowed to wander outside our home, even if there was nothing to do in the hut. How I yearned to be able to venture beyond the captivity of our hut to see the world outside and make some friends. The only time I could sneak a peek at the outside world was when I needed to go to the public bathroom down on the beach.

Standing in front of our hut, me and my friend, Q.
The cardboard sign over on the left corner said "Thanh Ha Tailor."

By the time we arrived at Air Raya in August, it was already flooded with refugees and an established settlement of straw huts and vendor huts. Sunken boats were disassembled, and their wood repurposed to make bars and shops on the beach. A pier was built to serve the daily boat trips to and from Letung Island, and to welcome boats from the Red Cross, the UNHCR, and other nearby volunteer agencies.

Merchants from Singapore supplied the refugees' demands for meat and alcohol. Hogs were shipped to the island regularly and processed daily in a slaughterhouse, providing us with fresh meat. I remember being awakened every morning by the squealing of pigs. Their distress calls created so much anxiety in me that I had to cover my ears as my stomach churned.

We soon settled into a routine at Air Raya. Early in the morning before the scorching sun was up, Dad took cousin Cao and my brother Viet into the forest to gather wood for our daily cooking. They were also responsible for picking up our daily food rations from the UNHCR and then checking for our names on the bulletin board for a possible interview.

Because Dad was a former military officer from South Vietnam, we were told that America was likely to be the country to sponsor us. People were sent to America either because they already had families there and/ or because the U.S. was exercising a moral obligation to those who had supported the war effort in South Vietnam. They now felt responsible to those caught up in the massive exodus following the fall of South Vietnam. I didn't know if that was true, but we were thrilled to hear it! America was the only place we wanted to settle, and we hoped they would grant us our wish. We had no idea how long it would take to process our papers, and we were concerned that our health conditions could be a deciding factor.

It rained a lot in the month of October, and my 17th birthday came and went, and no one noticed—not even me. I forgot that I was turning 17. No, in my new reality, according to my official papers, I turned 13. In the Chinese culture, and certainly in my family, birthdays were a significant day only for the elderly and for the very young. However, my parents and most Chinese made a bigger deal remembering and celebrating the death anniversary of beloved family members. The fact of the matter was that I hadn't felt like a kid since 1975. After the fall of Saigon, I started being Mom's apprentice and took on so many responsibilities that I learned to behave and worry like an adult. I never really got to be a teenager. Experiences, hardships, and loads of responsibility did give me wisdom beyond my years, I suppose. Someone once told me that I was "born an old soul." I'm not sure that would be true if I had been the youngest in the family.

Being Nosy

Life in Air Raya became a time for me to think very deliberately about how I might best be prepared to face my own future. What might I do during this waiting period in the refugee camp to prepare for the coming years, and what skills might I gain during my time here? Mom was happy that I kept working, but I felt like I was missing out on so much being cooped up at home with no big vision. I begged Mom to let me take some English lessons in the camp. Finally, she agreed. I sought out an English teacher and so, twice a week, I had a legitimate reason to be out of the house for an hour.

My English teacher, Mr. Dat, was a young man in his late twenties. He lived with a 16-year-old girl and a 10-year-old boy who were not related to him. Being nosy and curious, my new friend and classmate, Hong, and I made it our mission to find out more about our teacher's relationships. After snooping around a bit, we learned that the girl and the little boy were siblings and Mr. Dat was a friend of their older sister who had left Vietnam much earlier. The plan was for the siblings to escape with Mr. Dat and be reunited with their older sister. The conditions at the camp were very crowded and, as was true in many of the small shelters, everyone slept in the same bed. Was this girl being taken advantage of? Did she have any say in this? She was our age but already she was cooking and serving Mr. Dat as she would a husband. It disturbed me to think how many young people in refugee camps were separated from their families due to difficult, desperate circumstances, and there was no one to look out for them.

This made me think of what my own situation might have been. Mom had almost sent my brother Viet and me to escape with her pharmacy friend and her family. Mom thought that if she couldn't escape with her family to a free life with the hope of a better future, then maybe she could give a couple of her children a chance for that. Luckily, Dad had been able to strategize and save enough to buy passage for all of us. Dad said, "We either all live together, or we will all die together. None of my children will die at sea with strangers." And I was so grateful for that.

It is a parent's instinct to protect their children, make sacrifices for their children, and do all they can to secure a hopeful and happy future for their children. Most often, this future is realized as parent and child walk hand-in-hand together into a shared future. But what if a hopeful future for the child can only be realized by letting go of their hand, and pushing them into an uncertain and perilous escape that may be their only chance of hope for a better life? And what scars are left behind when the hand is released? Many a difficult and painful decision was made by loving, caring parents and families, and every person in that camp had a story that involved difficult decisions.

Uncle Ho's Mausoleum—Lăng Bác

Limited living space on both Kuku and Air Raya Islands forced people to build their huts very close to each other. Each row of huts had a small walkway for traffic to get through. Our hut was away from the beach and closer to the mountain, so very little cooling breeze was able to penetrate our palm leaf covered walls. On the other hand, by being away from the beach we enjoyed more privacy, were less likely to "lose" stuff, and we stayed drier during a heavy rain.

Our hut was a little bigger than the porch we had rented in Letung, but in place of a clean linoleum floor, now we had a sandy floor. We put two sheets of plywood together that served as a worktable for me during the daytime, and the bed for five children and Mom at night. A small piece of wood off the ground served as a bed for Ngho, our former neighbor's daughter who now lived with us to help with the cooking and cleaning. There were four hammocks hung on four corners of the hut: one for Dad, one for cousin Cao, one for Uncle Long, and one for Uncle Dinh. None of them were related to us but they had all journeyed with us in the same boat and it was our custom to call our parents' friends *Uncle* and *Aunt*. They were just renting sleeping space.

For my morning routine, I would wake up with a jolt and quickly cover my ears to muffle the loud and frantic squeals of the pigs. I would then lead all my siblings down to the beach outhouses for their morning business. A row of toilets was constructed with tree branches and offered a privacy barrier only up to waist high. There was a long ramp to get to the squatting hole/toilet. It was embarrassing. When you squatted down to do your business, you could still see people standing in line, and the line was always long. I hated toilet times in the refugee camps. In Vietnam, we were told that Ho Chi Minh's mausoleum always had a long line of people waiting to get in, so the term, "visiting Uncle Ho's mausoleum" was widely used as a euphemism for going to the toilet. During high tide, you could see floating feces washing ashore into the swimming areas. Not very appealing, but that's how it was.

Row after row of huts were built to accommodate the continuous influx of more and more people. With so many refugees living in such proximity, sanitation was a major problem. Trash and rubbish accumulated faster and faster. Flies, mosquitoes, and swarms of insects seemed to multiply at an exponential rate. The water available from the streams and the crude wells was untreated. At one point my sister Phan and I both got sick with a high fever at the same time, probably from drinking polluted water. Fortunately, we both recovered, but after that, my parents made sure that the water was boiled before we drank it. Many families were quite careless about purifying their drinking water and the result was often diarrhea, which, when coupled with malnutrition, often led to other illnesses.

My parents did their best to shield us from the outside world, so I had no idea how severe the situation was in the camps. However, sewing clients brought me many tragic stories of what was happening outside my straw walls in the rest of the camp. Mrs. Pham told me of her neighbor who had just lost a baby girl from a high fever and vomiting. She didn't know what the cause was, but they couldn't get any medicine even though a new clinic was being set up in the camp. There were not enough doctors nor medications to meet all the camp's demands. Another client, Mrs. Chau, told me that her father-in-law was ill with the very same symptoms. She worried that he would not be well enough if they were called for an interview and they might miss their chance for a resettlement screening. Unfortunately, he died within a week of the symptoms appearing. No one was aware of the disease called *malaria*.

Working so intently at sewing had kept me occupied and made the waiting time pass a little faster, but now business was slowing down for us in Air Raya. That bleak feeling of not knowing when or even if we would ever get out of the camp was torturing our family and tens of thousands of others. The dream of getting off the island quickly had faded. Living in the horrible cramped conditions in the camp made people realize how uncertain their future was. Spending money on new clothes became a low priority. People spent their money supplementing their meager diets of rice, cabbage, and soy sauce provided by the Red Cross and United Nations.

Our family was having a difficult time adjusting to the grim condition of our existence. September and October had been extremely rainy months and the thin thatched roof took turns leaking in various spots. We left the front wall of our hut uncovered to improve the ventilation, but now the wind and rain would splash through onto the plywood. We had a heavy green blanket from Dad's military gear which we hung up for more privacy at night. Now we left it up all day as well. Our tiny hut felt dark, wet, and stuffy. Heavy downpours created an unbearable humidity and it seemed that everything was covered with sticky wet sand. The whole island was steaming with human sweat and garbage smells from the angry earth.

I lost interest in creating and sewing clothes and instead became lethargic and pensive. Rather than drawing clothing designs on outdated newspapers, I scribbled random words and perfected my signature. Mom scolded me and criticized me for wasting time. I missed going to school, missed the freedom to move around. I missed living a regular, teenage life. Time had stopped for me. I felt trapped!

Air Raya Nightlife

Life in the camp during the day was bleak, harsh, and tedious, and people were eager to find ways to break the daily monotony. And so, a nightlife began to take shape on the beachfront, reminiscent of the pre-1975 life in Vietnam. Scraps of wood were salvaged from the escape boats and recycled into a nautical beach-themed cafe. Tiki lights adorned the tables and, for a moment, people could escape their rotten refugee camp huts and gather in a beachside oceanfront café under a sky bejeweled by millions of stars.

By the end of October, on days when it wasn't raining too hard, we would hear loud music from the beachfront cafes echoing throughout the night. Several of the refugees who were singers, musicians, and songwriters formed a band and performed music to entertain the people in the camp. Beer, alcohol and soda made their way into the camp by way of merchants in Singapore and local indigenous islanders who saw this as a way to make some money.

Hong, my English classmate, reported to me that the cafes on the beach were crowded with young people who congregated nightly for drinks and music. I wished I could be there to witness the fun! I would listen to the loud music every evening in the candlelight of our hut, and imagine what it would be like to be there.

One of the songs frequently sung was composed by Truong Hai in 1979. He was a popular singer/songwriter in Saigon, but then was living in the Air Raya camp waiting for resettlement. "Rain on Air Raya Island" beautifully expresses the sentiment of Vietnamese refugees, and to this day, whenever I think of the beach of Air Raya, I hear this song playing in my ear. "Does anyone know the feeling of the stranded?"

Truong Hai's song: https://www.youtube.com/watch?v=7ASqmP4NZcI

End of Sewing in the Camp

One late morning after my English lesson, I needed to run to Uncle Ho's mausoleum because of the chronic acid grinding in my stomach. I returned to the hut to see Dad in a rage, swinging a chair over the sewing machine and screaming curse words. I hid in the corner of the hut, wondering what had happened this time. I wasn't that surprised, but you never get used to it, and it just rekindled an all too familiar fear. Apparently, Dad was upset because Mom was always worried about "making money!!!" He shouted, "NO MORE SEWING! Do you plan to be the island queen and stay here for the rest of your life?"

It was embarrassing to have people gather around our hut to watch the drama. In my life I had witnessed many such episodes, but that never made it easy. Dad stormed out of the hut and disappeared until dinner time. I knew that sewing wasn't the reason for Dad's furor. Dad was jealous. He thought Mom was flirting with Uncle Dinh, but as always, he didn't tell her the real reason he was mad. Sadly, I think Mom knew why Dad was always lashing out. Was Mom starved for attention? And was negative attention better than no attention at all? After this incident, our sewing business abruptly fell apart. I was sad about the way it ended but happy that now I had more time to learn English and explore other things.

There were two sisters, Lan and Mai, in their early twenties, who lived across from our hut. Every morning the sisters went to the beach to swim. Some mornings, after Dad left to gather wood or watch his friends play chess, I would plead with Mom to let me tag along with the sisters to practice swimming. Surprisingly, she let me go. Mom was taking a risk letting me go because not only could I get into trouble, but she could as well. I treasured those moments where I could be out in the water and spread my arms and swim free. There was a tiny island with big boulders about a few hundred yards from the beach. I would follow Lan and Mai out to the rocks, swimming back and forth. I was always very cautious and careful not to have any accidents. If anything happened, I was more frightened of the severe punishment I'd receive from my dad than from any injury itself. I had grown up under an extremely protective father, and I wasn't sure how he would respond.

October came and went. We were anxious to hear news from sponsoring countries and how they planned to disperse the refugees. My friend, Hong, had several sisters in her family, and they were interviewed and accepted by Australia. I didn't know if it was true, but Hong told me that families with pretty young girls of child-bearing age were the main criteria for being accepted by Australia. "The country needs females, especially pretty females," she told me. I was happy for her departure but felt restless for my own family.

People who had relatives in Europe or the United States were often sponsored by those countries. People who had been in the military or government services in South Vietnam were given priority by America, the country that took in the most refugees. Every day, Dad stood in long lines waiting to check the bulletin for our names on the departure list. Finally, the long-awaited day came! We had spent exactly 98 days in Air Raya refugee camp, but now we were leaving to begin our new future.

7

Galang, Pinang, and Singapore

The Third Island—Galang

On November 25, 1979, while Americans were celebrating Thanksgiving Day in the United States, we departed from Air Raya on a ferry to go to another refugee camp called Galang Island. Galang was part of the Riau Archipelago, near Singapore. The camp was established in 1979 by the United Nations High Commissioner for Refugees (UNHCR) to temporarily house the boat-people refugees and asylum seekers. The camp covered about 16 square kilometers and was at its early stage of development when we arrived. We were told we would only have a short stay on Galang Island and would soon be transferred to another island. Most refugees there had already been assigned to a sponsoring country and were awaiting their next step to resettlement in the U.S., Australia, or one of the European countries.

Several large barracks had already been built to house refugees and more were under construction. They were made with aluminum and were extremely hot during the day. As I understood, each barrack housed up to a hundred people, so a dozen or more families all shared the same building. This island and campsite were much bigger than the previous islands we had seen. Construction of the barracks and water lines was still in the early stages. The roads were sandy with red clay and it was often very dusty from the traffic of excavating machines and trucks.

Our family was in Camp One. Camp Two was still under construction. The camp was far from the beach, so the lack of sea breeze coupled with the sun beating on the metal roof made us constantly feel like we were drowning in our own sweat. Inside the barracks, there were two rows of bunk beds. The space between the beds was where we put our belongings and did our cooking.

After every meal, we would walk miles to the water pipes for drinking water and would then carry buckets of water back to the barracks for basic cleaning and cooking. Dad's job was to get food rations from UNHCR while Mom took care of little Nam. The other three siblings became my shadows everywhere I went.

We were thankful we only had to stay in Galang for 20 days. Every day, I was resigned to walking miles to get water, cooking a little rice to eat with canned food, and then walking miles again to stand in line to get buckets of water for showers. I remember parading my brother, Viet, and my two sisters, Phan and Que, to wait in line for a bucket of water. I would wet all three of them down from head to toe with their underwear on, lather them with a bar of soap and then go back in line for a round of rinsing. By the time we got back to the water pipe, the soap on their bodies was all dried up and we would continue going back in line until everyone was thoroughly rinsed and washed.

I brought a big towel along and used it as a sarong for changing out of our wet clothes right there on the spot. There were no changing rooms anywhere. It normally took us two to three hours a day just to get clean. By the time we got back to the barracks, the clay and dirt from the roads had already found its way back onto our bodies.

As much as I hated going to the bathroom in Air Raya, I hated going to the restroom in Galang even more. The toilets were extremely dirty and smelly from the heat. The flies would flock to your bottom during the day, and the mosquitoes would drain your blood at night. I often wished I was a male, so I would only have half the problems to deal with. Three weeks felt like a long time, but we sensed the worst of our ordeal would soon be over. Our last physical exam in Galang indicated we were all shipshape and ready to advance to the next place.

Even though we only had a short stay at Galang, I heard that people arriving after us were sometimes detained for years, having to learn English and a vocation before being able to leave for their adopted country. The site was becoming a small city with permanent buildings: a hospital, school, church, Buddhist temple, youth center, and even a cemetery. All this infrastructure was planned, built, and governed by refugees. Had we arrived several months later, after the camp was well established, we might have been stuck there for months, or even years to learn English before we could qualify to get out. It was a blessing after all.

One afternoon, Dad came back with some documents and he wanted help filling them out.

"Pa, the paper asks, 'if we had a choice, which state in America we would prefer to settle in?'" I said.

"Pick some place warm!" Dad replied.

We both agreed that Hawaii was the top choice for our family, so I checked the box and handed it back to him to submit.

On December 15, we said goodbye to Galang Camp, and it was the happiest day of my life!

The Fourth Island—Tanjung Pinang

After yet another ferry ride, we arrived at Tanjung Pinang, a refugee camp on Bintan Island. It was a short boat ride to a place that was clearly designed to only be a temporary stop. Compared to Galang, it was a breeze. No bad memories. We stayed in a big tent by the beach and every day we stood in line to get a ready-cooked meal. Knowing that within a week we would be leaving this camp made any discomfort there might have been, bearable. Despite the perilous conditions in Indonesia, I was grateful for their humanitarian efforts in doing all they could for the boat people. Without their help, our family and many others would have perished at sea. Thank you, Indonesia!

Singapore—The Paradise

On December 22, 1979, we boarded a cargo ship with many other refugees and headed to the well-known, tiny, prosperous nation of Singapore. We were elated to get out of the hellhole refugee camps where we had become afraid our stay would be indefinite. Now, we were going to paradise. This was truly a Christmas gift from above, and we weren't even Christians.

Singapore was for us the glimmer of light at the end of a long, dark tunnel. It was the first time since we left Vietnam that I felt truly hopeful, happy, and relieved. When the bus pulled onto 25 Hawkins Road, Sambewang, I couldn't stop smiling. There were two signs at the entrance: "Hawkins Road" and "Vietnamese Refugee Camp." This felt like the gate to heaven on earth.

Here, refugees were granted some freedom to go shopping or even work. The gate was open during the day and closed at night. Restricted curfews were set up for refugees, but they were free to explore the city as they pleased, and some even took daily jobs to earn a little money.

At the camp center, there were bins of donated clothes, shoes, and hats that we could pick through and take what we wanted. Like many others, I was like a kid in the candy store. The dresses in the bins were so beautiful, and were in perfect condition. I took half a dozen and couldn't wait to wear them. Life was colorful again!

The next day, Dad took a bus trip out of camp with some of his friends to explore the city and to shop for some "luxury" items to bring with us to America. He came back with an electric rice cooker, a piece of cookware we missed having all those months. Almost everyone I knew in Vietnam had a rice cooker. It was so good to not be eating burned rice! Dad also bought his favorite delicacy: strewed pig's stomach and chicken intestines in soy sauce. It cost 50 cents a kilo in Singapore money. That night we felt like we were partaking in a feast. Our life was almost back to normal, like we were waking up from our long nightmare.

When we left Vietnam, we brought with us a small radio/cassette player. Now Dad brought home a giant, two-foot-wide, 16-inch-high replacement. He was ready to rock-and-roll in the new country. When Dad was in a good mood, everyone in the family was happy. I was speechless when Dad presented me with two amazing gifts: a watch and an Olympus mini camera. He even included a roll of film for me to capture the beautiful moments in Singapore. The next day, Mom and I took the kids and walked around the campus taking pictures with my new camera.

After months of helping people feel pretty, I finally felt pretty myself, with all the fashionable clothes I picked up from the center. We changed into one outfit and then another and took pictures of ourselves. We walked out to the street and took pictures posing with random parked cars and pretended that they were ours. The day we had dreamed of for so long would now soon arrive, but still we didn't have a clue where our future home would be. What would it look like? Where would we be going? Would it be the American paradise we imagined?

It was around Christmastime and the atmosphere was very festive. I was delighted to meet three lovely college students who volunteered at the camp. They were thrilled to find out that I was able to speak Mandarin Chinese. They asked me, "Little sis, have you ever been to a zoo?"

"Yes," I said, "we used to go to the zoo during Lunar New Year in Vietnam, but I am sure the zoo is much bigger and better here in Singapore." So, they invited me to spend a day with them out of the city visiting the zoo.

I went to bed that night so excited, I could hardly sleep. In this group, I would be the baby for a day. There would be no little kids that I had to care for following me around. Instead, *I* would be the little sister with three big sisters to spoil me. They were poor college students, but they were rich at heart. They treated me to lunch, and we had a fantastic day at the zoo. The new camera Dad gave me came in handy. I took lots of pictures of animals but regrettably forgot to take any pictures of us.

After lunch, one of the girls gave me a piece of gum (this was before gum was totally banned in Singapore) and immediately reminded me to give the gum back to her when I was done chewing it. I was confused as to why she wanted it back. She explained that if I tossed it on the ground, she would get a heavy fine. I said, "No worries, I won't spit it out on the road. I promise to put it in the trash can." Over the course of the next hour, they repeatedly asked if I was done chewing the gum. I felt a bit paranoid and acutely aware that they did not want to take any chance of me making a mistake. So, I put the gum in the trash to ease their concern. I have never seen anyone so concerned for the cleanliness of their city as the people in Singapore. It was the cleanest city I have ever seen.

Singapore felt like heaven to us, and we were not at all eager to leave. It immediately became our home country away from home. About one third of the population in Singapore was Chinese and communication was easy for us. Dad had so much fun window-shopping for new electronic gadgets and brought home his cherished pig and chicken organ delicacies every day. It was cheap and they were delicious. Mom stocked up on herbal medicines and Chinese ointments to bring with us.

It felt like we were on vacation. I told my parents that someday I would come back to retire in Singapore. It was a dream that I cherished for a long time, and I was glad I could come back to visit 40 years later. Our week in Singapore went by way too quickly and before we knew it, 1979 was over and we were told to get ready to depart for America on January 2, 1980.

On the day before we left, Dad bought a bag of a new delicious fruit called persimmons. We had never tasted fresh persimmon in Vietnam. They were crunchy and juicy, like a peach or a nectarine, except sweeter and tastier. We enjoyed them so much that Dad bought another bag to bring with us. Unfortunately, no one could bring fruit on board the plane, so rather than dump them in the trash, our family ate the entire bag of persimmons before checking in. To this day, we remember the "persimmon story" as a happy ending on a high note of sweet abundance after living the life of scarcity in our arduous refugee journey.

Good times in Singapore (December 1979)

8

Onamia

The First Flight

Exactly eight months to the day after we boarded our homemade boat with an uncertain future, our family of seven walked forward to board the airplane that would take us to America.

We were stunned to see the behemoth plane up close. Words cannot begin to describe the feelings we had as we walked across the tarmac towards the huge double-decker passenger plane, a Boeing 747 jumbo jet. I'll never forget its enormity. I've read that the Wright brothers' historic flight was shorter than its wingspan. After all that we had been through in the prior eight months, our sense of awe and excitement was a welcome change.

As we boarded the plane, my thoughts went back eight months to the feelings I had as we boarded our little boat, obscenely small in comparison but just as significant in our journey to a new life. My dad was filled with "oohs" and "aahs" at the size of this amazing airplane. As for me, my heart was beating faster and faster, anticipating with excitement all I imagined America would bring: freedom, prosperity, any number of mysteries…all good.

We were ushered to the second deck of the plane, which was mostly occupied by refugees, none of whom we knew. The first deck was filled with regular patrons who I suspect were all experienced fliers. But for our family and the other refugees on the upper deck, this was our first time on an airplane. Everyone could hardly contain their excitement. Our hearts were as light as the air that was about to lift us into the sky. I sat by a window, and as the plane sped along the runway and took flight, I took one last look at Singapore, making a promise that I would be back.

I had loved my time there, but I was giddy with excitement to leave for America. Of course, my emotions were mixed. As I said goodbye to Singapore, I also said goodbye to my old self, my 17-year-old self. In my new life I would no longer be Le Thanh Ong; now I would be Le Khanh Ong, the name of my deceased sister. I would also take her birth year as my own, just cutting off four years in one fell swoop. My father thought that presenting myself as a 13-year-old would give me more time to acclimate to my new life, become proficient in English, and have additional years of education. And so, as a new adventure began, another chapter in my life ended as my whole identity officially changed.

I was now a new, hopeful person of a new era, of a new country, and would be literally reliving four years of my life. I spent my 13th, 14th, 15th, and 16th years in Vietnam. And now I would live my 13th, 14th, 15th, and 16th years all over again in America. Can you imagine? Subtract four years from the age you are now and picture yourself living those four years over again, though you remember everything you experienced the first time! I understood there were advantages, but I was not prepared for the emotional conflicts that came with it and the psychological impact reliving those years would bring.

I gazed out at the pillow-like clouds and let my mind wander. It was amazing how far we had come. For the past eight months, our family just did whatever it took to survive and followed any instructions we were given by authorities in our temporary encampments. Each day we faced something new, never knowing what the next day would bring. We lived too long in uncertainty. We didn't know which country would sponsor us, how long we would be waiting before we got there, what the climate was like, or what it would be like to be living as refugees in a new country. We didn't realize how tiny Vietnam was compared to the vastness of the United States.

Now, here we were flying to America. It did not feel like we were on a vacation, it was more like one big adventure into the unknown. But one thing I was confident of: we would no longer be country-less refugees. We were on a path to becoming citizens of a FREE country that valued freedom of thought, human rights, and the rule of law. My family had lived in a free-market society and then, after the takeover, under communist rule, so we knew the difference. I shudder to think how ruined all our lives and descendants' lives would have been if we had not succeeded in our escape.

The 16 hour plane ride from Singapore to Los Angeles did not seem that long. The many drinks and meals being served to us throughout the flight made us feel like we were already living some other life in a new world. I napped here and there, but it was hard to settle into sleep. I was filled with the excitement of the mystery that awaited us. How odd it was to fly out of Singapore on the second of January, spend 16 hours in the air, and arrive in Los Angeles still on the second of January. Time was literally standing still for us as we entered our new country, our new world.

At LAX, the Los Angeles airport, all the refugees from the second deck of the plane disembarked and seemed to quickly disappear. They dispersed throughout the airport in many different directions to their own sponsored destinations. Our family was directed to another airplane that was heading to "Minnesota," a place we had never heard of until that very moment.

Beginning of a New Era

We were all in the dark about our destination, but we knew how to follow directions and we had great faith in whatever this new life would mean for us. It was now the evening and, by the time we boarded the plane, it was dark. For the first time in our lives, we were completely separated from people of our own race. There were no other Asian people on this flight, and we were the only refugees on the plane. It seemed we were the only people who could not speak English. We had always felt close as a family, but now we were also seven orphans being adopted by our new parent country. The four-hour plane ride to Minnesota seemed to take no time at all. Our hearts were already there, faster than any plane could carry us.

We had fled Vietnam on May 3, 1979. We arrived at the Minneapolis/ St. Paul airport at midnight, January 3, 1980, exactly eight months later. We quickly gathered together all our earthly belongings. Dad carried a cassette radio and a large bag with our brand-new rice cooker that he had bought in Singapore. Mom was holding Nam and carrying a small tote bag. Each of us children carried a blue *Care* bag with our clothing and belongings. We were surprised as we disembarked from the plane that we were walking across a covered bridge straight into the inside of the airport. We did not know what was going to happen next. We were all nervous, but this was the moment we had been waiting for since we boarded the boat to escape the tyranny of Vietnam. We were walking into our new life, right then and there.

I immediately saw a small sign with my father's name written on it, "Tai Ong," held by a woman alongside a tall man and two other women. On the floor in front of them were several boxes. They had spotted us before we saw them, and they held up the sign to get our attention. They approached us and greeted us in such a warm and welcoming way that we instantly felt more relaxed. We learned later that the tall man was Tim Rauk, the pastor of the Lutheran church, our primary sponsoring church. Next to him was Nancy, his wife, and two other women from the church. They were all dressed in heavy jackets, which seemed strange to us because it was very comfortable in the airport. We didn't understand that the airport was heated, and that the weather outside the airport was very different. Very, very different.

They opened the boxes and pulled out thick jackets, mittens, hats, scarves, gloves, boots, and earmuffs. They made sure each of us had a coat that fit us properly. While they were busy flipping and finding things in the boxes, I looked at my mom who was as confused as I. Why were they so concerned about being warm? We were perfectly comfortable with the temperature. I guessed it was maybe cooler outside in the night air, but I could not imagine why we had to cover ourselves with heavy layers like this.

Once we were fitted with our new winter wear, we followed Pastor Tim and the women to the garage adjacent to the airport. They loaded us into a station wagon and all our stuff in another car. Nancy asked us, "Are you hungry?" It was my first attempt to communicate in English to someone in America. I felt I should have understood something from studying English at the camp, but I didn't. So, she resorted to gestures to communicate with me. Those I understood.

Our sponsors tried talking slowly, hoping that if they spoke a little louder and slower than normal that we might understand. My dad tried to communicate with smiles and nodding, but we didn't know what anyone was saying. It was what our family would call communication between a chicken and a duck. One phrase that stood out to us was, "It's cold!" Dad turned to me and asked why they kept saying "bitter." (The English word *cold* sounds like a word meaning *bitter* or *suffer* in Teochew Chinese.) Dad was concerned that it must signify the bitterness of what we were about to face here in America.

The cars rolled out of the airport parking ramp and we saw, for the first time, the beautiful sight of something we had never witnessed before. Snow! Light flurries had blanketed all the cars, and there was a beautiful stillness to the scenic landscape. As our cars left Minneapolis for a two-hour ride to our new home in a small town called Onamia, we prepared ourselves for another important step in our journey.

Tired from 24 hours of plane travel, my siblings fell asleep quickly in the car. I sat quietly looking out the window. A peacefulness engulfed me. I thought back to the vastness of the sea, first from the boat, and then from the long flight over the ocean. And now, the vastness of the snow-covered landscape of rural Minnesota. So different from one another, yet how similar they were. They brought me an inexplicable peace, and at the same time a nervousness as we faced an uncertain and unknowable future in our lives.

As we drove into Onamia, the sign outside town reported the population to be 720 people. Our new town looked like a postcard; a perfect small, charming, rural Minnesota town, buried under a fresh covering of new snow. But as beautiful as that picture was, coming from a tropical climate, where it was wet or dry, hot or hotter, we weren't prepared for how dramatically the cold weather would affect us. Dad kept talking to me in Chinese as if I had the power to translate it to the new foreigners. He said he now understood the meaning of his recent dream, where he was looking down at a beautiful new watch from Switzerland. It must signify that we would be residing in a super cold place. I nodded in agreement just to keep my dad happy.

The cars stopped in front of a white Cape Cod style house, at 319 S. Oak Street. My heart skipped a beat. This was our new home. As if forcing the idea to sink in, my mind said: THIS is our new home. This IS our new home. This is OUR new home. This is our NEW home. This is our new HOME.

The house was brightly lit and warmly heated, awaiting its new residents. Getting out of the car, we gasped, inhaling the crisp, cold air. For some reason, this made me tremble with joy. The single-digit freezing cold temperature gave us a hard welcome which stiffened our faces. We lugged all our belongings into the house with the help of our sponsors. It was almost three o'clock in the morning, and none of us had gotten more than a few hours of sleep in the last 36 hours, but we were not sleepy.

Pastor Tim and Nancy were eager to show us where our bedrooms were so we could finally get some rest, but none of us were interested in sleep. We wanted to explore our new HOME, a place we had yearned for since we left Vietnam.

Our American sponsors told us that they would come back tomorrow afternoon, leaving us all morning to catch up on our sleep. "Feel free to eat whatever is here. There is milk, eggs, and vegetables in the refrigerator, and cereal, bread and fruit on the countertop in the kitchen." We did not understand a word Pastor Tim said, but based on his pointing, we totally understood his message.

My family gazed at everything with awe. The house was probably no more than 1,500 square feet, but our impression was that it was large and spacious. It was completely furnished with donated furniture, decorated with details of love and affection. In the living room was a small TV, a comfy sofa, and two good sized chairs. A giant heater was placed at the center of the hall leaning against the wall. To the right was the master bedroom and to the left was the entrance to the dining room and the kitchen which looked cheerful with its white cabinets and deep red colored Formica counters. Across from the kitchen, and adjacent to the heater, was the precious bathroom. Finally, we would have the privacy that was completely missing at the refugee camps. Now we could shower and do our business in private without always feeling like we were on display. Next to the bathroom was a door leading to an unheated mudroom. A stairway led up to two small bedrooms on the second floor, heated only with a vent in the floor which conducted heat up from the main level.

As soon as Tim and his entourage left, we all scattered in different directions to check out the house. There were note cards posted throughout the home. "Wall," "refrigerator," "stove," "lamp," "table," "chair," "window," "door," "closet." Everything was labeled and carefully taped to secure the vocabulary cards in the proper places. How thoughtful!

Mom and Dad went straight to the kitchen. The cupboards were filled to the brim with food: all sorts of canned goods, dried foods, and even a large bag of rice was there. Rice! They somehow knew how much we loved rice. We were also surprised to find a bottle of fish sauce in the cupboard. How did they know how important these foods were to us? Everywhere we looked we found treasures waiting to be discovered. In the corner of the living room, there was a basket of children's books, toys, and stuffed animals that could entertain my young siblings for hours. It was another heaven on earth, but this was not temporary. This was ours!

I went to the closet and found clothes, tons and tons of clothes in different sizes and different styles for women, men and children. There was even an old sewing machine. This was unbelievable! During our first week in our new home, Mom and I had so much fun mixing, matching, and altering clothes for the family. The summer dresses and clothing we brought with us from Vietnam and Singapore were in no way suitable for the Minnesota winter. But we would be fine, thanks to our benefactors who had filled our closets with warm clothing and coats.

Mom took out a small pot, cooked some porridge and opened a can of sardines. Was it breakfast or dinner? We weren't quite sure what time zone our bodies were in. It was about 5:00 a.m., and our bodies suddenly submitted to the sleepy ghosts that started inhabiting all of us. My parents and little Nam went to the downstairs bedroom. Viet and Que shared the front bedroom that Phan and I had to walk through to get to our back bedroom. Each room was just big enough for two twin beds with an aisle in between. That was plenty for us, and we were grateful to have a private bed in our own private family space.

As I fell asleep that first night, I felt safe and secure in our new home. We could have been confined there, buried by a three-month Minnesota blizzard and it wouldn't have mattered to us. We had food, TV, toys, and clothes. Life felt so complete for our family of seven. We had been through a terrible ordeal for the past eight months, and now, we were home.

*   *   *

It was early afternoon the next day when the sound of the doorbell awakened me with a jolt. For a moment I felt disoriented. I ran downstairs to open the door with my parents standing behind me. A gush of cold air blowing off the blanket of white snow reminded me that I was no longer in the tropics. A woman handed us a casserole and a plate of cookies. Everything was still warm, fresh out of the oven. We thanked her and invited her in, but she said something, and then left. It was remarkable to us that not only had our kitchen been well-stocked with more than enough food for all of us, but in addition, a stranger had come out in the freezing cold weather to bring us a hot, home-cooked meal. If our Lutheran sponsors wanted to make an impression about how charitable and kind Christians were, they were doing a great job by showing us generosity like none of us had ever seen before. We were very grateful.

The first week had its challenges. Because of jetlag, we tended to sleep during the day and were up like a pack of rats at night, foraging for food and exploring the gadgets in the kitchen. During that first week, we did not have to do much cooking because there was an influx of food dropped off from neighbors and parishioners from all the churches in this little town. Sometimes we would hear the doorbell and find bags of food at the front door. It was like magic!

Pastor Tim and Nancy would stop in from time to time to make sure we were comfortable, that the house was warm, and the heater was working properly. They taught us how to operate the washing machine and drier. The washing machine was in the house, but the drier was in the mud room which had no heat. It was so cold out there that Dad nicknamed that room "the morgue." No one was keen on using the dryer, which was in the morgue, but when the clothes were done from the wash inside the house, we had to bring them out and get the drier started immediately or they would freeze! It was a torturous, but fun thing for my brother and me to do.

Looking out the windows, we were fascinated by the snow. To face the cold, we put on thick clothes: jackets, ski masks, mittens, scarves, and boots. We were covered from head to toe before we dared to venture out of the house. We weren't outside more than 15 minutes before we'd run inside to stand in front of the big heater. The cold wind was somehow able to get through all the thick layers of clothing and whip our bodies and faces. The hot, humid days and nights in Vietnam and Indonesia gradually became a distant memory.

Scabies

One of the first orders of concern was to evaluate what impact our ordeal as boat people and refugees might have had on our health. Many people volunteered to be a part of our health care team, looking after our physical needs. One of the couples that visited us regularly was Andy and Sharon Stevens. Andy was a radiology technician and Sharon was a nurse at the hospital. Their role was to schedule all of us for physical and dental checkups. There were a lot of medical trips for our large family.

Of immediate concern was a terrible rash that Phan and Que had on their faces and all over their bodies. Mom tried treating it with an ointment we had bought to treat blisters, but they didn't get better. At the Onamia clinic, it was diagnosed as scabies. Scabies is a skin condition that is caused by a microscopic, eight-legged mite that results in itching and rashes. Scabies is terribly contagious and can spread very easily from person to person through close physical contact. When this was explained to Mom and Dad with the use of pictures of the offending mites, they were horrified. Dad wanted to make sure to communicate that this infestation was the result of the conditions of the camp. But Mom and Dad clearly understood that this needed to be treated immediately.

Pastor Tim's wife and Kay Mickus, the head nurse that the Onamia Hospital, volunteered to administer the treatment, which involved a thorough disinfecting of all our clothes and bedding with a special soap, and an equally thorough bathing of the whole family. Nancy and Kay were prepared to help in the bathing of children. We all gathered at Nancy and Tim's home and Kay brought a box of towels from the hospital that could then be properly disinfected after the treatment. But Mom would not let anyone else take care of what she saw as her duty as a mother. Each of my siblings were brought into the bathroom, and Mom made sure there would be no remaining infestation on any of us. Soon after, the blisters and rash went away, and we were then given tips on how to moisturize our skin in the dry cold climate of Minnesota. A change in soap and the discovery of lotion that had remained untouched and unopened in the bathroom brought additional comfort to everyone in the family.

Otherwise, we were all in good health, which was rather amazing considering all that our family had been through. We had survived four years of chaotic domination under the communist regime in Vietnam, followed by eight months of turbulence in our journey to escape. And then life seemed to come to a slow stop in Onamia. I loved the feeling of peace and quiet, watching the overcast sky drop a blanket of fresh snow that covered up the footprints and everything on the ground. It was as if the chaos of the past was being covered over with the serenity of a new start. I think our whole family felt it. Mom and Dad quarreled less. My father talked to us more and screamed at us much less. We had never spent this much time together as a family. There were no familiar forms of social life as we had in the busy city in Vietnam, so all we had that was familiar to us was each other. It was good, but we felt very isolated.

Citizens of Kindness

Certainly, the feeling of isolation was not because of the people of Onamia. To our surprise, our walkway always seemed to be cleared of snow. We had no idea how many neighbors and people in the town had taken turns to shovel our front sidewalk. Looking back, there were so many acts of kindness that we had not even been aware of because everything was so strange and new to us. From the severity of the climate, to the American lifestyle and culture, everything was a learning opportunity. We were overwhelmed with what would have been obvious had we lived in Onamia all our lives.

After spending about a week at home and re-regulating our bodies to adjust to the new time zone, we began to feel ready to face the world outside our cozy Cape Cod house. Dad was offered a job at the Community Mercy Hospital as a janitor. Every morning, he put on his uniform and would wait for a ride from a gentleman who also worked at the hospital. We did not have a car, so we relied on others for transportation.

Viet, Phan, and Que were enrolled in the elementary school as fifth, fourth, and third graders, respectively. I went to school at the junior high as a seventh grader. My fake birth records indicated that I was 13 years old. Because I was petite, no one suspected anything, but I felt awkward being placed with kids who were four years younger than me.

It was a huge cultural adjustment for us to make. Suddenly, we were living with people who all looked very different from us. The kids in my class at school were mostly tall, blond, blue-eyed children of northern European descent. There were a few Native Americans in class who, at first, I thought were Asians, but soon found out that we were not at all alike. We did not share any trace of DNA. I was the only Asian person in my class, and probably in the entire school.

By the second week after we arrived, a routine started to set in. Dad's ride would bring him to work at the hospital and we kids would prepare for a day at school. Mom would wake up early to cook hot rice porridge for breakfast and we ate with the TV on while waiting for the bus. We would layer up with clothing and winter accessories to protect every bit of exposed skin we could cover. The only thing visible was our eyes. It was too cold for us to stand in front of the house to wait for the bus, so we waited by the front window. As soon as the bus could be seen, we turned off the TV and ran out the door. America had introduced us to cartoons such as *Tom and Jerry*, *Bugs Bunny*, and *Popeye*. We all loved them, even Dad. We never tired of watching cartoons and it made getting up in the frigid cold weather for school a little bit easier. As we ran out the door to catch the school bus, Mom and little Nam remained at home where Mom sat by the stairs to look out to the snow, hoping every day that the mailman would bring us news from Vietnam.

One day after school, we found Pastor Tim and a reporter at our house. They were there to take some pictures for an article they were writing for the *Mile Lac Messenger*. The pictures featured me holding some Chinese ointments, Mom and her precious rice cooker, and Dad holding the phone. It is a blessing to have those articles to look back on after all these years.

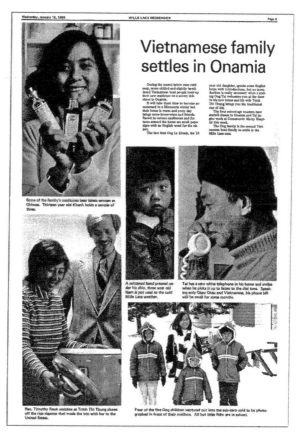

Possessions that I guarded with my life since leaving Vietnam were my English/Vietnamese, Vietnamese/English dictionary, my English/Chinese, Chinese/English dictionaries. I carried these two thick dictionaries with me everywhere. In Vietnam, I had seven years of schooling, so both my Chinese and Vietnamese language skills were adequate. But English was a very, very different language. If I got stuck on an English word, I would often check both dictionaries to get a better understanding of the meaning. These two dictionaries became my best friends that first year as I worked to learn to speak American English. I used them constantly in my communications with people in Onamia. I found myself being forced more and more to think in English. Often my translation was a bit clunky, but I was learning quickly.

At home, whenever the phone rang, it was my job to answer. The phone was in the kitchen and had a long cord. It was used mostly for local communications, and I was pretty much the only one who spoke on the phone with my dictionaries always close by. Whenever the doorbell rang, it was my job to answer the door. Whenever there were documents or papers that needed to be filled out, I was the one to do it. As the eldest child, I suddenly had so many adult responsibilities. I was the Chief Translator, and everyone relied on me to talk for them. I had only started to learn a little bit of English in a refugee camp. As the one responsible for all communication to the community, I took my responsibility very seriously. Advocating for my family had become my number one priority. Sometimes I got frustrated at myself for not being able to express what my family wanted. Sometimes my parents got frustrated with me because I hesitated to translate what they said if I thought it was an inappropriate comment or question. And at 17, everything felt awkward and inappropriate. I would change their question to something that I thought was more suitable. I didn't realize until much later in life how much pressure I was feeling during this first year being in America.

Nancy Rauk had helped us open a checking account so Dad could deposit his paycheck from the hospital job. In addition to everything else, it became my responsibility to write the checks and balance our checking account. Every month, I would send out checks for rent and utilities. When we went shopping, I wrote the check. So, in addition to everything else, I was also the family accountant. Our checking account was a teeny tiny account, but it was still yet another thing on my plate.

Mom could have taken on this role or at least worked with me, but she preferred to take a back seat and gave me that responsibility.

Saturday mornings were grocery shopping day. It was a family adventure out into the cold. All seven of us would put on layers of warm clothes and parade down a back road, across the railroad tracks, and walk through a parking lot to get to the grocery store on the main street of town. We would then parade back home, all in a row, with everyone except Nam carrying a bag of groceries. Through the parking lot, across the railroad tracks and down our backstreet we would march, all in a row like ducks. Sometimes Dad would let us buy a pack of bubble gum that included a little prize. Mom would then fix a wonderful home-cooked meal after our shopping journey that would remind us of the food we enjoyed when we were a family in Vietnam.

One other thing that reminded us of our home country was watching reruns of the TV show, *Kung Fu*. This show starred David Carradine who played a Chinese man, though he didn't look at all Chinese to us. We also enjoyed watching Chinese Kung Fu movies on Saturday afternoons. The lip movements never matched the words, but we didn't care. It was the family time that we all enjoyed. Compared to what we had gone through, this was a beautiful, worry-free period for our family.

Life in Onamia

The Softer Dad

During those months in Onamia, I noticed a big change in my dad. He seemed much more mellow. I think this must have been the most peaceful time for him since his childhood. There was no hustle and bustle of a crazy, unpredictable life. There was no business to take care of, no ration lines to stand in, and no cutting wood from the forest as he had to do in Indonesia. The world had slowed down tremendously for Dad. But there was no one for Dad to talk to except us, his children and wife. This must have felt very strange to him. We were the only people who could understand him. But now, his temper seldom flared up. He went to work, and then he came home to be with his family. We saw the softer side of Dad. He would joke with us. He watched TV with us. He would walk around the house with a blanket wrapped around him like a Buddhist monk.

Dad's short crew-cut hair grew long, and the gray hair became much more pronounced. He looked so much older than most 44-year-old men. I know Dad felt lonely. Long distance phone calls were costly, and Dad used the phone sparingly to try to locate friends and relatives who settled elsewhere in the United States. He was eager to find out about other cities where his friends were.

Our whole family had much to learn about this new country. Everything was new to all of us. We were in many ways all on the same playing field; but, we were all interpreting everything through different lenses, based on our own life experience. For the children, everything was new and exciting. For my parents, it was new and scary. I know they were worried about us. That's why they left Vietnam in the first place. Now, though, I could tell that Dad was concerned that his children would lose their culture and their roots in this brand-new world. To us children, Dad was still the most powerful person in our universe, but he worried about those forces that we faced as children that he was not able to control. The western world was such a dramatic change for him, and he was frightened for his children.

Slowly and surely, we began to feel more and more comfortable in our new community. There were routine visits from the church members and other volunteers in the community. We felt out of place in our new country, but we also felt shielded by all the people who cared so much about our well-being. Onamia became our northern bubble of ice and snow, filled with warm caring people.

It Took a Whole Village

There was quite a full-team effort to make us feel welcome, loved and supported. It really took an army of volunteers and many unsung heroes to care for our family. I wish I could remember all their names. Three churches had sponsored us: Bethany Lutheran Church, led by Rev. Tim Rauk, the Onamia United Methodist Church, and Holy Cross Catholic Church, led by Father Jim Hentges, had all recruited numerous people to take part in this helping-hand effort.

We quickly began recognizing the recurring presence of many of these helpers, but we had trouble pronouncing and remembering their names. Dad would affectionately give them nicknames based on a Vietnamese word that helped us recognize amongst our family who we were talking about. For example, on Sundays, there was a very nice elderly woman we called "Mrs. Chewy." She often volunteered to give us a ride to church. Dad gave her the name "Mrs. Chewy" because she was so chatty. After the service, she would talk endlessly with everyone in church. We would sit and wait for her to finish her conversations before giving us a ride home. We adored her but wondered what there was to talk about for so long after church. We loved "Mrs. Chewy" for her friendliness and generosity, but we often prayed that she would come late on Sunday so we could finish watching *The Three Stooges*, our family's all-time favorite comedy.

Another volunteer who came to our house one night a week to teach my parents English was Karen Helle. Taping vocabulary cards identifying the objects around the house was Karen's great idea. This helped us to recognize the objects so much more quickly. Karen was a new mother of a baby girl named Christine. She often brought Christine with her to our house. My siblings would sit and admire this gorgeous blonde-haired, blue-eyed baby, who would cry loudly if one of the black-haired people picked her up. We were just fascinated seeing a white baby for the first time in our lives.

Andy and Sharon Stevens were another couple who played a large role in introducing our family to American culture. They had two children; Becky was 13 and David was a few years younger. The Stevens family came to visit our family almost every other weekend, more frequently than anyone else.

One weekend, Andy stopped by to visit and saw what we had for lunch. He asked, "How was your tuna sandwich?" I told him that we'd had chicken, not tuna. He looked at me and said, "That looks like tuna to me!"

I pointed to the can's label, which said, "chicken of the sea."

"Then why do they call it chicken?" I asked, in my earnest attempt to learn more about my new country.

We had many amazing experiences with the Stevens. During the frigid months of January and February, Andy drove his snowmobile to our house on the snow-covered roads and gave both Mom and Dad a ride. It was a thrilling experience for Dad, but fantastically frightful and freezing for Mom. Neither of them could stop talking about it afterward.

Another interesting person who made a positive impact on our family was an elderly man in his eighties named Mr. Clyde. The first time we met Mr. Clyde was one afternoon, when he came to the house and rang the doorbell. We rushed to answer the door. He warmly announced that he wanted to welcome us to Onamia. Mom and I had just finished baking cookies with the new recipe I got from a lady at church. We left the cookies in the oven a bit too long, so they came out a little burnt, but that was all we had. We invited Mr. Clyde to have some cookies along with some Chinese tea. I felt embarrassed when I realized he had no teeth, but Mr. Clyde dunked the cookies in the tea, let them soak a bit so they were soft, and told us that they were very tasty. He invited our whole family to come to his farm for a sleigh ride! We could hardly imagine the idea.

The following weekend, he came to pick us up and drove us out to his farm. Mr. Clyde had two beautiful horses hitched up to a sleigh, ready to take us on a ride through the majestic snowy woods surrounding his farm. He taught us to sing: "Jingle bells, jingle bells, jingle all the way. Oh, what fun it is to ride in a one-horse open sleigh." I can still feel the warmth of his heart and the smile on his face as he sang and saw the joy we had on that ride.

Back at the house, Mr. Clyde proudly showed us the two tombstones he was carving for himself and for his wife. "They are all ready, except for the dates to be filled in later, of course." He revealed that he was 84 years old and his wife was 82. "I know she'll probably not be going too far behind me, so I might just as well get hers ready, too," he joked. I remember thinking how practical Americans were. Independent until the day they die.

There is a concept in Chinese Buddhism called, "filial piety." Filial piety is considered a key virtue in Chinese and Asian cultures. It is a virtue of respect for one's parents, elders, and ancestors. In more general terms, filial piety means to be good to one's parents; it is your responsibility to take care of them, and to show them love, respect and support. So, it would be considered a bad omen to talk about death when you are getting close to dying. Asians expect their children and grandchildren to have an elaborate burial tombstone to express their love for their parents. The bigger the ceremony, the more filial piety is demonstrated toward their parents. How strange and different our two cultures seemed!

I thanked Mr. Clyde for a memorable experience and promised to see him often. I only saw Mr. Clyde one more time, but I did correspond several times with him after we moved to Philadelphia. His first letters were hand-written. Eventually he began sending typed notes. He revealed that his eyesight had gotten so bad and he could not hold a pen anymore. In 1983, I got a letter from Mr. Clyde that his wife had passed. It was a short note. He said he was feeling too weak to write. We felt honored that Mr. Clyde took the effort to write to us, difficult as it was. He had left a memorable footprint on my heart. Every Christmas, when I hear the song, "Jingle Bells," I think of Mr. and Mrs. Clyde, they were special people.

Ice Fishing

Every weekend, the Stevens introduced us to completely new experiences. One freezing cold Saturday, Andy called and told us that he had an adventure in mind. "Be sure to dress warm," he said, "I'm going to take you and your Dad fishing." I wasn't quite sure how to explain this to Dad. In this icy cold climate where everywhere you look is frozen solid, Dad and I could not picture where there would be a body of water where fishing was possible.

Andy pulled up in front of our house with what looked like a small cabin being pulled behind the car. We hopped in his car and off we drove. We left the tree-lined highway, turned onto a road and drove out onto what looked like a huge field covered with snow. I would have guessed it was a corn field in warmer months. It was a vast open space, but we were not alone. We saw many other cars parked behind small cabins like the one Andy was towing.

Andy referred to the cabin behind his car as his *fish house*. "We're now driving on top of a lake," Andy explained. This seemed crazy to me, and I wasn't sure what Dad would think. Andy parked, unhitched the fish house from the car, and directed us to all step into the cabin. "We're going to go fishing now," Andy said to us. It was something I could not comprehend. I kept smiling and nodding my head, pretending that I understood. *This is so, so strange*, I thought.

Inside the cabin there was a wood stove and several stools placed around a hole in the middle of the plywood floor. When I saw the hole in the floor, all I could think of was the toilet hole in the refugee camp. The thought of that shocked me. While I was running these crazy thoughts through my mind, Andy was busy talking and starting a fire in the wood stove to keep us warm. He then took out what he called an *ice auger* and proceeded to drill a hole through the ice underneath the hole in the middle of the fish house.

I still didn't really believe that we were standing on top of a lake. How can you drive so many cars out onto a lake and park there? Andy explained that it was very safe because there were several feet of frozen ice on top of the lake. But this was something I couldn't quite fathom. *Even if the ice is thick, how could it hold all this weight?*

It took some time to drill the hole successfully, because indeed, the ice was very thick. The hole was about ten inches in diameter. When

Andy finally reached the water below the ice, the water gushed up to the top of the hole. Andy took out a short fishing rod, put some bait on the hook, and dropped the line into the hole. Then, as he patiently waited for a fish to bite, he poured us some hot chocolate from the thermos to keep us toasty warm. Within minutes, we saw the line moving and Andy pulled out a beautiful perch. Dad and I were wide-eyed, fascinated by the whole process. Andy asked me to open the door of the fish house. He unhooked the fish and tossed it outside to the snow. In no time, the poor fish was frozen solid. Instant freezer to seal in the freshness. That's the beauty of ice fishing, I learned that day. It was an experience my father and I treasured for the rest of our lives, something we could never imagine doing by ourselves.

For as long as we live, we will never forget many acts of kindness shown to us by the people in Onamia. It has inspired me to give back in my life in the same way I received such blessings from the Onamia community. There were so many incredible experiences that touched our souls and that taught me about Christian love at the deepest level.

With Tim and Nancy Rauk

Mom at Women's Club

Spring boat fishing with the Stevens

Fellowship at Bethany Church   *Picnic with the Stevens*

Schools in Onamia

While the volunteers from our sponsoring churches introduced us to our new community, we were also being introduced to American culture through the Onamia school system. Now we kids were with a whole new group of people and our parents weren't there to shield us. Most of the kids in school were kind and understanding, but some viewed us as a novelty and maybe with some suspicion.

Based on the official age, I was put in the seventh grade. I would often look at the high school kids and wonder what it would be like if I could reveal to them that I was really 17 years old. But then, they all looked so much bigger and older. Often, I was glad that my false age had bought me four extra years to learn more English and master all my academic classes. And besides, my physical size was indeed more like that of an American 13-year-old.

The first big difference I encountered in American schools compared to what I had experienced in Vietnam was having a locker in the hallway for my books and my coat. And in America, each teacher had their own classroom with desks for each hour-long class of students. Here, students were the moving parts and changed classrooms for each of their subjects. And in America, students could randomly sit wherever they wanted!

In Vietnam, students were assigned to a single classroom and had the same desk for the entire school year. We had drawers under our desks for books and we kept our book bags by our side all day long. The seating arrangement was mostly based on height, with the girls and the boys separated. Boys sat on one side of the room, and girls on the other. Shorter kids were placed in front of the class and taller ones in the back. I found it unfortunate that because of my height, I was almost always placed in the front row. We sat in that same desk the whole day, while teachers would rotate into our classroom to teach various subjects. The teachers were the moving parts, not the students. Teachers had their desks in the teachers' office room.

The classes seemed very informal to me, not stiff and tense like the Asian school system. Everything seemed to be the opposite of what I had learned in Vietnam. So much was unfamiliar to me. The one thing that felt familiar was that the classes were an hour long and every hour you had time to reset between classes. Thank God for that!

On my first day of school, I was led to a class where there were about 18 students sitting in individual desks with no apparent order. I was placed in the middle of the class surrounded by boys and girls of random heights. Physically, they all looked older, but they were only 12 and 13-year-olds. My teacher was a kind, friendly woman named Miss Wendy with a very soft voice. Unlike the students in Vietnam, the kids in class here seemed more demanding, and far less reverent toward their teachers. The highly irregular attitude was immediately apparent to me. I was floored when a boy sat down behind me and put his legs up on the table. He waved his hand to Miss Wendy and said, "Wendy, come here!" I almost fell out of my chair. This would never be tolerated in Asia. In Vietnam, students always raised their hands and asked for permission from the teacher to approach them. No one would dream of ordering the teacher around like that.

I wondered if all the schools in America were like this. My first impression was very mixed. There were several students in my class who had a darker skin tone, more like me. At first, I thought maybe they could be Asian. I was hoping to find more Asian families in the community. I soon learned that these students were Native Americans. The boy with his legs crossed on the desk was one of them. He appeared tough and hostile and it seemed that the teacher did not want to upset him. This same boy later walked by me when I was at my hall locker and addressed me with a string of "ching chong cha, ching-dong…" He then let out a big laugh and walked away with his friends.

At first, I didn't realize that he wasn't trying to talk to me in any language, but then, it registered: He was mocking me. He was making fun of me as a foreign newcomer. Yes, I was the only Asian, but how sad that I would be picked on by another minority student. I was afraid of him and his friends, and tried to avoid them at all costs. He had succeeded in intimidating me. For the first time in my new country, I felt unwelcome.

Becky Stevens was in the same grade and we saw each other in class from time to time. She introduced me to her friends, Debbie, Dawn, and Beth. They were all very nice to me and let me hang around with them during lunch. I told Becky about the bully and she told me to just ignore him. I was so grateful to have Becky as my first American friend. She was a good companion, and she really looked out for me.

One of my favorite classes was "English as a Second Language" (ESL). The class was taught by Mr. Dennis Dunn. Thanks to Mr. Dunn, my accent and pronunciation improved dramatically. Before this class, every time I would say the number "six" or "sixteen," it came out "sick" or "sickteen." Through his kind corrections, I gradually learned to improve my English pronunciation. I am indebted to Mr. Dunn for tuning my ears to the "x" sound and so many new distinctions in communication I had to learn.

I was doing well at school in most subjects. My drawings and artwork often got displayed in the hallway and the front lobby of the school. Math was a piece of cake. Being older than my fellow students, I had already learned many of the math concepts in Vietnam. But I sure struggled socially. I was shy and lacked the confidence to ask questions or initiate conversations.

Mr. Dunn was my ESL hero

First School Field Trip

Only a few weeks after starting school, I was told that the seventh graders would be going on a field trip to spend several days at cabins in the woods in the middle of winter. I was super excited. This would be my first opportunity to explore new things for a whole weekend by myself. I wanted to learn to be like the other kids in the school. I saw that most of the girls had their hair curled in a certain 1980's style. I gathered all my courage and asked Dad if I could buy a curling iron for my hair and a new pair of jeans for the trip. I knew how much money we had in the bank and waited for the right time to ask. To my amazement, Dad said yes. He let me buy those two luxury items which I know were unnecessary but meant the world to me! I was also learning that deep down inside, Dad was a very reasonable and loving person.

Since settling in Onamia, Dad had become noticeably more relaxed and less temperamental. I did not really understand why I was so afraid of him. I regret now that I wasn't brave enough to be close to him then. All the years of growing up in fear had put a barrier between my father and me. Communication with Dad had always been more like taking orders, reporting what had been done, and answering questions when asked, but I see now that there was another warm, loving side to my father.

The field trip was amazing. We hiked in the woods. We crawled into an igloo alongside the trail. There was cross-country skiing and snowshoeing. I learned to build a snow man and make snow angels. I stood outside and sketched trees in the forest, and listened to deer moving through the cold, still beauty of the winter woods. I was engulfed in a totally different world. I had been on many adventures in Vietnam and Indonesia. Previously, they were frightening and threatening adventures, but on that school retreat, it suddenly became clear to me how completely different this adventure was. It felt like I was in heaven.

All the suffering and pain we went through to get to the United States dissolved into my past. I finally began to feel that maybe all that could be put into our past and forgotten, and we could move on into our new life. In Vietnam, I could never have imagined the dramatic new turn our lives would take. None of my classmates here in Onamia had the slightest idea what the life we had in Asia was like. They lived the kind of life that I think everyone in the world would want to live, and I was now blessed to be living that life myself. I inhaled it in and made mental pictures of all my new experiences for my keeping.

At night, the teachers and students played games, sang songs, told stories, and drank hot chocolate. It was one first experience after the next for me, overwhelming but in a wonderful and truly memorable way. I pinched myself often to remind myself that this was real. I could live and dream and have a great future here in this God-loving country.

In elementary school, my brothers and sisters were settling in nicely with the guidance of Ms. Watson. All evening long, I would hear them say "Ms. Watson *this*" and "Ms. Watson *that*." This was someone who obviously had made a huge impact on my siblings. They were clearly excited and happy with their new school, but they too had a fair share of being teased. Phan came home with stories of being laughed at when she ripped her pants climbing over a fence. Sadly, her teasers were also mostly the Native American children.

Adapting well to American life

Back in Vietnam and in the refugee camps, my father was always very strict and protective of his children. We were never allowed to sleep at a friend's house. But in Onamia, when Becky and Andy asked if Viet and I could come over to sleep over at their house, Dad gave his permission. I was surprised. Had this totally new culture been changing Dad into a new man? There was something more relaxed in Dad's attitude. He was very trusting of the Stevens family and so he let us go to their home for a sleepover. It was a shock to us children to see Dad putting his protective guard down a little. I was very happy to have the opportunity to be a child like other Onamia children, exploring some of the world outside our house.

Staying at the Stevens, I had the chance to witness the American lifestyle in a real American home. I felt like I was envisioning my future life through the lens of their family. I discovered appliances and gadgets I had never seen, some that I never knew existed. Just in the kitchen, there was the electric coffee maker for brewing coffee, an electric can-opener, and a dishwasher. I was fascinated with the flat electric cooktop that got bright red as it heated the stovetop. And it was always clean. It looked so modern, futuristic and luxurious. Right then I started to dream of having such things in my own future home for my own family. I firmly believed that with hard work and tenacity, that opportunity would eventually be mine.

For now, I was content to play with Becky's pet hamster and listen to all her stories. She seemed to enjoy telling me things that she correctly assumed I would know nothing about, being a stranger in a strange land.

I remember she even taught me to watch out for yellow snow, and not to eat it when I was thirsty. Actually, I understood less than half of what she said, but I loved to bask in the kind, accepting way she befriended me.

At first impossible to imagine, it wasn't long before I had an experience that all the Minnesotans around me seemed to take for granted. That is, fun makes you forget frigid. One of the new experiences Becky introduced me to was to try cross-country skiing. She let me use her old skies, and practiced in the woods behind her backyard. It wasn't easy, skiing up the slopes and across the lake, but slowly I got the hang of it. It was so cold, but as we returned home, cold ceased to be an issue because we were having so much fun, laughing and skiing.

I don't think the Stevens family could ever realize how much their warmth meant to our family. It seemed that every weekend they would include us in a new activity. My parents appreciated this so much as they could tell it helped all of us to feel like we were assimilating, becoming more and more comfortable in our new world. We all appreciated the Stevens; no family could be more perfect as American ambassadors.

Searching for a New City

At school and outside the house, I had to play the role of a 13-year-old. My language skills, to be sure, were lacking, but I knew that I was more mature than the kids around me and that was beginning to wear on me. I knew I was living a lie and that went against my nature. For someone else, maybe that would not be so painful, but for me, the stress germinated seeds of resentment.

I would try to tell myself that I should simply be grateful that I no longer had to deal with the black market or worry about the family's safety. Now, I can be a kid and reclaim those four years of my life that living under communist rule had stolen from me. Why couldn't I just pretend those four years never happened, that I really was only 13? But I couldn't escape the fact that I was living a lie. Four years in the life of a teenager makes a big difference, and I began questioning if lying about my age really did bring me any advantage. I struggled with this internal conflict daily in everything I did and said. It took me years to come to grips with it.

Mom and Nam were getting used to being at home during the day. Nancy Rauk sometimes brought her boys, Jerod and Adam, over for a play date. Other women in the church also invited Mom to their Women's Club for art and craft making, tea times and social get-togethers. However, they could not find a job for Mom, and depending only on Dad's paycheck meant that financially, things were really tight.

As the bookkeeper for our family, I would write the monthly check for our rent to Phil Hanson for $200, and then the checks for our electric bill, the heating oil, water, telephone, and groceries. That would pretty much eat up Dad's $600 monthly income. Yet, Dad would always find a way to send a box of gifts to his two poor sisters in Vietnam. They appreciated it, but probably expected no less. They had no idea what our new life was like. They couldn't understand the cold weather and the feeling of isolation, or what it was like to try to make ends meet in a completely new country.

These were quite valuable experiences and skills for a teenager to learn. By making me the bookkeeper for the family, Mom and Dad were teaching me the value of being frugal and always saving for the future. No matter how tight our budget was, my parents tried not to touch the life savings that the pirates had missed on our boat trip from Vietnam. They were reserving that only for emergencies.

Mom was ready, willing, and able to contribute to household finances, but the opportunity had not come along…until one day when someone from church came by. They told her that if she wanted to, she could start making fishing lures. She would be paid a certain amount for each completed lure, and it was work she could do at home where she needed to be with little Nam. This little bit of income helped with the family expenses. All of us (well, mostly me) helped Mom after school, and we earned about $50 to $70 every couple of weeks. Unfortunately, the day came when the need was fulfilled; enough lures were in stock for the upcoming fishing season and the job ended.

We continued to try to find Mom a job. Dad was itching to have his own car so we could become more independent and not have to rely on the people in the church and Dad's coworker for transportation. That would require making more money. There were other things we started to think about wanting in order to build a more convenient and independent lifestyle. It began to be clear that we would need to look for opportunities outside of Onamia. Mom and Dad began spending more and more time exploring what those opportunities might be.

Dad reached out more to his circle of friends who had settled elsewhere in America and Canada. The most promising possibility came from a conversation with my cousin Minh Thu's brother-in-law, Tong, who lived in Philadelphia. He told Dad about Chinatown in Philadelphia, and said that Dad could possibly find a job as a sous chef in one of the many Asian restaurants. They suggested that we apply for government assistance while finding jobs that paid under the table to fund the financial gap. My dad said he would think about it, and hoped that Mom could find a job as well.

Tong also offered to let us stay at his house for a few weeks if we decided to move. He said he would take Dad around and help with whatever he could. My parents discussed it intensely and I could see they were somewhat excited with the idea. But I also know they were uneasy about leaving behind the people who had cared so deeply for us and were so nice to us. They were torn. And I was torn. We decided to sleep on the idea for a while longer.

By early March, the temperature began to improve, moving into the thirties and forties. We were able to pack away our thick ski masks. The worst of the cold climate was over, and it was now the season of Lent. I remember my parents dreading the extra mass we felt obligated to go to every Wednesday night in addition to the regular Sunday mass. Mrs. Chewy was so enthusiastic and never missed a beat picking us up both Wednesday and Sunday. I admired her for the Christian love and devotion.

My poor parents tried to act as if they were interested in going to church, but the truth of the matter was that they were bored to tears. They didn't understand anything at all during mass. Dad was tired from work and sometimes fell asleep, snoring loudly during the sermon. We had to elbow him to wake him up. It was funny and embarrassing at the same time. And it was just as hard for us kids to stay alert during the mass. We had been raised in Buddhism and trying to learn about a new religion, in a whole new language, was just more than we could handle. However, the reward after the mass was the fellowship we enjoyed with parishioners in the basement of the church. There, we enjoyed visiting with people and sharing whatever refreshments they were serving.

Sometimes, I babysat Pastor Tim's boys to earn a little money. In the early night, as the boys slept, I would sit in front of the large glass picture window and dream of my future as I looked out on the blanket of white snow. Would this be the life I would have as an adult? This was peaceful but I wanted to see more, to do more, to experience more and have a taste of what life was all about in a big city.

I still lugged the dictionaries with me everywhere I went, but I was becoming more confident and comfortable in speaking and interpreting for my parents. As spring came to Onamia, I began feeling more and more that I wanted to spread my wings and explore the choices and opportunities that might be there in this amazing country. Onamia was a great little town with warm-hearted people, but we were beginning to feel that our long-term opportunities for growth were too limited. I decided to help Dad speed up his decision by saying that I didn't mind moving. I knew he was waiting for me to share my feelings, even though he was reluctant to indicate that my opinion mattered at all.

So, the decision was made, and it fell to me to tell our sponsors that we were looking to move. I explained why we wanted to move and about our family connection in Philadelphia. I first told Pastor Tim and then Andy Stevens so they could relay the information to the church communities at Bethany Lutheran, United Methodist, and Holy Cross Catholic Churches. To our surprise and relief, they were sad but very supportive of the decision. They knew we worked hard, and job opportunities were scarce in Onamia. They did not blame us for wanting to go, but also let us know that we would be missed.

I was very touched when Mrs. Chewy came over one Sunday with tears in her eyes. She said, "Why would you want to go to Philadelphia? It's the dirtiest city in America, and no one would care for you the way we do here!" I hugged her and we both cried.

"We're so sorry," I said, "but that is the only place we have friends who can help us settle. Mom and Dad were told about good job opportunities there. But, please know, we will never forget you and all the people here who helped us so much."

Word got around quickly. And once again, the people of Onamia began exploring ways to show their concern for our family. They wanted to come up with a way that the community could help us accomplish our next step in settling into our new home country. Ideas began circulating. Someone suggested the idea of putting on a dinner. "Maybe you could cook a Chinese dinner and we could sell tickets to people who wanted to try an authentic Asian meal?" Mom and Dad were onboard and planned and oversaw the preparation of a full Vietnamese/Chinese dinner. Becky even helped me put together a Vietnamese cookbook from Mom's recipes to sell at the event.

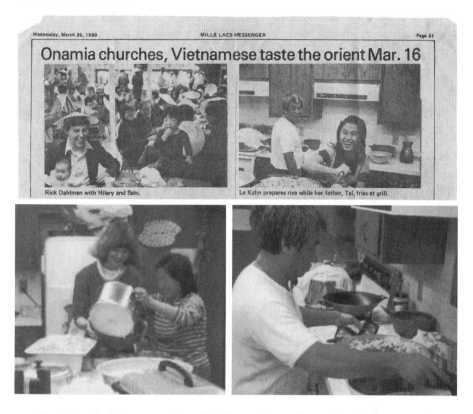

Onamia churches, Vietnamese taste the orient Mar. 16

Rick Dahlman with Hilary and Sein.

Le Kahn prepares rice while her father, Tai, fries at grill.

On March 16, over a hundred people gathered in the basement of Bethany Lutheran Church to enjoy an evening of Asian food, fun, and deep feelings of goodwill. Tickets for the dinner were sold for $3.50. The menu included fried rice, egg rolls, pork, chicken, stir-fried vegetables and soup. We raised over $300. The money would pay for the Greyhound bus fare for our move.

Dad felt that it would be best to wait until the school year was over in June before we moved, so we did our best to get back to our normal activities. I participated in Girl Scouts with Becky and even built up my courage to go door-to-door selling Girl Scout cookies. When Easter arrived, my brothers and sisters enjoyed the novelty of hunting for Easter eggs. By May, the ice and snow had melted, and our big brown backyard turned into a beautiful meadow of green. We had never experienced an American spring, and it was lovely.

Not long after the green carpet of grass appeared in our backyard, we awoke one day to see our yard covered with beautiful yellow flowers. Becky told me that they were called dandelions. "Wait a few days and all those flowers will turn into fluffy balls. And when the wind blows, the fluffy white balls will be scattered in the air. You might even think it's snowing!" It was so much fun. We ran around the yard, picking one flower after another, offering us hours of play.

We discovered two bikes that were waiting for us in the shed. We enjoyed taking the bikes out into the neighborhood for a spin as the weather allowed it. The bike gave me the opportunity to deliver the Girl Scout cookies to the neighbors. I was getting familiar with the community and had come to like my new home. Soon it would be time to leave. I know it was right for our family, but I had moments of sadness.

It was May and the weather was warming up quickly. We were able to pack away all our winter clothes. The Stevens brought us to a small lake for a picnic and swimming. This was the first time we had ever gone swimming in a lake in America. What I noticed immediately was the stink: the strong odor of dead fish. I didn't want to offend our hosts, so I went into the lake, holding my breath all the way. Then I ran back out of the water in disgust. I wish now I could have been brave enough to speak up and be more honest with what I was feeling. I continued to do things because I was afraid of displeasing other people. I am pretty sure now they would not have been offended if I did not want to swim in the lake smelling of thawed, dead fish.

After the picnic, Andy took us to a nearby dam and showed us how to catch fish swimming upstream using nothing but a net. It was as fascinating to us as ice fishing. The fish seemed to jump voluntarily into our net! We caught so many fish that Mom and I spent the whole day cleaning fish and making fish floss. Fish floss is made by cooking fish fillets in oil, with garlic, shallots, soy sauce, pepper, and sugar, until the fish are dehydrated and shredded.

There were so many new experiences in Onamia that my family will never forget. The generosity and affectionate love the people gave to our family was completely genuine. Our time in Onamia brought our family a measure of healing from the cruel and inhumane treatment we had seen and experienced in the poverty of our native Vietnam, and of course from our harrowing experiences as boat people. I was worried that we might not experience this kind of support in a big city like Philadelphia. Were we making the right decision to leave the people in Onamia who cared so deeply for us? Were we making a mistake by moving?

But the decision was made and on June 17, 1980, we closed our bank account of $206.32 and bought our Greyhound tickets. Pastor Tim, his wife Nancy, and Andy and Sharon Stevens came to take us to the bus station in Milaca. We said goodbye to the people we had grown to love as family over the past six months. With little more than what we had come with, the bags containing our belongings were tucked neatly under the bus luggage compartment. A two-day bus trip with a connection in Chicago brought us to Philadelphia, where Mr. Tong Lam received us at the Chinatown bus station.

And so, our search for the American dream continued. We kids were scared. I can't imagine what Dad was feeling. He felt responsible for the well-being and future of his family in this new world, but he was clearly excited about the new opportunities in spite of the uncertainty in the days and years that lay ahead.

 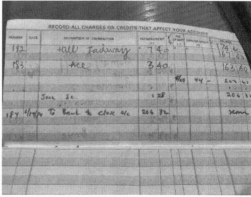

Minnesota—January 3, 1980 – June 1980

9

West Philly

Funkytown

It never crossed our minds that sharing a single bathroom with 12 people might be more than a little challenging. The Lam family had been sponsored by a Baptist Church and had lived in West Philly for almost a year before my family moved there from Minnesota. Despite the fact that they had very little, they very kindly offered to let our family of seven stay in their cramped apartment until we found a place of our own.

Tong Lam is the brother-in-law of my mom's niece, Minh Thu Trinh (my cousin). He was a few years younger than Dad and, though we had never developed a close friendship, he was known as our distant relative. He, his wife, and their four young children lived in a two-bedroom apartment in a large complex at 45th and Walnut Street. Tong's parents had a three-bedroom apartment across the hall where they lived with three of Tong's younger siblings. Residing on the third floor was Tong's sister and her family who also had four young children. The entire apartment complex was occupied by Asian refugees: Chinese, Vietnamese, Cambodian and Laotian, many of them related to each other.

We had all lived in refugee camps, so overcrowded conditions were very familiar to us and we understood the "luxury" of having a proper indoor bathroom, even if shared with such a large family. We were definitely in violation of occupancy codes, I realize now, but what we didn't know then didn't apply. Our family was very grateful for the Lam family's hospitality.

The night we arrived in Philadelphia, we got off the bus carrying our belongings and moved into the Lam's apartment. Across the hall I heard loud music blasting. How ironic that the song being played was "Funkytown" by the band Lipps, Inc. The song is about moving to somewhere more fun and exciting than Minnesota. What a nice way to be welcomed to Philadelphia! It turned out I had arrived just in time for an end-of-the-school-year disco party organized by Tong's younger brother, Liang, who attended South Philly High School. As soon as we settled into the apartment, I was invited to come across the hall to join the party.

I was exhausted from the 20-hour bus trip to Philly, but I was excited, curious, and didn't want to miss out on the first Asian party of my life with people my own age. Finally, I was free to be my 17-year-old self! I so much wanted to meet new people and to make new friends. The music was so fun and uplifting that "Funkytown" instantly became my favorite song. My parents and siblings were all so dead tired that they had gone to bed. I accepted the invitation without even asking permission.

Liang and Keow, the youngest brother and sister of the Lam family whom I had just met, walked me around the party and introduced me to their friends from high school. In the corner of the room, a few girls with poufy, permed hair smiled at me. I smiled back and walked over to make small talk. The music was very loud and the blinking disco ball hanging from the ceiling was so distracting that I could hardly hear or see them. I did my best to scream loud enough so they could hear me.

"Hi, nice party!" I said, of course in Chinese.

"Hello, I am Lan and this is Phuong."

"Nice to meet you. Do you both go to South Philly High?" I was very interested in their school.

"Yes, we go there. We are neighbors and live in South Philly. You should register to go to school there with us in September. It's really fun. There are lots of Chinese and Vietnamese students and we have a party almost every month," Phuong said.

"Is South Philly the only high school?" I innocently asked.

"No, silly. Philadelphia is a huge city, but South Philly has the largest Asian population. There is another high school in this area called University City High School that also has a lot of Asian students, but they have more black kids and maybe, well, I've heard there are some drug problems. You don't want to go there. And we have some handsome Italian kids at South Philly."

"And we have way more fun!" Lan added.

I discovered that my new friends had been in the area for nearly one year. It felt good being able to speak Chinese and mingle with boys and girls my own age who shared a common heritage. Yet, something didn't feel right. I could see that this group clung together, hung out together, partied together, and dated each other. They embraced a complacency that would prevent them from breaking out to try things individually. They did everything as a pack and their behaviors were similar, even the way they dressed and talked. In the days to come, I got to know my teenage neighbors more, and while I was glad to feel so welcomed, I resented being stereotyped and thrust into a group based solely on where I had come from.

All I was hearing about were parties and fun. I knew that if I got too comfortable hanging out with only Chinese friends that I would miss out on continuing to grow in my ability to integrate into the mainstream society of my adopted country. For the past six months, I'd had the privilege of being immersed completely in the American lifestyle in the small town of Onamia, and I wanted more, not less, assimilation into the mainstream. I knew I had to venture out from the comfort zone of the Chinese diaspora from Vietnam.

It would have been easy to enroll in South Philly High School, where I could be surrounded by a lot of Asian friends, but something was telling me that doing this would create a barrier to reaching my goals. I had dreams of being an exemplary student moving forward with my education. I wanted to surround myself with ambitious, academically focused individuals. I felt as if I was standing at the door to my entire future, and I wanted to define and walk my own distinct path.

I realized at that moment how significant our first few months in Minnesota had been. Being thrust into a world where we were the only Asians forced us out of our comfort zone, but we thrived. Talking with these teenagers, I knew I had to walk away. To me, they represented the old society and old way of life, as if nothing should change, and I wanted more. The next day I phoned Tim and Andy that we had arrived safely. It was nice to hear their familiar voices.

I had only a little more than two months to research new schools both for my siblings and myself. My mind was constantly racing to find solutions. I couldn't wait to get everything lined up and to be confident that we were all ready to begin our new school life.

First Apartment

While I was eager to branch out, my Dad was ecstatic when Tong took him to the "Chinatown" area of the city. Dad was so happy to be surrounded by a large population of Chinese people, even though most of the restaurant and shop owners were from Hong Kong and Taiwan. Even so, he was told that more and more Chinese from Vietnam were starting to open their own restaurants and grocery stores.

We learned that we could apply to the NSC, the Nationalities Service Center, on Arch Street, to obtain immigrant benefits once we had a permanent address in Philadelphia. The goal of the NSC is to welcome refugees and put them on a path to self-sufficiency. The Refugee and Community Integration (RCI) department of the NSC provides a wide range of services to meet the needs of new arrivals. For two weeks, my parents reached out every day to the Asian Baptist Church for help while I frantically searched the local newspapers for a rental home to establish our own permanent address. Most of the low-income apartment complexes like the one Tong's family lived in were overcrowded with refugees and had no vacancy.

I was also actively talking with everyone I met about schools in the area. West Philly was a run-down part of the city with chronic problems. We had no idea how bad it was. When we were in Onamia, Mrs. Chewy had remarked how dirty the city was and how hostile the environment was. Her warning was now beginning to sink in.

It was summer and the heat reminded me more of Vietnam than anything we had experienced in Minnesota. Just before the Fourth of July, as luck had it, I stumbled onto a posting in a local paper for a furnished apartment located just a few blocks from where we were staying. The apartment was a stand-alone unit in a row house on 44th and Chestnut Street. I called the landlord and arranged for my parents to look at the apartment. With dictionaries in hand, my parents and I walked the three blocks to 4405 Chestnut Street. There were two separate units in the row house, and the apartment was on the upper level on the second and third floor. On the street level, there was a laundromat, perfect for our family of seven to do laundry without having to walk a long distance.

The landlord, Mr. Rothenberg, was a Jewish gentleman in his late fifties or early sixties dressed in a tidy light-colored suit. He was quite friendly, and opened the door to a stairway leading to the second-floor apartment. As we climbed the squeaky stairs to the top landing, a wooden storage trunk gave my parents a jolt. It looked to us like a small casket. The place was very dark and gloomy, as if death was lingering. The apartment was messy, and stacks of old magazines and faded newspapers spilled out into the hallway. It was not ready for rent.

We toured the apartment, pleased that it would come fully furnished. That meant there wouldn't be much we would have to go out and buy. The living room had a beat-up sofa and a set of chairs that were comfortable enough, despite some rips on the seats. Accompanying the sofa and chairs was a three-piece coffee table set, a set of intricate statue lamps, and in the corner, a tall, old TV set that was a major piece of furniture. Every surface (chairs, tables, floors) was covered with old books, magazines, and knickknacks. We could hardly find a path to walk through. Underneath it all, the beige floor was filthy, but we were thankful that it was linoleum and not a dirty, dusty carpet which would have been nearly impossible to clean.

At the front of the living room, there was a window and a door leading to a small front balcony with white railing. I loved sitting there sometimes just to watch the street below. It reminded me of the balcony of my old house in Vietnam. The old existence's heavy floral-patterned drapes blocked out the light, making the room quite dark. The dining room contained two china cabinets filled with chinaware and figurines, and a large dining room table filled up the space with five odd chairs around it.

"Don't lean on the table. One of the legs is broken and I haven't had a chance to fix it," Mr. Rothenberg warned us.

The kitchen was small, just big enough for two people. The sink, countertop, cupboard and stove were all small, but the refrigerator was quite large. It sat empty, quietly waiting to be plugged in.

"The apartment has been vacant for a few months and it got a little dirty," Mr. Rothenberg explained. "My mom lived here for many years, but she passed away. I was going to have someone haul everything away before I rented it out, but I got so busy with business." Mr. Rothenberg walked us to the master bedroom which had belonged to his mom. It was furnished with a queen-sized bed, a dresser, and a night table. This would be the bed my parents would sleep in. "I am renting it as is. This floor is fully furnished, and you are welcome to make use of the furniture and everything else in the apartment. Rent is $350 a month and I would reduce your first month's rent to $200 if you were willing to clean this place up for me."

To Dad, I translated what Mr. Rothenberg had offered. A subtle smile came to my father's face, and I immediately understood. Inside, my parents and I were jumping with joy, but Dad wanted to appear calm and not show too much excitement. But we all were thanking God for this perfect opportunity. This meant we didn't have to spend what little money we had to buy furniture and household items—all we owned was what we had carried with us on the bus. A fully furnished apartment was ideal, and we saw great potential for this to become our home.

But Dad had an important question. "Ask him if his mom died at home or at the hospital." I knew the answer to this question was important to Dad. Asian people are very superstitious about death, and if Mr. Rothenberg's mother had died at home on this bed, it could break the deal. (Anything associated with the dead carries the potential of bad luck.)

I was nervous to ask the question and tried to think of a way to close the deal. We were desperate to move out of Tong's house and this was our golden opportunity. So, I didn't ask Dad's question. Instead, I asked Mr. Rothenberg if he could give us money to buy paint and we would paint the house for him before we moved in. He agreed. Then, "translating," I turned to Dad and said, "His mom died at the hospital and he will give us money to buy paint if we paint the place for him." It was the first time in my life I had lied to my Dad. In my defense, it may have been true that his mom did not die in this house, but I didn't know and didn't want to find out. I wanted what was best for our family. If we walked away, we would have lost a lot, and I figured that what we didn't know couldn't hurt us. I hoped and prayed that the old lady died peacefully and would not come back to haunt us.

It took our family two weeks to clean out the apartment. We took bags and bags of trash down to the dumpster, but were able to salvage many usable items, like the sheets we washed and were able to use to cover the sofa and chairs. I was very happy we didn't have to buy any new bulky furniture. It would have been a difficult job to carry furniture up the narrow hallway stairs. The only new thing that Dad bought was a bunk bed, and new mattresses for Phan and Que in our upstairs bedroom. I got a small cot with a thin, soft mattress. I loved how it sank down to fit my little body. Nam also had his own cot that was set up in my parents' room. Viet occupied another small bedroom in the front side of the upstairs. For us, this was a perfect arrangement, and we were all happy.

Several cans of paint were delivered from Mr. Rothenberg and we transformed the gloomy apartment into a bright, fresh place of our own. Unlike Onamia, every day now was hotter and muggier than the last. The apartment was like a brick oven and had no air circulation. Dad was thrilled to find a used air-conditioning unit from the second-hand store on 52nd Street for our living room. Mom took an old blanket and made a thick curtain to hang in the hallway door to keep the cooled air inside the living room which became our sanctuary on many hot, summer nights.

*Me with the
three-legged table*

*Mom and her new
Juki sewing machine*

The Jungle of Philly

West Philadelphia's crime rate was above the national average. Living in the city and being poor meant that frequent stories of robberies, rapes, and murders kept us a bit on edge, but we were happy with our new home. In Philly, it was common to see houses that were abandoned, infested with critters or drug addicts. Evidence of this was our next-door apartment: 4407. It had been totally abandoned and not fit to live in. My brother Viet and I kept peeking over our balcony to see if there was any sign of construction or renovation. Nothing! It remained abandoned the whole time we lived there. We often wondered what happened in that mysterious place which was separated from our apartment by a wall.

On the other side of us was apartment 4403. It was rented to either a Cambodian or Laotian family. I wasn't sure because we didn't understand their language. Between our buildings, there was a narrow alley with a fire escape. There was a small yard in the back of their building, and the windows on the side of the house and in the back facing the alley all had metal bars welded to the windows. It made it look like a jail. We had been city dwellers in Vietnam, so we were very familiar with the need for the metal bars on windows. It didn't bother us a bit.

Because of the abandoned place next door, it was impossible to keep our apartment free of pests. No matter how much I scrubbed the floors and the kitchen counter, we often had giant cockroaches and mice as visitors. I was terrified of them. We didn't know we had the right to ask the landlord to exterminate the apartment. There was so much we didn't know that we didn't know! We just dealt with the pests the way we did in Vietnam, by killing them with traps and sprays. We hung sticky tape from the ceiling to control the fly population. It sounds gross, but believe me, we were grateful to not be living in a flimsy hut with a dirt floor as we had in the refugee camps. It's all in your perspective.

Chestnut Street was a very busy road. Big trucks and cars came in waves and the traffic got very noisy at certain times of the day. Trucks roared by in the middle of the night, and our 100-year-old building rumbled and shook as if we were having a mild earthquake. When we first moved in, it was very distracting, but gradually, it became the rhythm that was rather fun for us. When the weather turned cold, the radiators that heated our apartment would clang and bang and whistle throughout the night. It was like being surrounded by an out-of-tune symphony of radiators! But we accepted this as part of our new urban life. Not one person in our family complained about being disturbed.

Once we had our own address, we began applying for help from the NSC and the Welfare Department. In Philadelphia, we had no one to hold our hand and guide us through each step of the way as we had when we lived in Onamia. We were thankful to the Lams for the help and guidance they could provide, so generous with us in many ways. They taught us to get around Philadelphia with public transportation, using the subway, buses, and the El (elevated train). We were also thankful that it was summer, so dealing with snow and ice would no longer be a barrier to our freedom.

I accompanied my parents on many trips downtown to file the necessary paperwork for assistance. I sat through endless appointments at the Welfare Office waiting to meet with social services workers. And every chance I had, I talked to people at the Asian Baptist Church, trying to discover which schools would be best for my siblings and me. The public schools would always be an option, but I also wanted to explore what other choices we might have.

Time to Rip Those Pants

One day, I ran into an old neighborhood friend from Vietnam at the Baptist church. Hue Man was two years younger and her brother was a grade below me in Vietnam, but we had never hung out in the same circles. Hue Man's family had arrived in Philadelphia a few months before us and she was also looking for a school. She had been talking to a Vietnamese Christian brother who helped Vietnamese refugee children to get into Catholic schools. My ears perked at the words "Catholic school." I asked for the contact and immediately started picturing myself in a school uniform like I wore back in fifth and sixth grades at Thanh Tam, the private Catholic school in Vietnam.

Brother An Phong Tran was a Catholic priest from the La San Order. He was known as Frere Phong. He was a young man in his early thirties who had dedicated his life to educating the youth in the spirit of faith, charity, and fellowship. Through the year, he helped transform hundreds, if not thousands of children's lives, mine included.

My heart pounded with joy when I met with Frere Phong, as I felt I had made the right connection to secure advice and help for my siblings and myself. "We just moved here less than a month ago from Minnesota and I am desperately looking for some good schools for all my younger siblings and me, could you help us?"

"Yes," Frere Phong, assured me. "That is what I do best. I help immigrant children integrate into the American school system, while also maintaining their heritage and enjoying a close-knit Asian community."

"But we are Buddhists, and we don't have a lot of money for tuition. Could we still join?" I asked anxiously.

"Of course, we don't discriminate against any religion. Christ loves everyone the same. If you really want to attend, we will work with your parents to find a monthly tuition plan you can afford. We just need to get some paperwork in order to matriculate your brother and sisters into St. Francis de Sales Elementary School. We can also apply for some financial assistance if you are eligible."

I breathed a big sigh of relief. "Yes! Let's fill out the forms. And, yes, we will need to apply for financial help since my parents don't have jobs yet. We are waiting for government assistance to be approved. All we have right now is an address and a phone number."

When I took my parents to meet with Frere Phong, he told them that Viet, Phan, and Que would be registering to go to St. Francis de Sales School on 47th Street near Springfield, which was about eleven blocks from our house. They would be in grades seven, five, and three, respectively.

"What about Le Khanh?" Dad asked, nodding to me.

"Le Khanh would be in a special situation. I need her to commit to one year of private school with me and nine of her peers. The classroom is inside the rectory building, located in front of West Catholic Boys High School on 49th and Chestnut. She then would be evaluated to see if she qualifies for admittance to West Catholic Girls High School the following year as a sophomore. We need to accelerate her English skills and American history before she is ready to attend full-time in a more competitive environment."

Frere Phong continued, "These are my conditions if you want me to help. The children must participate in the Youth Group, sharing their time, and fellowship together most weekends at the Youth Center. They need to pick up extra homework and tutoring during off-hours as needed, and during the summer, they need to concentrate on getting ready for the school year in the fall."

As Frere Phong was talking, his "conditions" were music to my ears. And I know Dad was very pleased as well. He was happy that his flock would be cared for by a Christian community. Dad would have far fewer worries knowing that we would have a faith-based place to learn and to be able to have fun with people of our own heritage. It would mean becoming disciples of Jesus and learning His teachings. Without hesitation, Dad said, "That's all fine with me!"

"Terrific," Frere Phong said. "And one more bonus—the girls' high school is only one block from where you said you live on Chestnut. You've probably walked by it many times."

I was excited about the prospect of being in an accelerated program taught by Frere Phong. Also, I didn't have to pay tuition for this special program this year, so my parents were thrilled with all this good news. They placed a very high value on their children's education. I could not contain my big ear-to-ear grin. Being able to attend an all-girls school with a formal uniform and no distractions from the boys was a dream come true.

I recalled what I told Mom before we left Vietnam: "All I want is to be able to wear my school uniform again and make up for the educational years I lost in the communist era." I could hardly believe that this deepest wish was coming true.

For my three siblings, the monthly tuition installment was about $120 a month. Dad and Mom discussed it and I heard Dad say, "Break open Nam's pants for the cause." Apparently, besides using the embroidered patch on my clothes, Mom had also hidden hundred dollars bills in the clothing of all five children before we escaped Vietnam—and there was about $500 hidden inside the seams of Nam's pants alone.

All that money survived the pirate robberies on the boat and the precarious life in the refugee camps. Mom and Dad had known that there would be many days of uncertainty in the years ahead, so they held on tightly to this stash as an emergency fund. Now, this was the kind of thing where Dad was glad to rip up the pants to get the money out. When it came to his children, education was always the most important thing for my Dad. "No child of mine is going to be a blind ox!" he often said. So, the $500 they had brought from Vietnam was now allocated for tuition, school fees, uniforms, and school supplies.

I was delighted that now I had a good reason to be out of the house during weekends for the youth activities. All I had to say was, "I have to go to Frere Phong's for the Youth program activities," and I would be granted permission to go. He was like a godsend for my freedom. Well, after all the chores and household tasks were completed, of course.

My parents also had their own educational requirements to fulfill at the NSC. Mom and Dad had to take ESL (English as a Second Language) classes three hours a day, five days a week, to qualify for financial aid, medical aid, and food stamp assistance. Dad attended the morning class and Mom went in the afternoon. It was healthy for them to be apart from each other, plus, they could take turns caring for little Nam who was four years old. I was happy to see my parents adjusting so well. They were making new Asian friends and getting more comfortable exploring the public transportation. Dad was determined to find a job and save money for a used car next year.

One of the qualities I admired about Dad was his ability to provide for his family. He was a very frugal and thrifty man, spending nothing on himself. His family's interests and well-being were his first priority. He made sure we had plenty to eat, clean clothes to wear, and were well protected. My siblings and I had never felt a lack of material things growing up, even when we literally had very little to our name.

Most of Dad's wardrobe was from the second-hand stores on 52nd Street. It gave him great joy to find a good bargain, whether it was a winter hat, a jacket, or a pair of shoes. "This country is so rich," he noted, "you can always find treasures if you look hard enough, and without spending lots of money." It was a marked contrast to the Dad I knew in Vietnam. He was a successful businessman and always dressed the part. I would make weekly trips to the dry cleaners to drop off and pick up his custom-made clothes. Every day, Dad dressed in starched, crisp, white shirt and slacks when he went in to work at his business. Obviously, all of that changed after the communist invasion.

Despite Dad's great finds for himself at the thrift store, Dad never forced us to wear used clothes. As a matter of fact, he bought me a brand-new reversible white and beige fluffy winter jacket and a new pair of winter shoes. My brothers, sisters, and Mom also all got something new for the upcoming winter, when we heard it would be just as cold in Pennsylvania as it was in Minnesota. Well, maybe not subzero cold, but still extreme when compared to Vietnam!

By late August, the summer heat in urban Philadelphia was unbearable. Dad cranked the air conditioning unit to the maximum to keep the living room cool while the rest of the house was steamy hot. Weekends were our favorite family time at home. We enjoyed pizza night and watched Chinese *Kung Fu* reruns while sitting or lying on the cool linoleum floor. Sometimes we watched wrestling or old Chinese operas. We were happy to share this tiny room with each other, sleeping all night on the couch and on the floor to stay cool. We enjoyed the closeness and didn't mind that all of us were crammed together in one room.

To ease the struggle, one must reward oneself occasionally. Dad gave himself the small luxury of a few dollars a week for the lottery, one can of beer on the weekend, and one cigarette each time he did #2 in the bathroom. He did not feel like he was deprived. It was a ritual for Dad to have a beer and to pick his lucky numbers for the weekly Big 4 Pennsylvania Lottery. He kept a data book of all the winning numbers and meticulously calculated the probability of the next set of winning numbers.

Dad believed in taking reasonable chances, especially when you are poor. "You never know when luck will strike," he said. "And if you didn't participate, how would you know if luck was going to come your way?" Occasionally he had some tiny wins, but he never won anything big. But a small win was enough to keep him hopeful. The dream of winning big brought him some smiles.

I learned many important lessons from my parents who taught by example how to live in good times and in bad. Moderate spending and a steady lifestyle were always the model, no matter how rich or poor we were. We didn't lavishly spend one day and starve the next. Always save for a rainy day. Keep an emergency fund for the most important things, such as medical needs, moving expenses, and most of all, education. Always, always live within your means, and never be wasteful of ANYTHING.

September of 1980 marked a new beginning for all of us. It was a period of transitioning, and everyone in the family had to learn to adapt and adjust. Dad had his ESL class in downtown Philly in the morning. Mom stayed home with Nam and started up her sewing business again. When many of her afternoon ESL classmates complained that they couldn't find blouses that would fit, Mom offered her services, and they instantly became her clients. She brought a tape measure with her to school and took down all the necessary measurements so I could draft and cut the pattern pieces for her to sew at home. She was jokingly scolded by her teacher once that she didn't come to school to learn English, that she was there for the business. Mom tried to be a little less obvious after that.

Although Mom did not have business skills, she was very talented in her crafts and was able to make a living wherever she went. Mom took money from the emergency fund and bought an overlock serger and straight stitch sewing machine. She spent almost $200 for the set, but was confident the returns for the family would bring in many times that amount. Those machines and the sweat equity were indeed excellent money-makers. (I kept those machines for years through several moves as an adult.)

I was so excited to be starting school—but I was finding that in addition to my own schoolwork, I had to find time to help with my parents' homework, my mom's business, and my siblings' need for help with their schoolwork. There was so much more responsibility falling in my lap than I could have foreseen.

10

West Catholic High

Never Waste a Minute!

I was lucky to only have five blocks to walk to the rectory, while my siblings had eleven blocks to walk to St. Francis de Sales Elementary School. In Minnesota, the bus picked them up right in front of our house, but there was no bus for them at this parochial school. When the weather got cold and wet, I felt so sorry for those tiny, weary feet and their long dangerous trek through West Philly. They had to get up early for the 45-minute walk. But none of them—Viet, Phan nor Que—ever complained. They kept each other company and, in the wintertime, occupied themselves by making pretty footprints on the snow along the sidewalk. Like the new-fallen snow, their souls were pure and innocent as they began learning to navigate the hustle bustle world of West Philadelphia.

As for me, I spent the year with nine other teenagers, but it was hard to know everyone's real age. It was not unusual for the kids to reduce their age on their official documents by two or three years. In my case, reducing my age by four years was a little more extreme. We soon learned each other's real age and didn't dwell on what our documents said. Brother Phong never questioned anyone for their true age. He knew our circumstances, and treated us respectively as young adults.

There were six boys and four girls in the class. Eight were of Chinese descent like me. We got along nicely despite our different educational backgrounds and ages. Frere Phong taught the core subjects of English, math and American history. The goal was to learn as much as we could about English composition and comprehension. Every day, we worked on diagramming sentences, vocabulary, and the cultural differences between the East and the West. We listened to cassette tapes and tried to understand what we heard.

Me and other students from Frere Phong's Class

I was so relieved to be back in a classroom of academic focus and well-rounded education. We took a field trip to Washington DC, went on a retreat, and had many trips to the library. It was intense, fun, and I loved it. I made up my mind to do all I could to get into West Catholic Girls High the next year as a tenth grader. That was my non-negotiable mission.

In class, my left and right-hand buddies were Hue Man and Xai Nga. Both girls were younger than me, but according to my documents, I was the youngest. We studied together and hung out together in the Catholic Youth Group that had been established by Frere Phong in 1975. Most of the kids in the group came to America in 1975, had a five-year advantage, and were already settled in the American schools. The rectory and the gymnasium at West Catholic for Boys provided a wonderful place for sports and cultural bonding for diverse refugee kids like us.

Several times a year, such as at Christmas, Lunar New Year, or over summer vacation, the Freres would offer singing and dancing shows to entertain the Asian community. They set up volleyball teams and tournaments for kids who enjoyed playing sports. There was something for everyone. The group was led by Frere Phong, Frere Nhon, another Christian Brother, and two seminarians, Duc and Tu, college students studying to become LaSalle Christian Brothers. There would be anywhere from 20 to 40 youth, ranging in ages from six to early twenties, gathering during the weekends. This was something my siblings and I looked forward to when we were not in school. The social aspect was wonderful, and as a teenager, I admit I enjoyed the safe, fun environment in which I could get to know some nice and like-minded peers.

The group was made up of fresh-off-the-boat youth from different parts of Vietnam, and called themselves the Bum Brothers and Sisters. Many of the Vietnamese kids who attended had been in the United States for several years already. They understood American football, and were very interested in playing sports. They had their own volleyball team that practiced nearly every other weekend. Our Chinese group went for the social aspect. (We were not very athletic.)

About this time, Mom found a contract job hand-sewing neckties. For every dozen ties she made, she would earn $4.50. It was a flexible job that could be done at home, just like when we made the fishing lures back in Minnesota. So, if I wasn't doing homework, helping my siblings, washing dishes, or cleaning the house, I would be hand-sewing neckties for Mom. There were times that I studied my homework while sewing. Multitasking is a skill I learned at a young age as Mom's apprentice.

"Never waste a minute!" she always said. "You turn back and forth, the day is over!"

I'm not sure if it's the way I was trained, or if I inherited a hyperactive gene from Mom, but I tended to always have multiple things going on at the same time. I would listen to something while watching something else and maybe study or sew or cook as well. "Never waste a minute" was a message constantly playing in my head. Sometimes, I suspected I had ADHD or a compulsive disorder. I could never sit still or focus on just one task.

That fall, everyone in the family was getting very preoccupied in their new settings. My 18th birthday snuck up on me in October. For the first time, it hit me hard that I couldn't openly tell all of my friends how old I was. I revealed my real age to my close Chinese friends, but kept it secret from the Vietnamese community.

Before we knew it, the cold winter had brought us into the new year of 1981. We did not realize that Philadelphia would get so much snow. Maybe not as much as Minnesota, but snow was snow. It makes no difference when you are accustomed to 100° weather. Cold was just cold! We walked everywhere. Luckily, the Thriftway supermarket was just a few blocks down on Walnut Street, but that was only good for bread and milk. My parents liked to shop for fresh meats and vegetables at the Italian market or the Oriental grocery stores in South Philly. That's where they could find the spices and Asian items for our traditional cuisine. Mom and Dad would take public transportations to shop there, while always keeping an eye out for job opportunities. Restaurants and grocery stores often posted job openings on a bulletin board.

With the expense of monthly tuition, other fees, and uniforms, Dad worried that we would eat through the emergency fund that survived the pirates. Even though we had a small income from Mom's sewing, some public assistance, and maybe about $150 a month of food stamps, this was barely enough to cover the necessities. The cost of oil to keep us warm during the winter alone was putting a dent into our savings. But no matter how tight things were financially for our family, Mom and Dad continued to send boxes back to Vietnam of over-the-counter medications, fabrics, and other items for my aunts and uncles on both sides of the family. They knew how difficult the conditions were in Vietnam, so they tried to be as supportive as possible.

On one of the many routine trips to the Asian market in the spring, Mom and Dad noticed a job posting taped to a window. The Saigon Restaurant needed a part-time female helper. The job would be chopping vegetables, making egg-roll stuffing, and cleaning the kitchen. Mom wanted to apply for the position, but Dad would rather that Mom stay at home with Nam and he would work.

"But they want to hire a woman!" She pointed out.

"Let's both go talk to them and see if they could hire both of us in two shifts. Maybe they will try us out." Dad was being creative and optimistic, as usual.

Both of my parents went into the Saigon Restaurant, and the owner, Mr. Le, agreed to a trial period, hiring both Mom and Dad. His wife was the cook and they thought a woman assisting in their kitchen would be faster and more efficient than a man. They did not know my Dad was the king of hard work. He loved to cook and was a fast learner. He had endured many different jobs since he was ten years old. Dad taught us: "Always go an extra mile on your job. It does not matter if you work for someone else or for your own company. The rewards will always follow your work ethic."

As Dad predicted, after only two days of a trial period, Mrs. Le hired both my parents to help in her kitchen. She eventually let Mom go but retained Dad for a part-time position. She was very impressed with his skills and it changed her perception of men being able to handle kitchen work. Mom and I were still making clothes for clients and sewing neckties in our spare time, so things worked out quite nicely. The jobs were not bringing in substantial income, but it was steady work and it kept us busy.

As if school, house chores, making clothes for clients and hand-sewing neckties were not enough, I also helped my friend, Xai Nga, with her weekend cleaning jobs. I wanted to make every dollar I could find. If anyone needed their bathroom scrubbed, their kitchen cleaned, or their home vacuumed, I said yes. I understood that my parents did not have a penny to spare for allowances, so I aimed to be as self-sufficient as I could.

I was learning to take care of myself in many ways. There were dangerous things happening on the streets of Philly that I never told my family about. One morning, I was walking to school toward 49th Street, and a white car pulled up to the curb. I paid no attention at first, but a man rolled down the window and said, "Do you need a ride? Come on in, I'll give you a lift!"

You would think that I was old enough to understand that this was a threat. Instead, I thought: *How nice of him to offer a ride to a cold girl who was walking in thick snow.* I looked at him and politely said, "No thanks." He persisted, but after a while he finally took off. I later heard on the news that there had been several incidents of girls being kidnapped by strangers who had offered them a car ride. What a tragedy it could have been if I had trusted what appeared to be a kind offer. I thought of the incident years later, and believe I had received protection from above.

We never thought we were living in a danger zone. We often sent the three younger kids to run errands to Thriftway to get bread or cereal when things ran low at home. The chain of command would often pass from older to younger in my house. Mom would say, "Viet, go downstairs to pick up the mail," and Viet would then ask Phan to do it, with Que ending up finally doing the chore. Same with buying groceries. Que dreaded going, but as the last in line with Nam too young to run errands, Que would be given some food stamps and marched off to buy bread.

The reason she hated going was that it meant walking by a corner where several boys always hung out and harassed anyone they believed they could intimidate. They would not stop bullying her for the errand money they guessed she was carrying. Que was so scared that one time she accepted a ride from a young couple who didn't like seeing her walking alone in the dark. The couple drove her around the block and dropped her in front of our house. It could have been a tragic story of kidnapping or murder if they had been bad people. She could have disappeared without a trace. I thanked God every day for protecting our safety and well-being.

Blueberries and Egg Sandwiches

In late July, the blueberry farms in nearby New Jersey needed workers. Dad and Mom signed up themselves along with their four older children to pick blueberries. They thought the experience would be good for us, and Dad was hoping to speed up the dream of being able to buy a used car. My parents had gotten a taste of the brutal winter in Pennsylvania and were tired of walking to the El and subway stations. It took several transfers to get to school in North Philly and work in South Philly. Dad was yearning for a car to take my siblings to school on the freezing cold mornings, and to save his numbed feet from having to stand in the frigid weather waiting for the bus. He set his sights on having a car before school started back in the fall.

Mom sent my youngest brother Nam to stay at the Lam's house so she could come to pick blueberries with us. The Lams became our second family. They had kids Nam's age, and we often exchanged babysitting. Standing at the corner of Sansom and 43rd Street at 3:30 a.m., my Dad, Mom, Viet (12), Phan (11), Que (9), and I waited for the cargo van to pick us up to head to the blueberry farm in New Jersey. The van winded through the streets in the neighborhood, picking up an Asian workforce

178

of Cambodians, Laotians, Chinese, and Vietnamese. There were no seats in the van. We were packed like cattle for the two-hour drive from Philly to South Jersey. But nobody complained. Some dozed off, catching a few Z's during the trip.

Back in the 80's, there were no laws (or no enforced laws) to protect laborers working in the fields, and children could work with their parents. The harvest season was only six to eight weeks long, from late June to early August, so scores of workers were needed and refugees and immigrants desperate for money were happy to have a job. It was hard work, but that did not discourage any of us.

We were all hungry for a chance to build our lives, and we took advantage of any opportunity that might help us move forward. No drinking water or clean toilets were provided, and the pay was below the minimum wage, but we knew it was a temporary hardship. Anything is possible in America if you are willing to work hard. In those dark days of our boat journey, in the refugee camps, and now in the blueberry fields, my parents were teaching us resilience and determination.

In central Vietnam, there was a highlands place named Da Lat. It was a cool and beautiful locale that attracts lots of regional and international tourists. The mountain range was famous for their romantic waterfalls and its strawberries. Dad had taken our family there for vacations a few times and we got to taste the strawberries, eating them with salt to neutralize the acidity. But we had never before tasted a blueberry. We were quite curious about this new fruit.

We got to the farm before 6:00 a.m. and stood in line, waiting to be assigned a row of the blueberry bushes to pick. Our family worked in teams. Dad and Mom each teamed up with one of my sisters and I worked with Viet, my 12-year-old brother. While my friends from school were home sound asleep, we were fighting the wet, cold morning dew. We wasted no time. With a bucket hanging around our necks, we started picking berries. The shorter person of the team picked the bottom of the bush, and the taller one picked from the top. We helped each other empty the berries into a cardboard box, then carried the boxes of blueberries to the truck in exchange for a ticket. We were supposed to stay in our assigned row and pick each bush clean, then move on to the next, but my daredevil brother kept disappearing to pick the big berries from other rows. I was so worried that he would get caught. Being Viet, he defied the rules and always tested the limits.

I raced to pick as fast as I could before the blazing hot summer sun dried our skin. We had only a few hours of cool temperatures before the sun turned the field into a broiler oven. Annoying nags and flies breakfasted on our sweat and slowed us down. As thirsty as we were, we didn't want to drink a lot of water. Bathroom breaks were in a smelly outhouse in the field. It was not a place we wanted to visit.

At 9:00 a.m. we were already soaked with sweat in the thick, hot humid air. The sun was bright and squinting up into the bushes above our heads to grasp the berries was a challenge. Picking from the bottom of the shrub was no picnic either. To reach the berries, we had to struggle through branches that were sharp and prickly, and we were instructed to only pick the ripe ones.

Filling a tray easily took a full hour for inexperienced children like us. The fruit itself did not look appealing to us. The berries were small and dark blue, nothing like the bright, succulent red of the strawberry. The first day we tried eating a few for the first time, and they tasted horrible! Was the sour and bitter taste of the blueberry a reflection of this experience? For years, I could not bear the sight of this fruit. Besides, eating the fruit meant it would take longer to fill the bucket, so no one in the family ever ate any of the blueberries.

The highlight of the job was our parents allowing us to buy our favorite Entenmann's pound cake for lunch instead of packing homemade sandwiches. While minimum wage in 1981 was about $3.35 an hour, each 12" x 18" tray of blueberries we picked was exchanged for a ticket worth about two dollars. That was our day: fill the bucket, pour the full bucket to the tray, and trade it in for the ticket. I worked to maximize my speed, and carefully guarded the tickets in my pocket to make sure they were all there at the end of the day.

The long day finally ended around 4:00 p.m. Everyone stood in line to cash out their tickets. I remember holding a 20-dollar bill in my hand and feeling delighted and eager to give Dad my contribution. I expected to see a smile on Dad's face. Instead, he took the $20 and looked at me in silence, with tears welling up in his eyes. Not a word was spoken, but I understood. These were tears of pain caused by seeing his young children slaving for a pittance, and he was ashamed to take the money.

These were tears of a proud man who had endured great hardship in seeking a better life for his family in America. He didn't bring us here to work in these substandard conditions, no matter how temporary it was. After several weeks of blueberry picking, Dad decided that we would not return to the field anymore. I guessed it was too heart-wrenching for him to see his children in hard labor. He would just have to find another way to save up for the car.

The bittersweet blueberry farm experience is a constant reminder for me of what immigrants were willing to do to secure the survival of their families. For almost 20 years, I could not enjoy eating blueberries despite learning of their nutritional benefits. Even if they were plump and sweet, all I could taste was the bitter memory of seeing tears on my dad's face. I am happy to say that I have gotten over that feeling and today I love blueberries, but Viet still does not find blueberries appealing, even after 38 years. I came to understand the sweet and sour meaning of this fruit for our family.

Enduring the hot sun, scratches on top of scratches on our hands and arms, parched lips and tired feet, the six of us toiled all summer because that is what was in front of us to do, led by my father who worked harder than any of us. Where there is a will, there is a way. For that summer, this was our way. This was how we wrote our own destiny. The experience taught me the importance of my education. My parents talked about how plenty of opportunities would present themselves here in this free country and we did not have to settle for poverty.

Mom and Dad in Dalat (vacation spot in central Vietnam)

Paying Back Airfare

Around this time, we got a formal letter from Lutheran Social Services regarding repayment for the airplane ticket from Singapore to America. I wasn't sure who the loan was from, but we had a year to pay it back. It was about $1,400 for our family of seven people. Dad said, "It was worth every single penny! I am grateful they took a chance on us!" We didn't have to pay it in one lump sum, but we did have to start making monthly installment payments.

On top of food and rent, with so many expenses like the airfare payback, school, and winter clothes, my parents had to really scramble in order to avoid selling jewelry or depleting their savings. They did not want to destroy the dream of owning our own house one day. So, both of my parents quit their English classes to pursue more ways to make ends meet.

Mom started to intensively look for regular employment. She landed a seamstress position at Jacques Ferber, a high-end fur salon in downtown Philadelphia. Mom loved working for Ken and Pam, the young couple who owned the shop. Ken was the operations manager in the workroom and Pam was in management and sales. Mom's job was to hand-sew a label to the lining of each fur coat. Working with thick fur was something that Mom had never done before, but the job was a perfect fit for her. She became more and more useful to the operation thanks to her skill. Her favorite job was sewing mink tails together as an accessory for a coat.

As the winter set in, Dad was asked to work at the Saigon Restaurant full time. He usually left the house at 9:00 a.m. and either took the bus or commuter train. Either way, it took several transfers and over an hour to get to the Italian market in South Philly. Working in the kitchen generated a lot of stress and the heat in the kitchen must have stirred up Dad's temperament again. He worked long hours and often didn't get home until almost midnight. Dad was increasingly agitated with everyone and everything at home. Tuesday was his only day off and that was the day he and Mom would get into all kinds of arguments.

A Misfit Identity

By the fall of 1981, we had passed through the buffer zone, the transitional place where Frere Phong equipped us to be ready to integrate into the classrooms of West Catholic High. All the girls in Frere Phong's class were accepted to 10th grade, but were placed at different levels according to their test results. Both my friends, Xai Nga and Hue Man, were in Level 2 in most classes, while I was put in all Level 1 Honors classes. Our interactions were limited to the weekend activities at Frere Phong's Youth Center.

Here I was, achieving the dream of going back to school, which was supposed to open all possibilities for my future, and yet, I still felt lacking. While I appreciated being a student again, my social life was grey and uneventful. I didn't have Becky Stevens to make me feel included, and both my new buddies now went their separate ways. I felt completely alienated and did not see any way to fit in. I wasn't able to find a new bond or a connection with any of the girls in my classes.

Struggling with English and feeling like I could not string two coherent sentences together, I lived in fear of being ridiculed. I aspired to hang out with the smart girls who took AP classes, but was too intimidated by their presence. I shied away from the popular girls and those who excelled in sports. I admired one Filipino-American girl, Melissa, who was at the top of our class, but learned that having in common our Asian identity meant nothing. The privilege and advantages of being born in America were far different than for someone who was "fresh off the boat." Her circle of intelligent friends adored her every step as I looked on from a distance, wishing I could be among them.

There was also a group of polished, pretty girls with make-up, fashionable hairstyles, and jewelry. All they talked about was how fun it was hanging out at South Street, partying on the weekends, and at the Dancing on Air show. I didn't care to be one of them, but I enjoyed overhearing their conversations during homeroom. I was beginning to understand how clueless and petty some people were. These divas had no idea what real pain or suffering was in the third world. How I wished I had some of their "first world problems," all completely inconsequential in a world of war and deprivation. So, I kept to myself. I learned to nod and smile, but would rarely strike up a conversation except for some small talk with kids who were also shy and inhibited at school.

I felt inadequate talking about who I was and where I was from. Since I had no knowledge of sports teams, popular music, or celebrities, it was hard to find any common ground. They didn't understand me, and I didn't understand them. A lonely misfit, I longed for some real friendship.

In addition to my social challenges, I struggled with the tougher academic curriculum. It was harder than that of the school in Onamia, or at Frere Phong's expedited program. To keep up with the comprehensive level in English, I had to study several times harder than the other students. I always tackled math and French homework first because they were the easiest for me. That may not have been the most effective thing to do, but it felt good to complete something I understood. Writing was my most challenging subject. I had to check the dictionary almost every other word for translations when reading English literature. My biggest challenge was poetry. It was brutal. I would save it for last, and often stayed up studying well past midnight, sometimes even until one or two o'clock in the morning. I took pride in the work ethic I had learned from my parents, but it never seemed like I had enough time for everything I needed to do.

The contrasting worlds of who I was supposed to be at school and who I was at home were on two opposite ends of the spectrum. I was confused, resentful, and had an overwhelming internal drive to study hard and work hard. Although my life was one long "to do" list of chores and responsibilities at home, I was determined to be successful in school. My only focus was to fulfill the dream of higher education. It was the second chance that neither of my parents had when they were young. I had a constant sense of anxiety, telling myself, *I must not let my feelings bog me down, I must succeed!*

Chinatown Sweatshop—Responsibilities at Home

Between my studies, I helped Mom cook and clean and care for my siblings. We continued making neckties, but this work had been dwindling to a smaller and smaller contract. Mom and I also worked in some of the sweatshops in Chinatown to sew on weekends. Sometimes my sisters and Viet would come to work there, too. Nam again stayed at the Lams.

In the '80s, sweatshops were popping up like mushrooms everywhere. The industry was booming, thanks to the abundance of cheap labor from refugees who never demanded improvements to the working conditions, fair pay, or employee rights. They were just happy to have the opportunity to earn a buck to sustain their families. The sweatshops were commonly repurposed from vacant old warehouses. They were terribly hot in the summer, and freezing cold in the winter. They had giant fans that stirred up dust and the lint from fabrics; sometimes it was unbearable to breathe.

The sweatshop was owned by a family with three young children. We always saw the kids playing in the office during the summer. The wife's name was May, and she was Malaysian. I don't remember her husband's name, but he was Singaporean. They were a lovely couple who communicated with Mom in Mandarin, but with me in English. They would pay the children by the hour, but seamstresses like Mom got paid by "chain sewing," which was a few cents per seam. Mom had to sew hundreds of seams just to cover our bus fare and lunch.

We all did what we could. Phan did press-ironing, which was very hot and steamy work. In the winter, it was nice and warm to stand in front of the presser, but it was brutal in the heat of the summer. Que's job was to trim thread on the garments. Viet pushed the clothing cart from the sewing station to the pressing station or vice versa. And I would be a floater to fill in wherever I was needed. They don't call it a sweatshop for nothing. Even during those long, tedious work hours, Mom would never miss a chance to tell her fellow workers that we could customize clothes for anyone in the shop who was interested.

One day, May's husband called me into the office and asked what career path I was thinking about for my future. "I don't know," I said, "but my grandma had always wanted me to become a pharmacist."

"That is a good plan," he said. "Keep working hard because I see a great future in you. If you need any help, you come and find me. I am rooting for you." Tears almost began rolling down my face. No one had actually said that to me before. I thanked him, and said I still had a few years of high school to go, but I would keep that in mind.

Sometimes one small encouraging phrase is all we need to fuel us forward. It was a boost of confidence that I tucked away for the rainy day when I felt I was not enough. Years later, they opened a bridal shop where I purchased my wedding gown. For me, it was another way to thank him for that little talk.

In addition to the sweatshop on weekends, I also had to work to get financial aid from West Catholic Girls High. At school, I served drinks in the cafeteria. I had access to the soda fountain every day, and thanked

God I did not get addicted to it. I could have ballooned up because of the easy access to free high-sugar drinks. I also had to clean chalkboards and sometimes I would work in the library. The work wasn't hard, but it did eat into my free time. I had to be careful about how I allocated my time for extra activities, or the vital time to do homework.

On top of my studies, I was responsible for tutoring all my younger siblings. I routinely helped Que and Nam practice their math homework. I told Nam that if he wanted to be in first grade, he needed to know addition, subtraction, and multiplication. I taught Que about fractions, which was more advanced than she needed. All summer long, they diligently did what I suggested. Nam memorized all the multiplication tables. When he started school, he was shocked to find out that the kids in his first-grade class barely knew how to add two plus two. He came home to tell me that I had been wrong. And I agreed, but reminded him, "Now, everything is so easy, so aren't you glad you have more time to do other stuff?" I believe that helped him build his confidence as he breezed through his school year.

Looking back, I don't know how we juggled so many tasks and odd jobs and still managed to find time for leisure. But we did! Down at Drexel University on 32nd Street, the Chinese students offered free, cultural movies, mostly Kung Fu. We begged Mom to let us off one day of work so we could go to the show. I would string along all my siblings and friends, parading down the street. It seemed like such a treat; we didn't mind walking 12 blocks for a free movie. Sometimes we stopped by the arcade on 40th Street to play a few games of Pac-Man. I imposed a limit of four quarters on myself and then watched others play.

For almost all my years in West Philly schools, Mom made egg sandwiches for lunch for all of us. It was easy and cheap, but after so many egg sandwiches, I sometimes found them hard to swallow. I was cautious with every penny I spent, but occasionally I would splurge and buy something different to break the sandwich routine. My parents gave us no allowance money, but if we needed something for school, they would gladly provide it.

West Philly (1983)

Life in High School

I spent many hours with Mom going to her doctor visits. Ever since Nam was born, Mom had suffered from chronic dull pain which appeared in different muscles in her body. Her fingers would sometimes throb in pain due to consistently gripping the needle as she sewed at work. Some days it was in her shoulder; other days, her wrists, then maybe her calves or ankles. They were unpredictable pains that came and went like visits from an angry ghost. Mom was hand-sewing with big, thick needles at the fur salon five days a week, which seemed to trigger the pain even more.

We learned that she had fibromyalgia, a musculoskeletal condition that causes widespread chronic pain. There are no signs of injury except swelling. I didn't know where to go to research for more information. I would helplessly watch Mom struggle to change her clothes in the mornings. All they offered her were painkillers. Her employers, Ken and Pam Ferber, were so understanding and sympathetic. They could see that Mom was in terrible pain even though she dutifully came to work. After a few weeks, the Ferbers decided to change her responsibilities to babysitting their toddler, Rebecca, instead of letting Mom go.

By the end of my sophomore year, I signed up for a government-funded academic support program for low-income high school students called Upward Bound. Most of the students were from the local Catholic schools in Philadelphia, and the majority were from West Catholic Boys and Girls High Schools. We were provided room and board at Gwynedd Mercy College for the six-week summer program. I was excited beyond words.

It was the first time I would be independent and have time for myself without family obligations; no Mom nagging, kids bugging, or Dad screaming. No doctors' visits or welfare papers to fill out. No chores or sewing assignments. I was glad to have a break from all the odd jobs, the babysitting, toilet cleaning, and work at the sweatshop. I would be free during the weekdays to study, play, sleep, be lazy, do nothing. I would get to make my own decisions for what I wanted to do. It would be my first real experience with freedom.

By my junior year, I qualified for a needs-based weekly stipend for being on the Honor Roll. Every Monday, I received $12 for bus fare and my lunch allowance. It didn't matter that I lived only one block down the street, or that Mom packed me an egg sandwich every day. The $12 was all mine to save or to spend on personal needs or for school supplies. I felt *rich*. I wrapped the money carefully in an envelope and tucked it away for the future.

When not in my school uniform, I wore outfits I designed and made for myself.

11

Falling in Love

Who's that Guy—Duc Tran

In the summer before my senior year, Duc had come over to my house more than usual. I kept bumping into him. Every time I went downstairs, he would be there. When we greeted each other, I pretended to be busy with my chores to avoid chatting. I was shy and didn't know what to say.

Duc had just moved out of the rectory to an apartment complex across from my house on 43rd and Chestnut Street and decided he no longer wanted to become a Christian Brother as his mom wished him to be. It was his last year of college and he wanted to branch out to try the world on his own. I thought he was lonely. Because he had no family nearby, Duc often came over to our house to hang out with my younger brothers and sisters in the evenings or on the weekends.

Duc was welcomed by the whole family, from little Nam to Dad and everyone in between—except me. I felt awkward around him, never really knowing what to talk about. He seemed eager to talk to me, and yet reserved at the same time. I didn't know what to make of him. But the kids loved him, especially little Nam. My parents also respected Duc as a knowledgeable, educated Christian young man. He was quite handy, building a shelf for Mom and helping Dad change the oil in his newly purchased used car.

He once saw me all dressed up to go to a disco party with Hue Man and Xai Nga. It made me uncomfortable. Because Duc was rather quiet and serious, I perceived him as an authoritative figure. I hoped he didn't get the impression I was a party girl and I was worried that he would tell Frere Phong about it.

At that time, my brother Viet was struggling with math and Duc volunteered to tutor him. Viet would sometimes knock on my door and say, "Duc wants to know if you also need help with your math."

I always replied, "No, but thanks!" I was doing fine with my math, but after the second or third time, I had an inkling that this wasn't about math. *Maybe he likes me, and is looking for an opportunity to talk to me?* I started to wonder. *Nah. He's studying to be a Christian Brother, right? And Catholic priests don't date. What does he really want?* I was perplexed. At that time, I didn't know he no longer wanted to pursue the priesthood. I just had a gut feeling that Duc wanted to meet me.

But Duc is Vietnamese! I didn't think Dad would ever approve of me dating someone who was not Chinese. I paused and reminded myself I was getting way ahead of the game. He had asked to tutor me, not date me! I told myself to stop complicating things without having more facts. Besides, what made me think Duc would want to date a Chinese girl? He was just as aware of the long-standing differences between the Vietnamese and the Chinese. What would his family think?

Following my curiosity, I accepted Duc's help in Pre-calculus. At each tutoring session, Duc would bring an extra math puzzle to solve. From word problems involving toothpicks, to reading diagrams and interpreting graphs, he would leave me with the riddle and would then bring the answer to our next meeting. I used to dread having yet another problem to solve. He had a book full of puzzles that he could use to buy time with me. He later confessed that he was so nervous about meeting with me that he had to find something to talk about to occupy the time.

As we talked more and more, I was surprised to find out that he was only two years older than me. In our first heart-to-heart talk, I knew I could trust him. I revealed my real age to him and explained the dilemma I felt, living as a younger person.

There were other boys who had shown an interest in me, but I had never taken them seriously. Duc was different. As I got to know him better, I found him to be charming and attractive in his own quiet way. Duc had a kind heart. He was always helpful to my parents, and generous and playful with my four younger siblings. He was a family man, and a thrifty and conscientious spender like my dad. I loved how self-assured he was. He valued independence and wanted to be self-sufficient living in the jungle of Philadelphia. Duc had the self-confidence I was lacking.

Duc is the youngest son of nine children in his family. As a faithful Catholic, Duc's mom had dedicated her best-behaved child to God and told her son that he would make a great priest. Duc had left Vietnam with his eighth brother and his fifth sister (with her new family of three) during a time of panic and chaos. On April 30, 1975, as the communists rolled their tanks into Saigon, Duc and his siblings jumped onto a big commercial boat and got out of Saigon's Ben Thanh port just in the nick of time. He lived with his sister's family in South West Philly for a few years before moving out to establish his independence after high school.

Duc's oldest brother was an accomplished lieutenant colonel in South Vietnam, and was assassinated by Viet Cong in 1972. Four of his older siblings made it out of Vietnam on the last day and three stayed behind to look after their parents who had migrated to the south in 1954 to flee communists from the north. They knew the country would spiral downward, and did not hesitate to let their youngest son go. Duc was only 14 when he fled with his older siblings. In contrast, I had left as the oldest child.

After school started, we were interacting more with each other. I was beginning to have feelings for this very simple, wholesome person. "Am I in love?" I wrote in my diary. Thoughts of him occupied my mind more frequently. "Does he have the same feelings for me that I think I have for him?" To ensure my brother could not intrude on these private thoughts, I wrote in Chinese, which he did not know.

Duc came so often, he became part of the rhythm that was so natural to our family. Every now and then, he would disappear. It made me wonder. Just like the song "Tell Her About It" by Billy Joel: "Tell her about it, every day before you leave. Pay her some attention, give her something to believe…Cause now and then, she'll get to worrying, just because you haven't spoken for so long…" I was feeling uncertain throughout those late summer months. I didn't know if he was just being kind to me like he was with everyone else, or if he actually had feelings for me.

On the last day of October of 1983, Duc and I were finishing our math session and he challenged me to a game of Hangman. Three words. Only eight letters. I started with the vowels. No "A"s. Two "O"s. One "I" and one "E". Could it be? Next, I guessed "L" and the solution to the game jumped off the page. There it was. "I̲ L̲ o̲ v̲ e̲ Y̲ o̲ u̲," Blushing, I was stunned, confused, and not sure how I should react.

I paused with my hands on my face, but couldn't say a word. I looked at him, still speechless. He was shy and with a shaking voice, he said, "I didn't know how to tell you, so here it is." My speculation had been right, but I didn't know how to respond.

All I said could say was, "Are you for real?" and "Why me?"

There were so many thoughts racing through my head. My heart was pounding and my face and ears were flushed. I trembled with excitement. It was late. Since we didn't have school the next day (it was All Saints Day), we decided to meet to continue our conversation. It would be much easier without kids running around the house, interrupting our important discussion. I walked him downstairs and after making sure no one else was around, we exchanged our first goodbye kiss. It was a lightning-quick kiss, but it gave reassurance that this was real. I didn't sleep a wink that night. My world changed forever and for the better since that Hangman game! God had granted me a personal guardian angel. Duc is my earthly saint!

It couldn't have been more fitting than to have our first secret date on All Saints Day. I told Mom that I had to go to the downtown Philadelphia library near the art museum. It was the honest truth about the museum. We walked along the Schuylkill Riverbank, not quite knowing how we should act. We were both raised in a very traditional society and this was the first time we ever told each other about our feelings. We talked and talked for hours. It was astonishing to hear him participating in a conversation for that long. Duc was very philosophical and very much an idealist. His goal was not to change the world but to enjoy a quiet simple life. He said he would be perfectly happy leaving the city and living in the jungle like Tarzan, needing nothing more than the basics.

"Is that practical, living in a jungle away from civilization?" I asked with a raised eyebrow. "I lived in the jungles in Indonesia for eight months. Trust me, it was no fun! I am more of a city girl. I want my garden to be manmade and manicured, not wild."

I shared my thoughts with Duc as I had never done with anyone. I told him that I had ambitions to be successful in the mainstream of America and that I wanted a secure life with financial freedom so I could help my family. I wanted to escape from poverty and not be the parasite that many people think of refugees as being. I wanted so much for him to understand my desires and my dreams of being a contributing member of society. I wanted him to be clear on the path I planned to pursue. It was important to me that we were on the same page.

Duc assured me, "Falling in love with you is changing the way I think. I am willing to do what it takes to build a life together with you."

I know this probably sounds strange to be immersed in such serious conversations on the first date. The truth is that in Asian cultures, we take dating extremely seriously. We would not talk about love until we were absolutely sure that we would be partners for life. Duc and I both knew that we were establishing an unofficial contract and we needed to talk through all potential differences.

I was thrilled but also worried that my parents would never accept a Vietnamese boyfriend, much less a future son-in-law. There was a subtle and often not-so-subtle prejudice between the Chinese and Vietnamese people. It went both ways. Growing up I often heard negative comments about Vietnamese people, and I felt the bigotry of Vietnamese people directed towards our Chinese community. In Vietnam, it would never have crossed my mind to date a Vietnamese boy. I was very worried that my parents would object, and that the same would be true for his family.

"But we are so different. I am scared that our families will not understand," I said.

Then Duc asked me, "If two people are looking in the same parallel direction, how do they ever meet?"

"You are right," I said, looking into his eyes. "We will not look in the same direction but at each other. We will meet halfway, whatever comes."

And just like that, we began seeing each other in secret. We made many more trips to the library. Duc still came to the house and we acted as if nothing was different. He sometimes helped me thread needles while I sewed the neckties for Mom. I was sure that if anyone was paying close attention, they would see the exchanges of conversation, and the twinkle in our eyes as we exchanged glances. Mom was oblivious, but Dad, on the other hand, was very observant.

Even though Dad was only home one day a week, he picked up stories from Mom and was aware that Duc was there for a purpose. Dad said nothing and simply continued to observe. He would never have allowed Duc to form a deeper relationship with the family if he had doubts about Duc's personality and character. I had no idea that Dad had already checked out Duc's family background through connections at the Saigon Restaurant. He talked to people who knew the Vietnamese Catholic community and people who knew Duc's sister and her family well. Dad said nothing to me. And Dad said nothing to Mom.

Spring in Longwood Garden (1984)

12

High School Graduation

Heartbreaking Tuesdays

Dad worked 12 to 13 hours a day, six days a week at the Saigon Restaurant on Washington Avenue, and Tuesday was his only day off. We never knew which Dad we would get when he was home. He would either be the happiest person in the house that everyone loved, or a screaming, angry monster that everyone would avoid. We never knew which way the pendulum would swing, and did our best to ride the waves of uncertainty.

There were many happy family moments when Dad was in a good mood. He would cook a nice meal of steamed fish with ginger and mushrooms, or traditional Chinese dishes that he would sometimes share with friends he invited over to our home. He enjoyed taking the family on a shopping spree at the big K-Mart in South Philly to stock up for the week. Some days, we just drove endlessly after dinner on the West Chester Pike to look at the big houses in the suburbs pointing out the ones we liked—simple pleasures that were free and made us all happy because Dad was happy.

I struggled to make sense out of the many heartbreaking Tuesdays when Dad was home and the pressures of daily life once again bubbled over and exploded. To be fair, Dad was not totally to blame for his rages. Dad could be a logical, reasonable person when you were not stepping on his toes. Mom, on the other hand, could be quite overbearing, throwing sarcastic comments and making accusations that led to the bickering. My poor rebel brother Viet continued to be the primary scapegoat, too often making the wrong move at the wrong time. I, on the other hand, tried hard to tippy-toe, complete my chores, and remain under the radar at all costs.

Mom was always very hardworking, looking for more and more ways to earn money. She could never slow down and relax, and she didn't think Dad or anyone else in the family should rest, either. She would overload Dad with a long list of errands; places to go, things to do, asking him to drive to New York to drop off and pick up garments from the sweatshops in China Town. Many times, Dad would scream, "I have only one day off, and you won't even let me enjoy that!"

I can still hear him shouting at Mom, "Is your face plastered with money? I don't want to spend our whole life working for pennies with no long-term vision for the future!" It was always the same story, and they were like fire and gasoline, both contributing to the explosions. Most of the quarrels were about money, petty things, and Mom's endless complaining about everyone in the family. It certainly wasn't all financial, as any stressful situation could turn a simple conversation into a big argument.

When Dad didn't know what to do with his frustration, it would come out as a storm of rage on Mom, Viet, or me. We became casualties. Our family didn't know how to express our emotions without hurting others. Frustration was expressed in a harsh way, through foul language and putdowns. In America, it's called "verbal abuse."

One night, Dad returned home from work around 11:30 p.m. Something caused him to erupt at Viet like a volcano. He locked Viet out of the house all night and no amount of screaming and crying from Mom and me could stop Dad from his punitive discipline. Mom and I tried to let Viet back in the house, but Dad forbid it. He insisted that Viet needed to be severely punished and wanted to frighten him so he wouldn't repeat whatever it was that he had done. I was sobbing alone in my room upstairs, hiding out of sight, worried about Viet's safety. I know Dad was worried too, but he let his pride and his temper get in the way of being a compassionate father. The incident terrified everyone in the house. It could have ended so badly. But my prayers for his safety were answered; one of his friends let him stay overnight.

My relationship with my Dad was always a paradox. On the one hand, he was my hero. I was indebted to him for risking his life for his family. His personal needs were always secondary to the needs of his family. He was frugal, and he always had a vision for the future. On the other hand, he had virtually no control over his pride and hot temper. I did not respect how he let his anger and frustrations take over his whole being as he would become so noxious to his family.

Mom was also a paradox. She was totally committed to her family and worked tirelessly to see that all our physical needs were met. But she too could be a very difficult person to live with, and her negativity and sarcasm could trigger so much pain. She pushed all the wrong buttons that made her family feel bad about themselves. It often caused my father's temper to escalate abruptly. I don't think she realized how much she was pushing her loved ones away from her.

I began to notice the amount of anger and the number of self-centered habits that we imposed on each other. Many times, I felt lost and confused. I was no longer a seven-year-old kid who stood on the sideline and ran to my grandmother for help. I was a frustrated teenager who could not solve the problems of her parents' co-dependent, dysfunctional relationship. They both wanted me to take sides as an adult, to favor one over the other, and justify their behavior. As a result, I was torn, and I resented both of them for it.

Too often, my voice of reason was drowned out by my own temper. As I began recognizing the behaviors I had picked up from both of my parents, I felt the internal conflicts deep inside me. My whole life seemed like a love/hate relationship. The complex cross-cultural background that I inherited led me to believe I was unworthy, disconnected, and didn't belong anywhere. This unfortunately became the pattern that disrupted my emotional and mental well-being for years and years to come. I am sure all my siblings got a big load of this too.

I see that when a home is not a nurturing or happy place because of the constant battles between parents, children get caught in the middle and suffer from a lack of confidence. Our parents came from a culture of discipline, punishment, pride, and duty; not from a soft place of nurturing, gentleness, and praise. They didn't know how to express affection for each other. The pain they bore was transferred to them from their parents. Nobody taught them how to love, so they could only teach us what they knew: Tough love! And it ended up being more tough than love.

Senior Year

One Tuesday evening, Dad told me he wanted to talk to me after dinner. I was very anxious, wondering if I was going to be in some kind of trouble. He sat calmly in the big chair in the living room and pointed to the opposite chair and told me to sit down. He didn't shout. That made me even more anxious. He looked at me and said, "I know you are seeing Duc." I held my breath. "I don't have any objection. I think he is a good kid."

Oh my God!

I almost fell out of my chair. *Dad's never home, how does he know?* As if he was reading my mind, Dad said, "I can tell by the way both of you react when he comes through the door to visit. I have eaten more salt than you have consumed rice." It was a Chinese saying which means, "I've been through a lot more life than you." (Americans would say, "I wasn't born yesterday.")

Dad went on, "Did you think you could hide this from me? Your mom may not notice, but nothing in this house could bypass me." I stared down at the floor, not daring to look him in the eyes.

Did my father just give me permission to date a Vietnamese boy? My mind was racing. I was so excited to tell Duc. I could scream at the top of my lungs with happiness that Dad knew, and he was fine with it. My relief was enormous.

Dad continued with some preaching about dating and about focusing more on studying, and then he said: "Don't be greedy like your mom. She only sees what's right in front of her face. She's not able to see the long road ahead." I had great empathy for Mom whenever Dad was tough on her—just like how I resented it when Mom said bad things about Dad.

Within our family, Dad always had a vision, he saw the bigger picture. He didn't want me to waste time on short-term money-making ventures if it meant sacrificing the long-term goal. He would rather have me spend more time studying or joining an organization to learn skills that would help my career in the future than working odd jobs on the weekends.

But without Mom's diligent habits, we would never have made it this far. Mom was a workaholic, and frugal to a fault. She picked up jobs anywhere she could find them. Big or small, she was willing to work through the night and did not mind involving the kids to help. She worked hard to turn nine dollars into ten, tuck it away and save it for later. When Dad needed money for a big item, or to establish a business, she would give some to him. She told me that her mom taught her to always have some private money set aside from your husband. "You never know when you will need it if he leaves you one day." I'm not sure I believe that was from Grandma.

Dating Duc had become so much nicer and easier now that I had Dad's blessing. He was becoming part of the family. He was there to guide and tutor my brothers and sisters, and he filled in for me if Mom needed to see the doctors or social workers. He would fix broken furniture for Mom or navigate directions for Dad. Duc was getting increasingly involved in my siblings' activities and with our entire family in general.

Duc was calm, laid back, and the total opposite of how I was raised. He had an enormous amount of patience, and nothing seemed to bother him or make him angry. When I did something wrong, he would apologize first to get me to acknowledge I was also at fault. He taught me to put down my defenses, and that it's okay to say "I am sorry," a quality we lacked.

During the senior year of high school, I was pretty much on my own in picking out a college. My options were limited because of my lack of resources and knowledge of the process. My parents were not able to give me any guidance. Duc helped some, but he was also in his last year of college and busy with his schoolwork. I was eager for the freedom to think for myself, and to live as an independent young adult, not having to answer to my family. But the guilt of abandoning my family prevented me from looking at colleges that were far away. Luckily, Pennsylvania has the most outstanding universities in the area, and I worked hard to save money for college applications.

Being the eldest, I had a responsibility to my family. Unlike Americans, our parents didn't want us to be independent of them. They expected us to depend on them, and later on, be their caretakers. The seed of resentment was growing bigger inside me because I had seen how this played out before. In Vietnam, I witnessed the ongoing argument between my dad and his brothers and sisters about who sacrificed most for the family, and who should be doing more. Even though they truly cared for one another, the expectations fostered resentment and lots of unresolved issues.

I can still hear my uncle say to my dad, "I did more for this home and for Mom than any of you ever knew about!"

And Dad would say, "Yeah? And who took care of everyone when Mom passed away? Where were you?"

The culture I grew up in was filled with this type of guilt, needling, hidden anger, and resentment. The bickering and squabbling were never-ending, and it became part of our family history. I couldn't wait to break loose and be on my own, but I knew that I would never be completely detached from my duties as the eldest.

Since I was a child, the idea of being a pharmacist had been planted in my mind to fulfill my grandma's dream. She told me many times that

I had healing hands and that made me feel like I had a gift. I tried to make it work, and originally, the Philadelphia College of Pharmacy was my first choice. But the school was not in a safe part of Philly and I definitely didn't want to commute, so I crossed it off my list.

The Upward Bound summer program was a great help. My mentor and counselor, Nancy Lucas, volunteered to take a few of her students to visit Villanova University. I fell in love with the campus, which was an hour from home in the Main Line suburbs of Philadelphia. The location was ideal. It was away from home but close enough so I could come home on the weekends to help my family.

In the end, I applied to my top three schools: Drexel, Saint Joseph's University, and Villanova. To my surprise, I was accepted to all three universities and they all offered me partial scholarships. My heart was set on Villanova, not only because I was in the three percent minority in school and got a substantial merit scholarship, but also because they had a free tutoring program. Villanova has a strong science program, but they didn't have a pharmacy program, so I picked a general science major to buy me some time to think about what I should do next.

The spring of 1984 was full of hope as the independent life I dreamed about was getting closer to becoming reality. In June, I graduated with high honors. I should have been thrilled to celebrate my accomplishments, but instead, I was disappointed. I didn't qualify for the National Honor Society. Even though my GPA and academic standards tests were good, I was lacking in extracurricular activities such as community service, sports involvement, or leadership in school and the community. Had I known this was one of the requirements, I would have made an effort to fit it into my schedule. I blamed myself for not being on top of the game.

On graduation day, Duc was the designated photographer for the family. Several of my Chinese friends also attended the graduation. As I was walking down the aisle of the large auditorium in the Civic Convention Center, I knew my parents were very proud of me, especially my dad. This was the accomplishment for which he took all those risks: the opportunity to see his children achieving the higher education he dreamt he could have had.

In the short four years since we came to America, I not only succeeded in this difficult academic journey, but I was ranked in the top seven percent of my class and was listed as one of the outstanding seniors in the yearbook. In spite of all my challenges, late-night studies, and physical distress, I had finally completed this step on my bigger journey.

At the ceremony, I was seated with the top ten percent of my class on stage. It was a surreal feeling. Looking out, I could see the rest of my classmates sitting in the auditorium. *It's still not enough.* Even though I had made it this far, and done well, I wished I could have done better. I wished I had the advantage of growing up in a family that didn't require so much of my time for all the family's needs. I beat myself up for not getting a full scholarship because my SAT scores were only average. I wished I could have been born in this country, because I would have had the same advantages as my other classmates. If I wasn't so afraid of rejection, maybe I could have gotten into an Ivy League school like the University of Pennsylvania, but I settled for "no" as the answer before I even asked the question.

Looking back, I want to tell my younger self, "Don't be so harsh on yourself. Enjoy what you achieved. For what you have been through, you are enough!"

Me, first one in the front row on the far left of both pictures.
It was a pleasant surprise to be included in this group of "Outstanding Students."

West Catholic Girls High graduation (1984)

The Last Summer at Home

I secured a six-week summer job from the guidance office stuffing envelopes for a company that taught speed-reading to college students. The company was located across the Schuylkill River on Walnut Street. I worked from nine to five on the third floor, folding letters, stuffing envelopes, sealing, labeling, and stamping solicitations to thousands of students in universities around Philadelphia. I thought to myself, *It would be a waste of money if I took this speed training.* There was no way I could ever read quickly because I still had to stop every other sentence to check vocabulary in the dictionary. How cool and advanced I would be if I could easily comprehend what I read.

For those six weeks, Duc always waited for me promptly at the door at 5:00 p.m. on the ground floor by the elevator to walk me home. He was patient, consistent, and ready to listen to whatever I had to share. We had about 16 blocks to walk in order to get home. That was how we spent our dating time, and how we grew our relationship.

In mid-August, Duc told Dad that his sister's sister-in-law had a duplex home in Yeadon for rent. Moving out of the bad neighborhood of West Philly was something my family had been talking about for some time. It was an unsafe neighborhood. The tragic news that two of my classmates were stabbed and killed in their own homes helped us to speed up the decision. Phan, Que, and Nam would benefit from not having to walk over ten blocks to school in the cold, and Dad's car meant that transportation would not be a problem. It was decided we would move to the suburbs of West Philly.

Mr. Rothenberg was sad to see us leave, but he understood that we were moving to a safer, better place. As much as he liked us, he did not offer to give us any of his old furniture from the house. Trust me, Dad told me to ask!

The plan was to be out of West Philly before school started in September. Duc was between college and job searching so he had some free time to help my family move. I could tell that Dad was happy to have the extra help.

Two weeks before school started, we were out of the tiny apartment, leaving the rats and the roaches behind to advance to the next level of our American dream in the suburbs. I was both the happiest and guiltiest person on earth. I felt selfish for leaving my family who needed me in order to pursue my own dreams off at college.

But the sky had opened up for me! The school was only a 45-minute drive from our house, and I didn't tell my parents that staying at home was an option. I told them that room and board was a requirement. There was no way I could focus on my studies living at home and I wanted to enjoy a new freedom. With the family now living in the suburb, I could legitimately not worry so much about everyone. Unfortunately, I was so involved in my family's affairs that I could not easily break free even if I wanted to. I planned to come back home on the weekends.

Yeadon

Compared to our Chestnut Street apartment, our new home was gigantic. Our side of the duplex was a two-story, three-bedroom house with a small front and back yard. There were many advantages for our family, Dad being happiest about the street parking.

"We never have to put a dirty trash can on our front curb to reserve a space for the car! There is plenty of street parking here. I love it!"

The house was located on Cypress Street in Yeadon, Delaware County, a suburb on the outskirts of West Philadelphia. Yeadon is a quaint borough located at the edge of Delaware County, bordering the city of Philadelphia. We were less than a block from Cobbs Creek Park, a small wooded park on either side of a meandering creek, featuring walking paths and a playground.

With our new spacious interior, we had the task of buying many home furnishings as we only had our beds from our last place. Lien, the owner, left a wooden-framed sectional sofa for us, so we had a start on furnishing the living room. Mom bought a table and a few chairs at the second-hand thrift store and, voila! We had a dining room set for four people.

When the temperature dropped in the fall, Dad realized our heating bill was high because of the drafty windows. His solution was to cover all the windows with thick plastic sheets to keep the heat inside. Floor-length drapes would have been nice, but those plastic sheets were an upgrade from the metal bars on the windows in West Philly.

Instead of the clunking noise from the radiators, we now had a kerosene heater smack-dab in the middle of the living room, ten feet from the front door. The odor of burning kerosene oil hit you in the face as soon as you stepped inside. Like most people who used kerosene heaters at that time, we had no idea about the toxicity of poisonous effects it could have on us. Not to mention all the fire accidents on the news about the kerosene heaters. It reminded us of the big electric heater we huddled around in Minnesota to keep warm. The smell eventually became familiar and it gradually stopped bothering us.

Since we were there only two years and I was living on campus at school during the weekdays, I admit that I don't have many memories of that house. Even though I came home almost every weekend, I was so overwhelmed with my own experiences at college that I didn't pay much attention when I was back.

Our creative idea of plastic window treatments for extra insulation

13

Villanova University

Life on Campus

Villanova University was not cheap, but I managed to pull together enough scholarships, grants, personal loans, and income from various odd jobs to get everything I needed for school. Like many refugees and immigrants, my parents did not have the knowledge or the qualifications to be involved in college selection. They couldn't help their children navigate curriculum requirements and arrange all the things involved in being successful in college. We pretty much had to be on top of our game by ourselves. It never even occurred to me to ask for financial help from my parents. I knew if I had asked, Dad would not hesitate to sell everything he had to pay for my education; it was that important to him. But I was fine managing it on my own.

I was proud that I was independent enough to have done it without adding another burden to the family. I was fortunate to have Duc by my side to coach and mentor me about applying for government grants and loans. While I was busy settling in at college, Duc was helping my family cope with the challenges of moving and starting a new life in the suburbs.

I was happy to have the excuse of a higher calling: college. I was still obligated to come home every Friday night and stay until Sunday afternoon, but I selfishly tuned out many of the bad reports. I helped with the urgent issues, but kept my head in my books and focused on my own struggles, things I didn't even try to share with them. I started to dread coming home; it was such a troubling environment. I felt so helpless when I was there, and felt guilty that after the weekend, I could escape, and they couldn't. At school, the only thing I had to look forward to every day was a phone call from Duc. The rest of my time was applied to tackling mountains of reading and homework.

Not every Freshman could qualify to live in the upperclassmen's dorm, but I had won the lottery. I was assigned a room in Alumni Hall, one of the oldest buildings on campus, dating back to 1848. The building was renovated in 1920, had three floors, and housed approximately 110 students in single, double, and triple accommodations.

My room was a typical old dorm, only big enough for two twin beds or a stacked-up bunk bed, two small desks, and two dressers. It was roughly 12x12 with two built-in closets on each side by the door. There was a window facing the campus courtyard where I enjoyed watching the ROTC cadets march their routines in the early mornings. The peace and quiet of Alumni Hall were a complete contrast to the modern, loud, and chaotic freshman dorms located on the south campus. I was grateful for the quiet setting and short walking distance to classes and the cafeteria. It saved me a ton of time.

After I moved into the dorm, I met my first roommate, Cynthia, an African American sophomore student. Within a week, Cynthia transferred off campus because she found a new apartment somewhere else. I hardly had time to get to know her and now I was waiting for a new roommate. A few days later, when I came back to the dorm from classes, I saw someone had put some personal belongings on the dresser. There was a 13" TV on the window ledge, and the other bed was fully covered with sheets, spread, and stuffed animals. I assumed it was my new roommate, but there was no sign of anyone for days. I asked the Resident Assistance and she said not to worry and that I had a new roommate named Patricia, a senior nursing student.

Patricia showed up a few days later to introduce herself. She explained that she actually lived with her boyfriend, but needed to have a room just in case her parents checked in on her. My only job was to tell her parents that she was studying at the library if they called the phone in the hallway. She asked me to then relay the message to her, calling her boyfriend's phone number. So, in reality, I had the room all to myself!

Wow! Here I was, working so hard to stay on campus, and my new roommate was working just as hard to stay off-campus. This same room had two completely opposite functions for a Freshman and a Senior. I felt like I had just won yet another lottery, having my own private room. Certainly a first in my life!

While I appreciated having the entire space to myself, it would have been nice having that classic college roommate experience where we try new things and form a new friendship circle. I had no one to talk with or process the many new experiences, thoughts, and feelings. The isolation got to me when I saw groups of freshmen clustered together in their newly-made bonds, socializing as well as looking out for each other. And then I found Maria.

Maria–My BFF

During the freshman orientation in the big auditorium at Mendel Hall, I sat next to Maria Luisa Fernandez, who seemed out of place, like me. I still remember she wore a small-print yellow, ankle-length jumpsuit with a white T-shirt. Maria had a beautiful, angelic face and a friendly smile that drew me to her.

She took the initiative to introduce herself. "Hi, my name is Maria-Louisa Llanio Fernandez. I am from Bilbao, Spain."

"Hi, I am Le Khanh Ong. Nice meeting you."

"Do you know anyone here? I live in Sheehan dorm and am a General Science major." Maria was eager to dive into the conversation.

"No, I don't know anyone. Wow, I'm also a General Science major. Do you happen to have Chemistry with Dr. Ludwig on Monday morning?" I was hoping for a *yes*.

"Yes! Monday, Wednesday, and Friday, right here in this lecture hall."

"Great! Maybe we can sit next to each other and help each other out. I am not very good at English. I am from West Philly, but I came from Vietnam four years ago. Would you like to meet at the Pit for lunch later?" I immediately felt safe and comfortable with Maria.

"Absolutely! You remind me of my good friend in Spain. She is also petite and Asian." I was glad that she found something in me that was familiar and reminded her of home.

I was excited to find a kindred spirit—another freshman who needed companionship in a new foreign land. I had a feeling that Maria was also an old soul, like me. Her maturity was reflected in the conversations we had. We talked about cultural differences, like the differences in the high school education systems in Europe and Asia, and the brand-new world of college that we were experiencing in America.

It was a coincidence that we had the same birth month, that our birthdays were only three days apart. On paper, we were the same age, but

I didn't want to risk this new bond by telling her my age dilemma. Though our backgrounds were very different, we shared many of the same values and similarities in our upbringing. We both were the first-born, Maria had three younger sisters, where I had two younger brothers and sisters. We both were studious and took our responsibilities very seriously. We shared the same General Science major, and we both admitted to having no idea what would come of it.

We became best friends and ate together three meals a day at Dougherty Hall, nicknamed *The Pit*. It was the place I learned what "Freshman fifteen" means. It was food galore, with all you can eat, grilled bar, pasta bar, salad bar, sandwiches, pizza and anything you could think of—food heaven at our fingertips. I would've been happy to camp there all day, just trying all the different types of food. My favorite was the *Surf and Turf* meal twice a year, where we were given tickets to claim lobster and steak for dinner. Sometimes Duc came to visit and Maria would let him use her meal card when she had other dinner plans. I, fortunately, did not pack on the extra pounds, but many others struggled with yo-yo weight gain at the end of each semester.

The Pit was also the place where I met many of Maria's Latino friends, some from Spain, some from South America and other parts of the world. I loved her Latino community. Even though I didn't understand what they were saying to each other, I was always welcomed to hang out with her friends. I was fascinated by listening to their language and how fast they could roll their tongues, speaking a million words in one breath.

We shared new findings on campus and helped each other with many things, including correcting each other's accents. Their lives were far more adventurous than I could ever afford, financially and emotionally. Looking at them being so carefree and joyous, I felt out of place. I was at war with my identities, not happy with who I was, or the circumstances of my life.

I wished I truly was younger and had the courage and time to venture out and make new friends as she did. *You cannot fit in because of your economic background and the language barrier. You are an outsider of this culture,* I told myself

Being with them made me realize how different our worlds were. Their lives seemed so easy. There were times I wished I was born with all the privileges that seemed so frivolous to many people I knew. What fun would it be to breeze through life with my parents footing the bills? As much as I appreciated my upbringing and the hardships that we went through, there were times when I wanted to enjoy a carefree life, too. I found myself feeling the same feelings as I had in high school, but on a larger scale. I wanted to speed up to get to where I can be completely free to live a life for myself.

Soon after the semester began, Maria pledged to join a sorority. She would share stories with me while we ate together. I lived vicariously through Maria's stories and experiences. My room also became Maria's refuge when she needed to be away from the noisy world of Sheehan Hall, the overly active freshman dorm.

Every new semester Maria would come back with wonderful stories from Spain, Italy, France, and places where she vacationed with her family. She took a semester to study abroad in Germany and decided to earn a double minor in Math and Statistics. Maria introduced me to her circle of international students. It was my first encounter with the world of wealth beyond my scope of ordinary life.

By the second and third years, I saw Maria less and less as her social life had broadened. Nevertheless, even today, our friendship remains strong. Whenever we have a chance to see each other and we always pick up where we left off without skipping a beat.

I love and appreciate Maria because she was proactive in keeping our friendship alive. I would have let it go because of that crazy belief that I was not worthy or not good enough to be her friend. I told Maria I wanted her to be the godmother to be my first-born child. She said it would be her honor. And so, many years later when I had my son, Maria became his godmother. (By the way, I did not reveal my real age to Maria until decades after college. It was a relief that she didn't think less of me or seem bothered a bit!)

Maria sitting on Patricia's bed in my dorm room

Maria came to visit me in Pennsylvania, 1992

14

Crisis at Home

Chinese Takeout

A few months after we moved, Dad had a misunderstanding with his boss at the Saigon Restaurant. My father was a very proud and practical man with a high sense of integrity and an extreme temper. Apparently, he was upset about some putdown remark he heard from a third party, and when Dad got upset, his temperament was not easily soothed. His pride and ego had gotten cranked up into high gear and he couldn't downshift, so after a few days, he quit his job. He never bothered to try to clear up the issue with his boss.

He worked tirelessly for things that he wanted, but would rather starve than beg or ask for help. "Never live beyond your means. Don't flaunt it when you are doing well and don't act like a pauper when you are poor. Be steady and never, ever let people look down on you!" That was the principle he lived by.

Finances were tight for the family, and both my parents were constantly scrambling to find jobs. We were still on government assistance, unable to be independent because we needed medical benefits. There was no way we could afford health insurance for a family of seven, no matter how many jobs my parents had. Mom was transitioning to babysitting full time at the Ferbers while Dad looked for another kitchen position, all under the table.

It wasn't long after when Dad was approached by his friend, Mr. Lim, to talk about opening a Chinese food takeout restaurant in Southwest Philly on 63rd Street. Setting up a small takeout business in a poor neighborhood was a common business venture for immigrants and refugees.

The partnership was not fair from the get-go, but Dad was desperate to make things work. Dad loaned Mr. Lim $5,000 as an initial investment, and he agreed to work as the chef without a salary until the business got going. There was no written contract. He trusted that it would only be temporary until the takeout business grew. It was incredibly hard work for a one-man show. Dad had to juggle everything by himself in the kitchen. He had never cooked for a takeout food business before, and the pace and demand was much different than in a dine-in restaurant. Mr. Lim helped set up the restaurant, but then only popped in occasionally to check on things and to collect money.

My brother and sisters all took turns helping take orders after school, without pay. Most patrons were lower-income people who wanted cheap Chinese food and had little tolerance if something wasn't up to their American/Chinese fast food standards. Many times, Dad was forced to refund their money if they complained that the food did not taste like what they wanted.

Cultural differences also added greatly to the challenge. How was my dad to know American tastes and preferences? My Chinese father had to learn a new definition of "Chinese food."

My dad and Chinese people everywhere love eating fish, literally from head to tail. They will eat the bones, the head, the eyes, the gills—every part of steamed or fried fish. When a small fish is battered and deep-fried, the bones are soft and crunchy enough to be eaten. Dad was proud to be descended from fishermen in China who knew how to eat fish. But this is not how Americans eat fish.

Everything here is filleted, and one rarely sees that the fish they eat actually used to look like a fish. Americans rarely see any kind of meat that remotely looks like the animal that was once a living being. The possibility of choking on fish bones and having the eyes on a fish head staring back at you are repugnant to most Americans. So, when Dad served his first deep-fried fish sandwich (the entire fish from head to tail), the man had a disgusted look on his face.

His mouth dropped open and then he turned to my little sister who had taken the order and delivered the sandwich. "ARE YOU KIDDING ME? YOU CALL THIS F***ING THING A FISH SANDWICH!?"

Duc happened to be at the restaurant that night and saw my poor sister start to cry when the man was yelling at her. Dad quickly realized that what would have been delicious for him, was a big no-no for his American customers. The money was refunded, and the man vowed never to return. When I heard about this later from Duc, I felt bad that I had not been there to prevent such a disaster from happening or to diffuse the situation. It wasn't at all funny at the time, but years later, Duc and I could not stop laughing when we thought of that fish sandwich.

Needless to say, the business did not prosper. Time and money were lost, and Dad was overwhelmed and frustrated. About three or four months into the business, Dad finally gave up and took the loss. It was inevitable that it would fail. The neighborhood was infested with cockroaches and it was impossible to keep the restaurant pest-free. There were fines to keep up with and the business wasn't thriving. Dad did not understand the American culture of the Chinese takeout business. He had been working for free and whatever savings remained was disappearing. So, when Dad decided that he no longer wanted to continue with the takeout restaurant, it was a relief for everyone in the family.

Mr. Lim sold the place and never repaid the loan he borrowed from Dad. He said that he had sold the place for a loss. Mom was rightly upset and blamed Dad for trusting his friend and for not going after the money. Dad was angry and hurt by his friend's betrayal, but took it out on Mom. Her nagging did not help but agitated Dad even more. Everyone was defensive and every conversation became an argument. I was not at home, but I might just as well have been. I constantly got calls from my siblings or from Mom. My heart sank every time I got a knock on my dorm room door with someone saying, "Phone call for you!"

A few times when I got home and could not find Mom, Viet told me that she often went down to the creek and cried. After that, when I came home from college and did not see her, I frequently found her at Cobbs Creek. I could not stop imagining the worst, as the old scene of the bottle of medicine that Mom wanted to take after being battered from Dad reappeared in my thoughts. I was afraid she would do something foolish to harm herself or maybe be killed by some crazy guy down by the creek. I told the kids to keep an eye on Mom and report to me anything they saw.

Coping

The takeout restaurant fiasco had gotten the best of Dad, Mom, and my siblings. Because they were all stuck in the same household, every little issue and challenge at home became magnified. Mom was also struggling with her full-time babysitting job in downtown Philly. Public transportation was a beast. She had to walk down an icy hill in the cold winter weather to catch the bus, then take a trolley and the subway to get to her destination.

In the evenings, Mom put in extra hours of sewing. She brought the Juki industrial sewing machine from the old apartment with her and set it up in the basement to sew garments for the sweatshops in North Philly. She would subcontract some of her work out to her friends, but if they were sick or couldn't do it, she would have to stay up all night to finish the job. The drop-off and pickup of thousands of pieces of garments were due each week and the schedules could not be altered. Mom couldn't and still can't drive, so all the delivering responsibility fell on Dad and he did not like it.

Without me, Viet became the oldest in the house. Life was a real struggle for my 16-year-old brother. When he was at West Catholic Boys High School in Philly, he was an Honor Roll student. He surrounded himself with motivated friends who were also in accelerated classes. But after we moved, he felt totally lost trying to integrate into Penn Wood High. As a brand-new junior, he had no friends, no mentor, and no guidance. He got in with a bad crowd of kids and began neglecting his schoolwork. He would cut classes and started getting failing grades. He was always a rebel, but now he was at the peak age for teenage rebellion. He didn't want to talk to anyone, not even me.

One day, Viet rode his bike all the way from Yeadon to Villanova to ask me a question. He could have very easily picked up the phone and asked me (I can't even remember what the question was), but when I saw him waiting for me in front of my dorm, I was deeply concerned. I asked if everything was okay at home. He said yes, he just wanted to test out the ride and ask me something. Deep in my gut, I knew Viet was crying out for help, but didn't want me to worry.

I made him promise that he would never take such a dangerous bicycle ride on the highway again. He promised. The selfish part of me didn't want to know about the turmoil at home. I was just hoping it would go away.

Viet was looking for a place where he felt that he belonged and he didn't get it at home. He was rarely talked to except for being yelled at. My parents thought their negative put-downs, threats and demeaning insults were tools that would motivate Viet to comply. But unlike me, Viet had no fear of hard-core discipline and no instinct to go along in order to get along. I was shocked when he told me how he hung out with bad kids and regularly skipped class. When Dad discovered that Viet had forged his signature on a failing report card, all hell broke loose. Viet was again severely punished. Throughout high school, their conflicts escalated. It's a wonder that Viet remained living at home and did graduate.

Phan and Que and Nam were now fifteen, thirteen, and nine, respectively. They were such great kids. Always helpful and did what was told. Like it was ingrained in our DNA, they, too, never stopped looking for opportunities to earn extra money. All three of them started a paper route on the weekend. They helped each other and my dad helped with the evening delivery. Everyone in the family was chipping in to make ends meet by working constantly. The house was not a warm, fun, nurturing space of refuge, but a place of constant pressure to work, study, and work some more.

Que and Nam were trying to adapt to the new environment and did everything they could to help my parents. They were typical immigrant kids who had sat obediently at the takeout counter of Dad's failing business, taking orders from rude people who wanted fast, cheap Chinese takeout and did not hesitate to scream at the little ones.

My heart ached whenever I looked at my parents. Dad was aging fast and seemed crankier every time I saw him. I didn't know he was concealing the burdens and trying to bear those responsibilities alone, feeling frustrated and unable to share his worries with anyone. He had built an empire in Vietnam but now his hands were tied, and he had to rely on his wife and children to help him.

On the other hand, Mom was feeling trapped and her victim mindset was overpowering. Every time I came home, her eyes welled up with tears when she talked with me. Even though it went against every fiber of my being, I remember on several occasions saying to Mom, "Why don't you divorce Dad? This is NOT a happy place for you, for either of you. Why go on torturing yourself and us?"

That was when I knew my thinking process had fundamentally shifted. The new culture had influenced my attitude and even my core values. Traversing the new territory was not smooth.

Both my parents loved and valued raising us children but seemed to have no compassion for one another. Their love, their common thread of togetherness, was their children. We were the reason they worked so hard. And they didn't want others to laugh at them. Mom often worried, "What do outside people think of us? We will be the laughingstock for everyone we know." So, they continued to exist as co-dependents in this dysfunctional relationship. Good days or bad days, their only satisfaction was their family and their jobs. That's all they lived for, and neither of them were at a good place often in their life.

Each of us battled in our own way to help the family and we ended up getting on each other's nerves. We were facing conditions that were beyond what I could fix. I wished we could leap over this dark period and jump to the day when I would have a good job and could help lift my parents' burden.

Although Yeadon reminds me of many ugly incidents, there are some pleasant memories that I treasure with my siblings. When home from school on the weekends, I grew to love morning jogs with my sister, Phan. She started a morning running routine as her way of releasing stress and coping with everything at home. Phan was a morning person and I was more of a night owl, so it was hard getting me out of bed on a cold morning to go running, but I soon realized that the pluses far outweighed the minuses. Sharing a sunrise jog with my sister was priceless. All during our years in Vietnam, Phan had been my loyal buddy sister. I was proud to see the changes in her as a young woman. Her confidence was growing, and her routine morning run was a sign of that growing self-assurance.

My "babies" (Que and Nam). Yeadon 1984

The other delight that my siblings and I enjoyed together in Yeadon was the dollar movie theater on Church Lane. The movies were never current releases, but we were okay with that. It was an upgrade from the free Chinese movies at the Drexel Student Center in West Philly. These Saturday shows were the perfect low-cost entertainment that Duc and I could afford to provide for all my siblings. These times brought us closer together, and they were desperately needed.

15

Searching for a Career Path

Picking a Major

Back in high school, I had an assignment to interview a person in a career field of my interest. The pharmacist I interviewed was very discouraging. He talked about the negative aspects of his job and the struggles to maintain a traditional Mom-and-Pop pharmacy in the new competitive market. It sounded like it was all about pill-counting, paperwork, mundane tasks. It was very disappointing to me. One thing I would advise to kids now is to be wise about who you are interviewing for an important decision in your life. It is not wise to let one person influence your entire future based on one interview, but that's what I did. I walked away from pursuing a pharmacy degree based on the misery of this one pharmacist's point of view.

I had originally picked General Science as my major in order to give myself more time to decide what my best long-term option would be. Now a sophomore, I needed to make a choice.

I learned that a General Science degree would not get me a good job unless I was willing to go into teaching, so I had to switch to something else. I ruled out the medical field because I can't stand the sight of blood and seeing patients suffer. No nursing or medical doctor degrees here. I thought perhaps I could be in clinical research in the medical field, but I wasn't sure. I did not want to be in math or accounting because that was dry, tedious and boring. I told myself I wouldn't enjoy business because it involved sales and marketing, and trying to convince people to buy something did not appeal to me. And for sure, *no* to law and litigation—I was afraid of authority figures and there was no way I could do a job that involved being confrontational or public speaking.

Furthermore, I was afraid to seek out a mentor for help. I talked a lot with Duc but he was also struggling with the English language barrier and finding an adequate career path; he was treading water just like I was.

Both Duc and I were timid about confronting the outside world. Duc was introverted and content with the scope of his world. I, on the other hand, felt stuck. I could be an extrovert, eager to explore new and bigger possibilities, if only I were brave enough to speak up and courageous enough to seek out a mentor.

I am a creative person who has an analytical mind. I was already very skilled in fashion, both in designing and creating clothes. That was something I was passionate about. But I didn't feel I had the looks or the necessary connections to be in the fashion industry. I didn't think it would provide a stable and steady income for the fast-track professional career that I wanted to build. I was quite adept at talking myself out of all kinds of possibilities and opportunities. I regret that I didn't give these choices a chance.

Duc's sister, Tinh, was an analytical chemist. She worked at Wyeth Pharmaceutical Company, seemed happy, and made good money. I thought it would be much more interesting to make pills rather than count them. I had no idea there were so many specific fields in pharmacy or chemistry. The coursework didn't involve a ton of writing, and I was pretty sure I could handle formulas and memorizing the periodic table. If I wasn't going to be a pharmacist, chemistry seemed like a good next choice. So, I chose chemistry and hoped for the best.

On the first day of my chemistry class in Mendel Auditorium, Dr. Ludwig said something that still rings in my ears: "Every minute of class is a quarter that you give to me, whether you pay attention or not. This is college! You don't have to be here, but you paid to be here. You have the choice to walk out if you don't want to participate."

At that moment, I was determined to make every minute count! I wasn't going to waste any of the education I so gratefully received from the school and from the government. The Minority Scholarship from Villanova and the student loans from the banks gave me the opportunity to get the education I needed, and wanted, in this country. Every semester, I signed up for anywhere from 15 to 19 credits, the most allowed. You paid the same tuition whether you took 12 credits or 19 credits, so I made the most of it. It was like eating at a buffet where you pay one price no matter how much you eat, so I figured I might as well consume as much as they'd give me. I was determined not to waste anything I was given.

I spent all my time studying and working at Mendel Hall. It was a three-story science building with large lecture halls, classrooms, and research laboratories. It also housed all the professors' offices, and many graduate and post-doc research students camped there day and night. The building had a nickname, "Mental Hall," which I found insanely appropriate.

Coming from a small pond to a big lake, I struggled to catch up with other students and to keep up my grades. It was the first time I was fully immersed in an English-speaking world at home and school. Since I lived on campus, I decided I would focus more on speaking and listening to native English speakers as one way to help with my coursework. I was fortunate that Villanova offered free tutoring for low-income minority students who were struggling. Margaret, an upperclassman from Ireland, helped me immensely in English composition and with literature, in general. Margaret was a fair-skinned, red-haired, freckle-faced English and Theater major. I will never forget her soft voice and her kind encouragement whenever she helped edit my writings. I was able to get a B+ in English thanks to Margaret, but I stopped short of developing a personal friendship with her.

In high school, the subjects were all familiar and relatively easy for me, but now I was in completely uncharted territory. As hard as I studied, I always felt behind. The level of difficulty was ten times harder than high school. Every subject imposed a new level of challenge. I was trying to learn everything expected of me, from lectures, science labs, and mountains of homework assignments, but even though I was feverishly taking notes, I still couldn't grasp everything. My comprehension skills were lacking, and the teachers talked too fast, used idioms I didn't understand, references I didn't know, and told jokes I didn't get.

When it was time to formally declare my major, I decided on Chemistry. There were a whopping ten people all together in my major: me and four other girls and five boys. They all seemed to know for sure that chemistry was their passion. I, on the other hand, was still unsure of what I wanted. I just let the circumstances and guesswork determine my destiny.

The size of the classes for chemistry majors shrank down to less than ten percent from the General Chem class, which made me feel a lot more comfortable. Gone were the hundred-student lecture halls for the Biology and Pre-Med majors. The ten of us pretty much had the same chemistry courses and labs together for the next few years.

In my second year, I had hoped to get a job interning in the lab so I could learn more chemistry, but nothing was available. Instead, I took two work-study jobs, one at the library and one in the chemical stockroom. I worked anywhere from 12 to 20 hours a week, depending how much they needed me. I started going home less on the weekends and knew that having to work at a job would be understandable to my parents. I was glad to have justification for less exposure to the family environment at that time. Now that I was on campus during weekends, Duc came to visit and we were able to be together more. By claiming my weekends, not only was I being productive with my work-study jobs, I had more time to study and more time to relax with Duc. College life was improving.

Working in Falvey Memorial Library was an easy job. I helped retrieve archives, references, and maintained the microfilm department. The workload was relatively light, so I utilized the time to catch up on homework and reading.

The chemistry department stockroom, on the other hand, was not a fun job, but it was interesting. This was where all the extra chemicals and solvents for the entire department, undergrads and grad students were stored. The ventilation was not very good, and the bottles of chemicals sometimes corroded the metal shelves they were stored on. The toxic fumes were unbearable. Part of my job was to organize and clean up spilled chemicals on the shelves and reorganize them. I would hold my breath, do a little work, then run out to the hall to catch a fresh breath. I learned to organize the chemicals by their nomenclatures. It was a preview of what my future career would be like in a laboratory. I did not like inhaling the toxic fumes of the chemicals and solvents, but I thought it would lead me to a stable career with a good paycheck that could help out my parents. That was enough motivation to keep me going.

I told myself that I would get used to it and maybe even like it. To me, it was far better than the prospect of having to speak or write English all the time. How wrong I was! I learned later that no matter what major studies or career we choose in life, being able to speak, write, and communicate is a critically important tool to have in your possession.

Organic Chemistry

One of my favorite classes was Organic Chemistry. It was taught by Dr. Giuliano, a tall, dark and handsome Italian professor. One of the things I liked about Organic Chemistry was that I could see the structure of the compound through a drawing of the molecule. I loved the fact that you could actually see and identify how the properties of the compounds interact and how a new compound was formed. Sometimes mysterious byproducts were found in unexpected ways. I liked watching the transformation of the reactions, figuring out ways to purify the products and the process of identifying the molecules using different instruments. In our lab work, I found it gratifying to see the final crystal powder after many steps of the synthesis.

I was intrigued with this creative side of science. The chemistry lab was my kitchen. I learned to synthesize, purify, and identify chemical compounds that could be used for rubber, cosmetics, medicine, and for many other purposes to improve human life. I did not fully understand the magnitude of the impact of science, but I was starting to appreciate what I was learning from Dr. Giuliano. He was passionate about teaching chemistry and his energy was contagious. I ended up with a "B" as my final grade, but I knew I had tried my hardest in that class. Never in my wildest dreams would I have imagined that Dr. Giuliano would one day write very positive letters of recommendation for my first and second employment opportunities in the pharmaceutical industry. I don't think he realized how much he had infused the passion of organic chemistry in me during that year.

16

The Unimaginable

After closing the restaurant, Dad was recruited to work for a son of one of his old friends from Vietnam. He needed a chef for his Chinese restaurant near Cape May in New Jersey. It wasn't the most ideal position because he now had to room and board there six days a week. He wasn't happy that he was away from his family, but that was the only available job. Dad took the job while looking for other opportunities. Within months, he was able to find another job delivering goods in a grocery store. All of Dad's jobs were very labor intensive with long hours, but this one was the hardest. He constantly had to carry heavy boxes, but it was closer to home and he could commute, so he took it.

Since I wasn't home, I lost track of a lot of what was happening in the family. I knew Mom was still working very hard to recover the money that had been lost by the takeout business. Mom still provided childcare for the Ferbers during weekdays and was sewing non-stop in the evening and on weekends. Her goal was to save up to buy a small place for us. Most Asians feel like paying rent is like tossing money out the window.

Viet managed to graduate from high school despite his two-year struggle. I wasn't able to attend his graduation because of work. Viet decided to join the Navy right after graduation. No one in the family knew that he signed up. It was his way to get out, get away, and spread his wings. A blanket of sadness surrounded all of us when we heard the news. I could tell that Dad realized that his harshness had driven his son away. Dad was very sad, and his energy dropped. I heard him tell Mom, "It is better this way. I can't discipline him so maybe the military will." I think Dad said that out loud, hoping that he could forgive himself for the damaged relationship between a father and his son that was beyond repair.

Upper Darby Home

Viet left for boot camp that summer. The house was suddenly so quiet. It was around that time that we began looking for a house to buy in Upper

Darby which would be more convenient to the train and bus stations. Duc and I helped Mom house-hunt on the weekends. Dad became more reserved and spoke less after Viet was gone. He said that we should go look for a house and let him know the final pick. There was a dramatic change in Dad's behavior and that worried me.

One weekend I was home, cooking with Mom in the house in Yeadon, and I distinctly remember telling Mom about the recurrent nightmares I kept having.

"Mom, is Dad okay, working at the Chinese supermarket?" I asked.

"Yes, he is much quieter since your brother left. I think he's sad. Why do you ask?"

"I'm scared, Mom. I've been having bad dreams for the past few months, and each time it had the same ending with different scenarios. I cried myself awake each time."

"What was it?" Mom was curious.

"It's been the same dream three or four times now. Dad dies in the dream, and I cry so hard that I wake myself up and then I'm relieved that it's only a dream. So, I just want to make sure he is okay," I explained.

"If you dream about someone passing, you should never tell them. Then they will be okay. This is how they change their luck."

I breathed a little easier knowing that telling Dad was never something I would do.

I felt better having told Mom about the nightmares and hoped that was the end of it. We continued to move ahead to search for a home in Upper Darby. Dad did not participate much in making the decision to buy a house. He said it was up to Mom, Duc, and me. Whatever we thought was best—*wait! Was this my father?* I could not believe this was the same man.

Before long, we thought we had found what we wanted. It was a duplex with three bedrooms and one bath. Normally, my parents were very careful with numbers. They would make sure the sum of the house numbers added up to eight or nine for good fortune, luck, or longevity. But "226 Heather Road" was the address and 2+2+6 added up to ten. Ten was not preferred because it symbolized the beginning of a downfall.

"But the house was the best one we've seen so far," I said. Mom agreed, but was reluctant. "We can't let superstitious things like that stop us from buying a good house, Mom!"

"The market is hot, and the interest rates will be higher if we don't get the house now before school starts," Duc helped me explain to my parents.

Mom changed her tone and said to Dad, "Maybe this is America's 'perfect 10.' Maybe this has nothing to do with the Chinese 'ten' in Asia!" We all finally agreed to make an offer on the house.

The summer of 1986 came and went. Duc and I took one weekend off work to help move my family to our first purchased home in America. It was the perfect time for a school transition for the girls. Phan was finishing ninth grade at Penn East Junior High. She would matriculate to 10th grade and Que would start ninth grade at Upper Darby High School. Nam would start fifth grade at Bywood Elementary school.

Duc now lived with his brother's family in Lansdale, which was only about a ten-minute drive away. Duc came by often to help Mom make whatever fixes were needed to the old house we had just bought. Duc and his brother were both very handy. They enclosed our front porch to expand the living room and make it much larger. Duc also helped my parents board up a wall with wood paneling for extra storage in the basement.

Right around that time, the Saigon Restaurant reached out to Dad and apologized for the misunderstanding. They had just found out why Dad had quit his position and asked Dad if he would let the hurt feeling go and come back to work for them. Dad accepted the apology and went back to work at the restaurant in the Italian market area in South Philly. Things seemed to be getting back to normal, but everyone could see changes in him. He became easier and more somber. Maybe melancholy is the word. He mentioned often that despite their many confrontations, he was very proud of Viet for the man he had become. The only thing he was worried about was that they might send Viet to the front lines after training. Having survived growing up in a war-torn country, he knew that being a soldier meant being closer to death. I could tell Dad was living with guilt and worry.

I was happy to hear that Dad's hot temper flare-ups were less frequent. I think Viet's departure was his wake-up call that his children were growing up and he had no control over what their future would be. The kids were well situated in school, Mom could get to work a little easier, and everyone seemed to be a little happier in the new environment.

Analytical Chemistry

The third year was a tough year for chemistry majors. It was really an uphill battle at every turn. Besides the required elective courses of American Literature, Sociology, and Intro to German, I had both Physical Chemistry and Analytical Chemistry. Both courses came with three hours of lab work each Tuesday and Thursday afternoon. They were not my strongest suits. I was able to tread water in Physical Chemistry, a five-credit course, but I was drowning in Analytical Chemistry, also a five-credit course. That class was taught by the best and toughest teacher in the entire chemistry department at Villanova, Dr. Robert Grob.

Dr. Grob was a well-known analytical professor in his field of Instrumentations and Applications of Chromatography. I had no idea who he was at the time. He was nice, but firm. His class was no-nonsense and all business. During the first session, Dr. Grob made sure all ten of us understood that it would not be easy to pass his class. Everyone had to work super hard because his grading system was based on very high standards. Class was on Monday, Wednesday, and Friday, at 8:30 a.m. sharp! Lab was on Thursday afternoon from 2-5 p.m., and if you show up two seconds late, he would shame you in front of the class, no mercy! I was almost as terrified of Dr. Grob as I was of my father. I kept telling myself that if I could do okay this year with Dr. Grob, I could be a chemist anywhere.

I really struggled to keep up during class, pass the tests, and work on the experiments in the labs for both chemistry courses. It was so nerve-racking to follow procedure when I did not fully understand the direction. I sought out a lot of help from my classmates. Special thanks to Christa Laclair, who lived in my same dorm, for so patiently helping me get through the lab reports. I got the usual grade of "B" for Physical Chemistry, but even with all the intense effort I put in for Analytical Chemistry, I got a "D" at the end of the first semester. My heart sank when I got the report card. I thought my world had just ended! I wasn't smart enough to be a chemist. Who on earth would hire a student with a big fat "D" grade in one of the classes of her major?

I sought out Tarak Mody, a super smart classmate who always got "As" and "A+s" in every subject. But apparently not in Dr. Grob's class.

"Hey, Tarak, do you mind telling me what you got in Dr. Grob's class? I got a 'D' and I am thinking of changing my major because I think I'm doomed. Is it just me, or do you find that class hard, as well?"

"Oh, don't quit because of that grade. He will bump everyone up. I've heard from people who have had him that that's what he usually does. I only got a 'B' and that was my first 'B' ever."

I was also told by classmates that passing Dr. Grob's class was the ultimate test to see if you have what it takes to become a chemist. It was kind of like needing to pass Anatomy if you want to be a doctor. I felt better knowing that we were all on the same boat. There was a thread of hope to find a good job if he bumped up the grades later. So, I kept my chemistry major and hoped for a better grade the next semester.

I was working only minimal hours at the school library because I found a work-study job in the chemistry department helping two graduate students, Mark Baxter and Ani (from Armenia) in Dr. Shupack's lab. It was a good learning experience. I watched Ani grow crystals and helped with some minor experiments. I hadn't had any classes with Dr. Shupack yet, but it was a nice way to be introduced to him and his area of chemistry.

Bad Omens

In my college years, I got hooked on a TV soap opera named *The Young and the Restless*. It came on at 12:30 p.m. every day right after lunch. I always tried to catch at least half the show after lunch to unwind. By this time, I was fortunate to have my own dorm room in St. Rita. It was a tiny room, just big enough for a single bed, a dresser and a desk, but it was more than enough for me because it was all mine. Before that, during my second year, I had a roommate named Sandy. There were times I had to stay out of the room and go to the library because her boyfriend was there so much, and I was not very comfortable. I loved having a private room.

One afternoon, I was scrolling the channels during the *Y&R* commercials and something caught my eye that I felt compelled to watch. The *Incredible Hulk* star, Bill Bixby, was hosting a show discussing what people should know when they have a family member who is in a coma. What were the factors that needed to be considered when trying to determine when to remove life support from a loved one? I found it to be a very interesting topic and was drawn into the discussion about the pros and cons in keeping alive a comatose patient with no physical brain activity.

This raised a big moral question for me. How can anyone place a price on such a life and death decision? What about miracles where comatose patients wake up despite the doctor's prognosis? Was it fair to put pressure on the family to cut off the life support because of the high medical cost? I was uneasy for the rest of the day, but glad that I did not know anyone faced with that awful predicament. I told Duc about the show and the terrible conflict that it presented. We both hoped that we would never have to deal with anything like that.

The fall of 1986 was relatively quiet. Mom and Dad seemed more peaceful with only the remaining three kids at home. Duc and I started to talk about our future together. He planned to ask Dad for permission for an engagement in the spring because we wanted to get married when I graduated from college the following year. Duc had studied computer science at LaSalle College, but lost interest in that field during his senior year. So, he helped his brother work at the chemistry stockroom at the University of Pennsylvania for a little while, then found a job at the stockroom at Wills Eye Hospital in North Philly. Jobs were hard to find, so he settled for whatever was available at the time. Duc also went to a technical school in electronics in the evenings to fast-track his new interest. He found a better paying job at Bobman Chemical, so he changed jobs again, while pursuing electronics studies.

My parents accepted Duc and loved him as their son, so Duc had no problem getting Dad's blessing for my hand in marriage. Dad told Duc: "You clearly know how much Khanh helps this family. She is the eldest child, and by marrying her, you can't take her away from the family. You need to help her guide her siblings until they are done with school. Is that something you can do?"

"Yes, I love all the kids like my own brothers and sisters. I am happy to be part of this family," Duc assured him.

I was so happy Duc had the courage to talk to Dad and I was thrilled that our future was promising, and that I'd have Duc by my side. Everything happened according to plan. The whole family couldn't wait to celebrate our first Christmas in the very first home that my parents owned. Duc and

I went out to buy a small Christmas tree and set it up on the front porch. Being a Buddhist family, my parents did not celebrate Christian holidays, but did not mind at all for the cultural experience. We decorated the tree, wrapped gifts to put under it, and took a Christmas picture to send to all our relatives in Vietnam and Europe. When the film was developed, we could not find one picture of Dad smiling. He looked sad, very sad!

An Unfinished Conversation with Dad

Having bombed my first semester with a big fat "D" in Analytical Chemistry, I was planning to study a few chapters ahead at home during Christmas break, but it was hard to focus. The Monday before Christmas, Dad came home from work at about 11:30 p.m. and wanted to discuss something with me. I was certainly curious to know what was on his mind. I was now less afraid of him and glad that we were able to have an adult conversation.

The Saigon Restaurant where Dad worked was having a Christmas party on Thursday night after the restaurant closed, and they invited our whole family to be there. Dad also talked about what he had told Duc and about their discussion of plans for a traditional engagement party. Duc's older brothers and sisters would represent his parents and bring over trays of tea, wine, sweet cakes, and a fixed amount of dowry and then we had to choose a good date for the wedding based on the Lunar calendar. I nodded compliantly as usual, but then I saw this as a chance to talk to Dad about taking it easy on my younger siblings.

I mustered the courage to ask, "Dad, Phan and Que have been invited to their friends for a slumber party. Can they go?"

"No! They can attend the party but not sleep over."

"But that's the fun part, when they play until late in the night and then wake up together in the morning."

"We Chinese have to keep ourselves reserved. No kids of mine will stay at other people's houses overnight."

"But we live in America now," I said with much emotion showing in my voice. "We must learn to adopt some of the American culture. You don't want your children to miss out on being normal friends with their classmates here in America, right?" I was talking and crying at the same time, proud that I was sticking my neck out for my sisters, even though I never had the nerve to ask him for myself when I was younger.

The conversation went back and forth with many other issues being raised. Finally, I confronted Dad directly. "They are growing up fast now and you can't keep them by your side like they are babies anymore!" I could not believe how daring I had suddenly become. It was the first time in my 24 years that I debated with my father. I was shaking with fear, but felt good that I had said it. Dad paused, and then promised to be a bit more lenient. We ended our chat around 2:30 a.m. Dad had changed since Viet left home for the service. I think he was afraid of losing us too if he pushed too hard.

We all went to the Christmas party at the Saigon Restaurant and had a great time. I was able to get time off from my holiday job at the King of Prussia mall. There was dancing and singing. Dad drank some spiked cider and seemed happy in front of others. That was the first time our whole family was invited to their Christmas party.

It was Saturday, a couple days after the Christmas party. Dad came home from work around 11:30 and went to take a shower. I was in the room next door getting ready for bed and Mom was in their bedroom adjacent to the bathroom. We heard a loud thud and Dad's screaming voice. Mom thought Dad just needed shampoo and called out, "It's under the sink." But Dad had fallen before stepping into the bathtub. He yelled out my name to call 911 and told Mom to come help him get dressed. He said his arm went limp and he could not feel his leg. Dad had seen this happen to his boss and he knew it was serious.

I rushed downstairs to the phone in the kitchen and dialed for help, then called Duc to come over immediately. Fifteen minutes later, the loud siren of the ambulance arrived in front of the house. By midnight, Dad was on his way to the nearby hospital. They rushed Dad into the ER and wheeled him to the radiology department for a CT scan and MRI. No one in my family knew what that meant.

Dad was so nervous he was screaming my name in Chinese, "LiCheng, LiCheng, what are they doing to me?" His cry pierced into my heart. I was walking next to his gurney and they stopped me from entering the scan room. I was pacing back and forth out in the hallway not knowing what to do. I paced, and sobbed, and sobbed. Mom was out in the waiting room and was as anxious as I was.

All my life, I had been so afraid of Dad. He was the most powerful figure in the family and in my universe. Now he was begging me to help him. I could not fathom what was in his mind. Did Dad think they were wheeling him into a surgery room? Dad was claustrophobic and seeing the MRI machine no doubt terrified him. The medical staff did not give me a chance to talk to him, to calm him, or to explain anything to him. I had never seen Dad this frightened, not even when the pirates assaulted the boat nor when he found the leak in the hull of the boat. Now he was depending on me to speak for him, to defend him. I could barely stand, I felt so weak and powerless.

A doctor finally came out to me and said, "Your dad had a stroke."

"What is that?" I had never heard of this illness.

"He has a blood clot in his brain. We are administering medicine to dissolve the clot and he will have to stay in the ICU for a few days. You and your mom can come back tomorrow to see him."

"Can I go talk to him for a minute? Please?"

"Okay. But don't take too long. He will be okay."

Mom and I went in to see Dad. Half of his face was drooping, and his lips were not moving.

"Pa, are you okay? The doctor says you are going to be fine." I trembled as I talked.

Dad said in a low voice, "I can't feel half of my body."

"I know. The doctor says it will take some time to get back to normal."

Mom was crying and so was I. It was heartbreaking to see the sudden change in his physique.

"The doctor said that we can't stay. They want you to rest and us to go home. We will be back tomorrow." I assured Dad that he was going to be okay.

I saw fear in Dad's eyes. The only words he could say in English were *thank you* and *sorry* and not much else. There was no one to translate for him. Mom and I asked the nurse if one of us could stay, but they said no.

"We will be back first thing in the morning," I assured Dad.

Duc drove both of us home. I was scared and I had no clue as to the severity of the stroke. At only 50, Dad was young and strong. *Nothing should happen to him!*

A week later, Dad was out of the ICU and sharing a room with another patient. He was still the Commander in Chief to us, but Dad was now completely dependent on his wife and his children to fight for him. Things were looking up and I was back on schedule and working almost 40 hours a week at Stern's. Semester break was over and I was getting ready to move back to the dorm for the second semester of my junior year. Mom and I took turns visiting Dad in the evenings when we were off work. Many times, Mom tried to stay overnight to keep Dad company, sleeping on the chair next to his bed. Sometimes the nurse was easy and let her stay; other times, she was shooed home and Dad would be left alone in the hospital with a world of strangers by himself. Viet was notified, but he couldn't come home from boot camp.

Upper Darby High School was right next to the hospital, so Phan and Que would stop by to be with Dad after school until Mom got there after work. Que would stay the entire time to be with Dad while Phan went home to care for Nam. Que told me that she felt scared and didn't know what to talk to Dad about at first. But then her heart melted seeing Dad in such a helpless condition. Dad was very emotional, sad and crying all the time, which none of us had often witnessed.

In Vietnam, I had only seen Dad cry on a few occasions: once, when I was seven or eight and he was arguing with his older brother while drunk, and more recently, when we all had to pick blueberries to eke out a living. As frightened as I was of Dad, I knew he had endured trauma during his childhood, and his tough exterior was to conceal his pain. But now, he cried almost every time he saw us. My heart was shattered.

Que was getting more comfortable being alone with Dad and sometimes she wheeled Dad outside his room toward the entrance so he could get some sunlight. She reported Dad's progress to me. Mom told me how difficult it was for Dad when no one was around. He was not able to communicate with the nurse and often had to wait all day for one of us to be there to address his needs. Half of Dad's body was paralyzed, and his speech was slurred. After a few weeks, he had lost 20 pounds. Duc and I came over every weekend to visit. Finally, we heard the good news that Dad would be sent to a rehab center by the end of January.

Considering all Dad had gone through, to see his physical and mental conditions deteriorating before us—it was heart-wrenching. Dad missed Viet and mentioned him often. He said how proud he was of him and believed Viet would become a doctor to come back to treat him. He asked my siblings about school. He was kind and soft with Mom. His temper vanished, and he became melancholic.

The weekend of January 18, Duc and I went to visit Dad as usual on Sunday. That afternoon, Dad propped his weak body up in bed and looked at Duc and me.

"I am counting on you two to take care of Mom and your younger siblings," he said, his speech still slurred. "Can you promise me that you will do that? I don't know how long it will take for me to recover."

I cried and said, "You will be better in a few months, maybe by summer. Don't worry Dad!" I honestly believed that. Clearly, he was making progress. The doctor said so.

Dad began offering me his advice. "Find a job in your field which will help you land a good position when you graduate. Work for free if you have to. Don't get caught up just making money. Building credentials is far more important." I cried and nodded. I loved Dad's soft teaching moments. So different from the screaming admonishments. I wished he had done that more before he became sick.

Dad continued to engage in the conversation even though I saw how tired he was. "Are you going back to school tonight?"

"Yes, I have a Physical Chemistry exam on Wednesday, and I need to study."

"I hope I get better soon. I want to save money to buy you a computer after I get back to work." My heart ached to see how much Dad loved and cared for us, even when he was sick and unable to provide. I did not know that would be our last conversation.

Duc drove me back to school as Mom took over the shift. I felt depleted.

The last family picture with Dad

Viet was away in boot camp

The last picture of my parents, a few days before the first stroke

Random Kindness and a Terrifying Decision

The following Tuesday morning, I had difficulty picking out the right outfit to wear. Something seemed troubling to me. After ten minutes, I settled on white stretch pants and a white turtleneck shirt, layered with a black and white sweater. All day I was thinking about Dad and the conversation we had over the weekend. During the Physical Chemistry lab that afternoon, I could not focus. All I could think about was how much this stroke had changed my dad and how much his love revealed, even though he had so much trouble showing his real feelings. I wanted to do something special for him and spend a lot more time with my loving father who was no longer so scary.

Pears! Dad loved pears. *I'll go to Chinatown and buy some Asian pears this Saturday and then spend the entire weekend with him.* Feeling good about the plan, I had never felt so connected, and there was so much I wanted to get to know about him.

All I could think about how anxious I was to go see him and spend time comforting him and trying to cheer him up. Thursday afternoon was another long lab period with Dr. Grob in Analytical Chemistry. I was exhausted when I got back to the dorm. As I approached the door, I saw three big words on my message board: "Call home. Urgent!"

I ran to the hall and called home. Phan picked up the phone. "Dad just had another stroke. Duc is at the hospital with Mom. You should go to the hospital now."

It was in the evening in late January and the temperature had dipped down into the twenties. Snow had piled up a few days prior and hadn't melted yet. I didn't know how I could get home. It was too late to take the train. That would not be safe. Also, it would take too long to walk from the train station to the hospital. Crying, I grabbed my thickest coat and began running down to Lancaster Pike, the road in front of the dorm. I never, ever had considered doing something as bold as hitchhiking, but that was exactly what I had in mind. As I rushed out the door with tears streaming down my face, a girl approached me.

"Are you okay?"

"No, my dad is in the hospital and I don't have any way of getting to there."

I didn't know who she was, all I heard was, "I live in Saint Rita. Let me drop off my stuff in my room and I'll take you there. My car is parked across the street."

I was overwhelmed with relief and thankful to God for sending an angel to help me. I was so desperate, I really would have tried hitchhiking. I thanked her profusely and cried all the way to the hospital. When we arrived, I expressed my gratitude once again and assured her that I would be okay from there, but she chose to stay for a few more hours before finally taking off around two in the morning. A few years later, I searched and tried to find out who she was so I could thank her properly, but I have not been able to track her down. Her random act of kindness is one I will forever hold dear in my heart.

The second stroke had put my dad into a comatose state and Dad was no longer responsive. Mom was crying hysterically. She pointed to a burn on his leg. The nursing staff in the Cardiac Intensive Care Unit (CICU) was often under-staffed at night and something bad had happened. Mom continued to cry as she told me the entire story. That was the first time I learned of my dad's ongoing medical condition.

"Your father had been told by Bac Si Nghia [*Bac si* means *doctor* in Vietnamese] that he had high blood pressure. He was given meds to treat hypertension for the last few months since we moved to Upper Darby. But the medicine gave him bad side effects, it made him very uncomfortable and he got up at night frequently to urinate, which made him very tired when he worked during the day. He did not like that so he stopped taking the medication a week before he had the first stroke."

I put my arm around Mom's shoulder, encouraging her to continue with her story, though she spoke in sobs.

"Even though your dad was making progress at the hospital, it was very difficult for him to get comfortable after I left around 11 every night. The hospital was short staffed, and they did not take very good care of him when he needed to be moved or get a drink of water. I begged them to let me stay overnight to be with him, but they said no!"

I could see the anguish on her face as she shook her head. She pointed to Dad's leg.

"They had worked him really hard during physical therapy and his left leg was swollen. Apparently, a blood clot was forming. The nurse had

238

put a heating pad on his leg, and the next morning, his leg was burned. They had never come back to check on the pad!"

Mom cried another minute before she was able to continue. "When I came in the next morning, your dad was exhausted from a loud TV that was on all night from his roommate, and the pad had overheated and burned his leg. He had been complaining about a pounding headache since the night before and no nurse had come to check on him.

"Your poor dad, he was trying to tell me something, but I told him 'You are tired. Why don't you just close your eyes and take a nap. I won't go to work; I will stay with you today.' He tried talking but I could barely make out what he said. It was something about wanting your brother to become a doctor to treat him. He missed your brother and was sorry for driving him away to the Navy. He was terrified that Viet would be sent to the front line."

Mom looked away from Dad and straight into my eyes. "He told me that he was sorry for the way he treated me and for not being gentler with you kids," she said. "He told me that he would change, and he would save money to buy you a computer when he goes back to work. He said so much, but I kept telling him 'Go to sleep. You are tired. Talk later.' And now he is not waking up!"

Mom and I sobbed and sobbed when Dad's doctor, a female physician, came to talk to me about Dad's condition. A compassionate female doctor had been taking care of Dad since he was admitted. She was nice and honest with me.

The nice doctor said, "Your dad had another serious stroke and this time it does not look good. We are running more tests. The EEG will give us some news about his brain activity. We have valium in the IV to ease his pain, if he is feeling any. I can tell you more when I have the results from the tests. For now, he is in a coma. I am so sorry."

So, we sat and waited for more tests to be done. It seemed like an eternity. Finally, the female doctor came and gave us the most horrible news.

"Lea, I am very, very sorry to let you know that the EEG test shows that your dad has no brain activity. Basically, he is brain dead. The test ran for 75 minutes and he only responded to pain with slight hand and toe movements. We are pumping oxygen to his lungs to keep the body alive, but there is no possibility of him recovering."

Our hearts sank to see a breathing ventilator pumping oxygen into his mouth. He was lying calm, no anguish. Everything was quiet except for the pumping noise of the ventilator. Reality hit me hard. *How did we get here? Is this for real? Am I in a bad dream? Please wake up!* The room was eerily quiet, but my mind was screaming.

I did not know how to translate and deliver this terrible news to Mom. And then I learned that there was more to the story.

"One thing I think you should know," the female doctor said, "is that your father could have been saved if the nurses and the on-call doctor had followed my instructions. I wrote on the chart that it didn't matter what time it was, if the blood clot from his leg looked worse, I should be the one to call, not the on-call doctor. Unfortunately, they did not take care of the clot, but kept the heating pad unchecked all night and the on-call doctor did not address the problem."

Her words were cutting me to shreds. I could not speak, but she wasn't finished. "This is between you and me. I am an ethical doctor, and I want to tell you the truth. If you want to file a complaint or sue the hospital, I will be on your side."

I was drowning in all the information she told me and very confused as to what to do. I told Duc and he helped me explain to Mom the whole thing. But the focus was still on hoping for a miracle. The same miracle that got us out of the sea when we thought we were at the end of the rope. If only Dad would wake up from the coma and prove to everyone that they were all wrong. Mom said we didn't want to file a lawsuit for fear of retaliation. "It will not bring your Dad back."

There was a drop of hope as long as the machine was pumping and Dad's lungs were still working. His weight had dropped significantly since the first stroke and he was now down to skin and bones as he'd only had the IV feeding him. My heart shattered, watching Dad fading away. There on the bed was a strange, skinny skeleton that I called Dad.

The waiting was excruciating. For two days, we surrounded the bed and took turns massaging his muscles and talking to him. Suddenly I remembered: *School! I need to let the school know what's happening!*

"I need to call the chemistry department and report about Dad," I said to Duc.

"Tell them that you are not sure how long you may need to be with your family. They'll understand." Duc lightly touched my arm and gave me the strength to make the call.

I knew that I needed to go back to school to tie up some loose ends and to get some personal items. I went to Mendel Hall on Monday and bumped into Dr. Grob in the hallway. He had heard the news about my dad, and he stopped me and compassionately asked me how my father was.

"Young lady," he said, "I don't want you to worry about school at this time. You need to go home and spend as much time as you can with your parents. School can wait." My anxiety turned to a warm respect for my professor I once was so fearful of. My perspective of Dr. Grob completely changed. He was a very caring and loving teacher, just like my father. I was so grateful for the support from the dean, all my teachers, my classmates, and all the girls in the dorm who gave me hugs and strength at that time.

By the tenth day, Dad was deteriorating and fading before our very eyes. The hospital was pressuring Mom and me to let Dad go by stopping his life support machine. I protested and refused to make that decision. Mom, Duc, and I discussed this intensely, we prayed and took turns begging Dad to wake up.

In the meantime, we rushed telegrams to Viet and Soijek, Dad's youngest brother, to come if they wanted to see Dad one last time. Soijek had only arrived in Germany a few years earlier, having been sponsored by his children. These were the children, Dad's niece and nephew, who Dad took on the boat with us when we escaped Vietnam.

Mom was very confused and was barely able to function. She said she would let me make the decision about terminating Dad's oxygen supply. I detested the idea, and the TV show with Bill Bixby came to mind. Everything came back as I put all the puzzle pieces together—the dreams of Dad dying on multiple occasions, the episode on TV about making the decision to terminate life support for a comatose loved one. And finally, of all the multi-colors in my closet, I had chosen the white outfit. Why did I settle on the white color to wear on Thursday? White is the color of mourning. Did I already know that was the day Dad would leave us?

They were all there, forewarning omens confirming my sixth sense.

Despite the enormous hospital costs every minute, we continued to hope for a miracle. But there was also the painful reality of death. Now, they wanted me to be the one to make the final call about my Dad's last breath from the machine. What right do I have to make that horrible decision? I discussed this with Duc extensively. I told him there is no way I wanted to live with the guilt that I had permitted them to end my father's life. I bought time by telling the doctors that I needed proof. I wanted to see all the necessary test reports that said Dad's condition was hopeless. They gave me the test results and yet, I waited.

It was Duc's birthday, and no one remembered, not even me.

Soijek arrived in America for the first time to get the last chance to see his brother. As soon as he got to the hospital, Dad's lungs stopped taking in oxygen from the machine. It seemed that Dad had been waiting for his son or his brother, and once Dad heard his brother, he took matters into his own hands. The decision was no one's to make but his own.

Dad passed on February 9, Duc's birthday. It was like my father passing the baton to Duc, who soon became the male role model for all my siblings.

Within 43 days, my family's world had been turned up-side-down again. This time, we had no captain to steer the boat for us. I had been scared when we were on the escape boat, especially when we encountered pirates, separated by pirates. I had been scared when we were in the worst living conditions at the refugee camps. I'd lived in a home full of turbulent emotional ups and downs, but no matter what, Dad had loved us and protected us from the threats of the outside world. He had been the roof that we hid under. But now, he bequeathed that responsibility to me. I was not ready to rise up to take his place.

I felt an enormous obligation and a heavy weight on my shoulders. My whole world collapsed, and I was unsure of what to do next. My lifeline was my boyfriend, Duc. He brought strength and stability to me. I had to pretend to be strong to comfort Mom, who was hysterically crying all the time and needed me to help her make every decision. Viet eventually got home, but they missed their chance to reconcile with each other face-to-face. I don't know what was in Viet's mind, but I know one thing for sure, we all have unresolved relationship issues with our parents, and we had to come to terms with them sometime, somehow in the future.

My dad's death was unnecessary and preventable, but I was young and inexperienced. I felt so guilty. I trusted the hospital, doctors, nurses, and the entire healthcare system to do their job and treat their patient. It was a big lesson for me to learn, that we should always understand our loved ones' medical history and treatments, so we can stand up and advocate for them. It truly opened my eyes that we can only rely on ourselves to fight for ourselves and the people we love. No healthcare system can be expected to do that job for us.

17

Farewell Dad

Dad's unexpected passing hit us all like we were being crushed by an 18-wheeler truck. In my head, I knew the reality, but my heart refused to believe it could be true. It shocked everyone in the community. Dad was only a few months shy of his 51st birthday. "So young!" everyone said. He had not yet attended a college graduation or a wedding for any of his children. There were so many dreams he had not fulfilled, places to go, and loved ones with whom to reunite.

Dad had often wished that he had money and time to visit Soijek, his younger brother who lived in Germany. His ultimate wish was to visit Guang Zhou in China someday, where he was born and raised until the age of three.

The only vacation destination he had ever visited was Niagara Falls in Canada. We crammed nine people into Dad's silver Chevy—our family of seven, plus Duc to help navigate, and cousin Cao who came to visit us from California. I don't know how we did it, but for the ten-hour drive we drove with kids stacked on top of each other, no seat belts, having no clue that we were breaking the law. We did it refugee style. It was a fine trip with a cooler packed with home-cooked meals for the road.

Last year, Dad wanted to take Mom and my siblings on a road trip vacation to Florida. Dad had heard about Disney World and the warm climate in the south. But without me, Dad was hesitant about driving long distances without someone who could navigate directions and translate. The plan was to team up with his former boss from the grocery store to have a vacation together. The kids were super excited packing for vacation, but, unfortunately, his former boss cancelled the plan due to some urgent business and could not go. It was a big disappointment for my parents and my siblings.

As I closed in on attaining my college degree, I told myself I had to make money fast so I could take my dad's place and do the things he never was able to do for my brothers and sisters. I took solace knowing that I was more than halfway to finishing college. But how could I go back now? I could not leave Mom at home by herself to deal with the grief. I was afraid for her health. I certainly didn't want to lose the only parent I had.

When Dad's health began to deteriorate, my parents started appreciating each other more. Dad had changed from being a powerful figure to a dependent person. He became melancholy and emotional. Mom's fear of losing her husband made her appreciate Dad so much more. It is regretful that it took this huge crisis for things to change in the family. We never had the chance to fully reconcile our relationship with our father. I was just starting to feel brave enough to open up and have a conversation with him, and now death had robbed me from developing a normal father/daughter connection. I locked away the grief in a secret compartment in my heart so I could dutifully perform his role as he asked me to do. I wished Mom would have taken on that job, but she was too consumed with her own mourning. Every time I was around her, it hurt me to see how helpless Mom was without Dad.

It had now been seven years since our family arrived from Vietnam and I had never been to a funeral in the United States. Now my family was having one. Everything was an unknown. Everything required a decision. We had to choose a funeral home, select a casket, and find a Buddhist monk to chant a Chinese funeral ritual. Mom joined the Senior Chinese Association so Dad could rest in a cemetery with other Chinese people. She found a plot in Northwood Cemetery in North Philly. Dad was only the second person buried in the new section that the Senior Chinese Association had acquired. All his elderly friends thought they would get there before Dad. "What a pity, he was so young!" they all said.

We gave Dad a mostly Chinese Buddhist funeral, except instead of having the casket at our home as would have been the truly traditional way, we kept the casket at the Donohue Funeral Home. Mom bought white linen fabric and I quickly sewed nine sets of white clothes (symbolizing death) for the six of us, for my cousin Cao and his wife who flew in from California, and for Duc, the future son-in-law. These clothes are worn outside our regular clothes for seven days of mourning, and then for the seven-week transition of the soul after burial. No buttons or zippers are allowed, only sewn-in fabric strings can secure the garment.

Mom gave the orders and I did whatever she said to properly execute the Chinese rituals. Soijek stayed for the funeral, Viet was home, cousin Cao and his wife came. The Lam family, many Chinese friends, and Vietnamese friends from the community all came to give Dad their final respects. The Saigon Restaurant owners and the Ferber families all chipped in financially to help us give Dad the most complete funeral burial as we knew how. We were so grateful for their love and their support through our rough journey of losing the most important figure in our family.

Dad's sons, Viet and Nam, by his shrine

18

Marching On

College on Halt

After the funeral, our lives went on with a gaping hole. Soijek went back to Germany with a broken heart. Viet went back to boot camp with a heavy heart. My cousin and his wife left to return to their normal lives. Mom was melting away in her tears every day. I could not cry. I felt I had to be strong for Mom and for my younger siblings. I became good at faking my calm and being stoic in front of Mom, though I was crumbling inside. I knew it was up to me to get up, stand strong, and march on.

"Mom, I decided that I am going to take some time off from school and stay home with you. Are you okay with that?" It was my job now to step up and start taking care of everyone.

"Whatever you think, honey. You know what is best." I think Mom was quite relieved to have me home.

I felt that I needed to be home to provide financial and emotional support. I had a part-time job at Stern's and needed to find a full-time job quickly. But first, I had to go to school and take a leave of absence. I need to talk to Dr. Shupack and tell him that I could no longer intern in the lab.

Dr. Shupack was so understanding and offered to help.

"I can get you an interview at Sprouse Scientific Systems, a small startup company that runs data using infrared spectrum. Maybe they will hire you," he suggested.

"Thank you so much, Dr. Shupack. That would be ideal, to be able to gain experience in the chemistry field as my full-time employment. Yes, I would love to apply if you can introduce me to them."

Dr. Shupack not only got me the application, but personally gave me a ride to the interview. He knew I needed a little extra boost of confidence. On the ride there, Dr. Shupack told me that his father was also a first-generation immigrant. His father had to drive a taxi to put him through college, so he understood the struggles I was facing now with the death of my father. He was also the first in his family to graduate from college, and he wanted to see me succeed. I so appreciated his help, but I hesitated to ask questions. I was not comfortable with middle-aged men in positions of authority. They reminded me of my dad, and I was afraid to speak up to men.

I got the interview and was hired to make copies, mix solvents, and then eventually collect data and run tests using the infrared instrument. I kept myself busy working full time at Sprouse Scientific Systems (SSS), and also part-time at Stern's department store in the evening and on the weekends.

I moved back home, staying in Mom's room, sleeping in Dad's place in her bed. I had so much sorrow and grief that I was unable to express. I wished I could have gotten to know that man who was my father, who changed so drastically just before he died. I now didn't have that chance.

Based on Asian tradition that Mom believes, the louder your cries for your deceased loved ones, the more it shows you cared. During the funeral and for weeks after, Mom was going full force expressing her grief for Dad. Her crying was so hysterical that she almost fainted on several occasions. I was careful not to trigger her pain by hiding my grievance. I suppressed my emotions, and didn't validate my pain of losing Dad, and that stayed with me for years. I could not express it to anyone. Not to Mom, or even to Duc. *I have to be strong for everyone. It's my job now to hold this family together.*

Hiding my tears, guilt and anger, many nights, I cried in the bathroom with the faucet on to muffle the noises. Only then could I sob till my heart's content. Other times, I would cry and have a good scream on the highway driving back from work. I was sad, scared and frustrated! *I did not volunteer for this enormous responsibility of taking over his job.* He was supposed to be there to see my college graduation and walk me down the aisle for my wedding. We were supposed to start over with this new wonderful relationship. It wasn't fair!

Driving his car constantly reminded me about my dad. It was the only possession Dad left for me since I was the only one in the family who could drive.

It dawned on me how quickly everything had changed. What was I supposed to do with my life now that my family was officially on my back? At work, I would hide in the back of the building during lunch and just cry. Abu, the manager of SSS, caught me sometimes and expressed his concern, but I said I was going to be fine. I just needed to get it out of my system. I thought I just needed time. Crying in secret did not make me feel better. It simply added to the wound that I swept under the rug.

Changing Seasons

Forty-nine days of mourning passed, and we were no longer required to have a clip of white cloth on our clothes. We switched to black and continued to mourn for a year. I dreamed about Dad often, while sleeping on his mattress imprint, next to Mom, in their bed. "You need to go back to school to finish your degree!" he told me, in a calm but compelling manner. "I don't want you at home, missing out on your future," Dad said in my dreams.

Was that my subconscious mind talking to me in my sleep? I could imagine him saying these things to me because he had always prioritized his children's education. Should I value my own education less than what I had been taught to believe all my life? Was I disrespecting his wishes when I only meant to fulfill my responsibilities to the family he had left behind?

I missed my dad very much. The ache was intense for a long, long time. Memories flooded my mind all times of the day and night. I treasured the happy family meals he had cooked for us. My heart lightened for a moment when I recalled how all of us would watch *The Three Stooges* with him in better times in Minnesota in that small living room, all sitting around the one-unit heater. I missed his bright smile and even his loud voice. Yes, that voice instilled fear, but also feelings of security that he was there to protect us from harm. This sounds like a strange dichotomy, but that is the paradox that was my father. I imagine his relationships with other family members were as complex as what my dad and I had. There was fear, respect, love, hate, resentment, pride, and a whole lot more in the mix. My favorite memories are more recent, the conversations we had when Dad treated me like an adult.

In my junior year of high school, Dad and I took a trip to California. It was the only trip just the two of us ever took together. I wasn't sure it was a good idea back then, but now, I'm so glad we had that precious time together. It was the spring before we moved to Yeadon. Through letters from Vietnam, Dad found out that his nephew Cao was living in Los Angeles and that there were more opportunities for Asians in that area. So, he booked a trip and took me with him to California to check it out. He wanted me to give him my input and honest opinion before he made the major decision to move again.

We had the best time. We stayed on the same page throughout the trip and he did not lose his temper even once. He let me visit an old friend who was living in California, he even gave me money and permission to go to Disneyland with my friend! When we were leaving to head back home, he asked me what I thought. I told him that I had fun visiting but didn't like California enough to live there.

"Why not?" He seemed sincerely interested in what I thought.

"Well…" I hesitated. "There is too much hustle and bustle in California. It's almost like we're back in Vietnam city life. I can see that L.A. would be a fun place to live, and you and Mom can easily find jobs, but I think we kids wouldn't have as much of an opportunity to practice English. There are too many distractions in the Asian community. Besides, the East Coast has the best colleges and we would have fewer temptations and more opportunities there."

"Hmmm. Well, if that's what you think, then I guess we'll stay in Philadelphia."

I was stunned. Dad was willing to sacrifice his own happiness for us to have the opportunities I had laid out in front of him. He listened to my observations, trusted my choice, and valued my opinion. *What?* He actually made the decision based on my feedback. I was proud and hoped we would now have more conversations like this. I knew Dad could be a very logic-driven, practical person, but I could never predict when he would react irrationally and flare up. That was the million-dollar question when dealing with Dad. But back then, I was young and didn't realize that Dad's volatile temper was from the stress and the frustration of the financial burden he felt was his to carry. He bottled everything up, took all the responsibility upon himself, and then exploded from any agitation in the family. All that pressure affected his health and his ill-temper toward people he loved the most—especially his wife and his eldest son.

Many times, Dad came back in a dream and told me that I needed to get back and finish school. I knew dropping out of college would be a non-negotiable option were Dad still alive. It would have made him angry to hear me even mention it. "Education is always the priority in life when you can get it." I could (and still can) hear him in my head loud and clear. It was time to get my act together and get back on track to graduate on time. That's what would help the family the most.

I decided to make up for the lost semester by going back to school in the summer in order to catch up with my classmates. Mom neither discouraged nor encouraged me. She trusted me, and believed I knew what was best for the family and for myself. I pretended to be far more confident than I really felt because I knew how emotionally dependent Mom was on Duc and me. I was very nervous about the workload at school, but was excited about the possibility of graduating on time. I knew this was what Dad would have wanted. It would make him proud and I would live up to my promises.

In order to make up for lost time, I quit my job at SSS and did some major rearranging of classes. I loaded up both summer sessions with 13 credits, including the difficult courses of Physical Chemistry with a lab, Biology, American Literature, and World Religions. Out of necessity, I also continued working part-time at the King of Prussia Mall. I was afraid that an average below a "B" would limit my ability to find a good job, so I committed myself to that goal as well, and achieved that GPA. It felt good to know how resilient and tough I could be once I set my mind to succeed.

Soon enough, it was fall. In Pennsylvania, the season makes quite a showing: daylight becomes noticeably shorter, the air becomes crisp and cool, and the trees and ground turn flaming red, orange, and gold with leaves. I had caught up at school and soothed my sadness just a bit by imagining how my dad would be nodding in approval. There was an atmosphere of "new beginnings" as I came back to campus; I was ready and eager to start my senior year with full force.

I retook Analytical Chemistry with Dr. Grob and began Inorganic Chemistry with Dr. Shupack. I filled the rest of my schedule with Quantum Chemistry, Chemical Instruments, Biochemistry, Social Psychiatry, and The New Testament. I kept my part-time job at Stern's at the mall and applied for a work-study position helping grad students in the analytical lab under Dr. Grob. Ever since the day he told me it was important to spend time with my father rather than worry about the grade in his class, my perception of Dr. Grob had changed completely. I was still timid around him, but knowing that he was such a kind man made me less afraid of him.

Ironically, I did not like either Physical Chemistry or Quantum Chemistry, but I got an "A" in both courses. I was equally surprised to get a "B" in Dr. Grob's Analytical Chemistry class. I think it turned out to be true that he waved his wand of mercy and bumped the grades up for the entire class. Unfortunately, the Social Psych class bogged me down with tricky multiple-choice questions on the final exam and I barely passed. Every grade mattered a lot to maintain that precious 3.2 GPA, so in the last semester, I used my biggest asset to pull my grade up. I signed up for Intermediate Chinese and got an "A" to rescue me. I wasn't particularly proud of that, but it was nice to reconnect with the language of my origin and save my GPA at the same time.

Graduation time was approaching, and I confirmed that I had all courses fulfilled for a degree in chemistry, except I still needed an elective physics class for my final requirement. I was quite upset to find that the only offering of that class conflicted with the schedule of my required chemistry class. As uncomfortable as I was, I went to the dean of the chemistry department to ask if he would let me graduate and walk with my class. I promised Dean Ellis that I would make up the physics class in the summer to qualify for my diploma.

It was the first time I put "ask and you shall receive" to the test. Dean Ellis gave me the blessing of pseudo-graduating without a diploma until the physics class was completed. He was very encouraging and didn't think it would affect my ability to search for a job because I had fulfilled all the requirements of my major. My real diploma would say "Class of 1989." In the yearbook, I was in the Class of 1988. "It's just a piece of paper," Dean Ellis said. "Don't let that bother you."

I was grateful for the support of my professors, my dean, and all the people who helped me get through a tough four years of education. As a brand-new foreigner in this country, the challenges at times seemed insurmountable, but I did it. Dad would have been so proud.

But as I've learned time and time again, another challenge is always waiting around the corner. The next big hurdle would be to look for my first full-time professional job.

Though I can be a bit scatterbrained at times, when I'm on a mission, I become obsessive and laser-focused on that one goal. I can't sleep, my mind won't stop spinning, and I work tirelessly to accomplish what I need to do. My mission towards the end of my college career was to search for and find that dream opportunity of having a corporate job. By March, I had already sent out countless job applications all over the tri-state area and even one for a position in Florida.

By April and May, I had a slew of interviews lined up. There were a few government job openings in Pennsylvania and New Jersey in the water treatment facilities. I was told that government jobs might not pay well, but if you put in the years, the retirement benefits would be much better than in the private sector. Point taken, so I went to check them out.

As soon as I entered the plant site, it didn't feel right. The odor of the facility was overpowering. I could not imagine waking up every morning to go to work there. I thought the storage room at the chemistry lab in school was bad; entering the water treatment plant labs was ten times worse. I had a profound respect for the scientists who were working and serving the township in those facilities, but I couldn't see working there as my future. I admit that I was being rather picky. Even before the interview was over, I was thinking ahead to my next interview, hoping the environment there would look more like something I would see in the magazines: a clean lab in a modern facility.

The Engagement

It was almost 14 months after Dad's passing when Duc and I decided on April 3, 1988, for our formal engagement. In Vietnamese and Chinese cultures, engagement is a big deal before the wedding. It symbolizes the official confirmation of a relationship from both sides of the families.

The bride's parents usually request a certain number of gifts (in my case, eight trays of candies, fruits, tea, wine, and dozens of Chinese engagement cakes to give out to all the relatives to announce the good news). According to tradition, the future groom's parents also need to offer a pair of earrings, an engagement ring, additional jewelry, plus a set amount of dowry as gifts to the future bride/daughter-in-law.

In our cultural tradition, this was for the actual, formal engagement ceremony to take place, not an after-party. Duc's sister and brother-in-law represented his parents to ask Mom's permission for Duc to have my hand to be his wife. Incense sticks were burnt to the ancestor shrines to introduce the future son-in-law, so technically, Dad already knew about this and he was there in spirit with us the whole time.

Both sides of the family and all our friends gathered for our engagement at my parents' home in Upper Darby. Frere Phong and a few of our high school and college friends came to celebrate. It was a very nice ceremony, so wonderful to be surrounded by scores of family members and friends. Everything was perfect.

Except, I missed Dad's bright laughter!

Duc and Lea - engagement ceremony, April 3, 1988

A Sweet Taste of Tropicana

My quest for a good salary and a good place to work was the number one focus of that spring. I had interviews at various places like McNeil Pharmaceuticals, at a few small startup chemical companies in Lancaster, and at Wyeth Ayerst Research in Monmouth Junction, New Jersey. Out of all the interviews, the one that excited me the most was Tropicana, the orange juice company in Bradenton, Florida. They were looking for an analytical chemist for their quality control lab. I got the interview and was excited to go on my first airplane trip by myself—and someone else was paying for it!

It really hit me how far I had come. I could hardly wait to rush to the cemetery to talk to Dad before taking off for the interview. How I wished he was still alive for me to ask how I should prepare for the interview. How I wish we had a normal father-daughter relationship. Instead, I talked and cried with a tombstone, by myself, on a clear spring day. I knew he was proud of me and was watching over me with his bright shiny smile that he often gave to other people. I imagined him giving me that smile and it warmed my heart. I started to understand that I deserved it.

The plane landed at the Sarasota-Bradenton International airport. I picked up a rental car and drove to the hotel that had been booked for me. I had so many mixed feelings. I was filled with pride and a sense of accomplishment that I had been flown in for the interview. *I must be worth it.* But I was also feeling anxious. The interview would be the next day, but I did not know exactly when I would know if I would be offered the job. What would I do if I got the offer? Would I really move all the way to Florida? What would it mean if they did not choose me? Why would a good company hire someone just out of school?

There were lots of reasons I accepted the interview that had nothing to do with the job. It felt good that they wanted to spend the money to fly me down. That told me I must be qualified. Secondly, I had never been to Florida, so it was a free mini vacation to see a beautiful place that I had always heard so much about. Thirdly, I was curious about Tropicana, a well-known company that I had often seen advertised on TV. Also, I wanted to test my courage to travel alone. The list could go on, but I was afraid that none of these were the right reasons to take this job if they were to offer it to me. I could hardly sleep that night at the hotel.

I was met by someone from Human Resources early the next morning at the entrance to the plant. It was a nice clean facility and I could smell the tangy sweetness of orange juice miles away. Mr. H.R. took me to sample the fresh orange juice offered in the lobby to showcase their product. We chatted a little bit, just casual conversation, and then I got the schedule. I would be meeting four other scientists in the lab.

The interview was typical. What did I know about liquid chromatography and gas chromatography? Could I use the instrumentation of mass spectroscopy? What was my five-year goal? I answered all the technical questions to the best of my ability, but I stumbled on the last one. I didn't think telling them that "my five-year goal is to have a well-paying job and make sure all my siblings graduate from college" would impress them. What did that have to do with this opportunity with Tropicana? So, I made up something about having an ambition of rising to a management position in their company.

On a plant site tour, I saw truckloads and truckloads of oranges and got to see some of the operation. The workers in the citrus plant and the drivers of the trucks reminded me of the laborers in the blueberry fields in New Jersey. Without a college diploma, this was likely where I would be, a blue-collar worker.

I could see the TV commercial in my mind, "…fresh from the grove," but orange juice had never been appealing to me. All my life I suffered with a very sensitive stomach and the acidity of even the sweetest orange would cause GI problems within hours. The sight of so many oranges turned my stomach sour. I was very grateful for the tour and tried to picture myself in that work environment every day. The chemical labs were so much nicer and cleaner than the labs in the water treatment facility. The instruments I would be working with were similar to the ones I had learned at school: the Infrared Spectroscopy (IR) and the Gas Chromatography (GC). *This could work.*

After the interview with the director and the senior chemists in the lab, I was invited to have lunch with one of the chemists. I then circled back to meet with the H.R. manager for the concluding interview. To my surprise, I was offered the position on the spot. I was stunned. The protocol I expected was that I would go home, send out a thank you letter, and then wait for weeks to hear back from them. I really was not mentally or emotionally prepared to be presented with this decision that very day.

I was told that the panel really liked me and that, specifically, they were impressed that I was a student of, and intern with, Dr. Grob. He was a renowned and respected professor in the field of Gas Chromatography and because they thought so highly of Dr. Grob, they predicted that I would be a perfect fit.

This all seemed too good to be true. What should have been an affirming confidence-builder suddenly made me feel confused and frightened. I wondered what they would think had they known I was struggling in Dr. Grob's class. Why would anyone want to hire an immigrant with a thick accent? My chronic lack of self-worth was setting limitations in my own head. I was offered an annual starting salary of $23K, which was in a to-be-expected range but sounded amazing to me. I struggled to compose a response. "I am very honored by the offer, but I have to go home and discuss it with my mom and my boyfriend. I also have a few more interviews in New Jersey. I would like to see what other options are available. I will let you know in a few weeks." I answered politely but was shaking inside and not really sure that I heard what he had just offered.

He put in his final plug. "Well, they may offer you a higher salary, but remember, the cost of living in New Jersey is much higher than here in Bradenton. We can help you find an apartment near the beach. Work ends at four and you can be out on the beach by four-thirty."

I thanked him and promised I would keep that in mind. I was elated and my head was spinning. A lot of the exhilaration was from the fact that for the first time, I was personally experiencing the value of being an American citizen. Duc and I had become naturalized U.S. citizens six months before I graduated. We thought that would make it easier to find a job. My goodness, here I was being offered a professional position with a great salary by a top-tier American company. It was a lot to absorb.

It was time to set aside the refugee mindset where I saw myself as a victim. The freedom my parents worked so hard for was here, now, and I was the recipient who was now living out their dreams. I had worked hard to take advantage of the opportunity for an education and now I was experiencing the most-hoped-for outcome from that. Wow. Dad would be so proud.

I took the rental car for a spin to the beach and checked out the town. Might as well take full advantage of this free trip and enjoy as much as I could. The beach was truly beautiful, but no one was there. My family would love to run along the white sandy beach and dip their toes into the water. I would make that happen as soon as I could.

I was flattered that they had made me an offer on the spot, but it also confused me. There was no way I would leave my family and Duc to build a life on my own in Florida. But I had to wonder, what would my life be like if I hadn't come from the tragic circumstances of a refugee? What if my family didn't have to rely on me for everything? Would I spread my wings and fly all the way to Florida for my first job and explore a brand-new lifestyle here? What path would my life be taking at this juncture? I was 99% sure that I would decline the offer; nevertheless, it helped build up my confidence for the following interviews and it gave me leverage in exploring other opportunities. I thanked Dad for watching over me.

A week later, I put on my lucky outfit once again for an interview in New Brunswick, New Jersey, at Wyeth Ayrest Laboratories. The company focused on basic research, development, and marketing of prescription drugs. The interview agenda was intimidating, to say the least. I met with five sets of scientists, each in one-hour time slots. Each interview included a PhD that I would be directly working under, and another PhD who was the director of that project. The interview was a test of how much knowledge I had in applying chemistry to day-to-day work. I was terrified at first, but their friendliness calmed my nerves. It was five hours of interviews and I had a nice lunch with a peer host and her friends. I was impressed with the brand-new modern building that housed the research teams from the merger of Wyeth and Ayrest Research only a year prior.

It was a spacious, state-of-the-art building with large glass windows and bright wall colors. The tall ceiling in the lobby showcased a large stairway to the research offices and labs on the second floor and had bright red handrails. Everything was modern, new, and clean, with a top-notch air ventilation system. The place looked like a cover of a scientific journal. I felt like somebody important just from walking around on the tour, guided by my peer host. *I could really see myself here.*

I passed all the tests. A week later, I got a letter from H.R. saying that the Medicinal Department would like to hire me at a starting salary of $27K and I could pick a date to start after graduation. My spirits lifted higher than they had been in a long, long time.

I received a third job offer from a small lab in Lancaster, Pennsylvania. I had a 3.2 grade point average, and now had three job offers even before graduation. My life felt perfect. This precious milestone was the fulfillment of the dream my dad began formulating the day the tanks of North Vietnam rolled into Saigon. I knew it was Dad who had altered our future. It was Dad who had made the impossible become possible for me.

There was so much going on that spring before I left Villanova. It was all good and dramatically different from the year before. College graduation was a dream I had yearned for since my parents decided to take me out of school in Vietnam. Their decision did not mean that they didn't value my education, but rather that my parents had such an immense respect for all academic studies that they wanted it to be one of quality. We were frustrated and disgusted that my schooling devolved into propaganda and indoctrination once the communists took over.

Now, here I was, a part of this all-important ceremony walking down the aisle with thousands of other university graduates. My heart swelled with pride, but felt hollow without Dad. I looked as typical as any other student around me. No one knew all the blood, sweat, and tears that had gone into this diploma I so valued. I represented generations of suffering. I was honored to be the first one from both sides of my family to graduate from college. The sacrifices of my grandparents and my parents were all wrapped up in this single piece of paper I was about to receive.

I still had to pass a three-credit physics class to make my graduation official, but I was so glad I did not let Dad's passing derail the goal. Who would have guessed our family had yet crossed another ocean and this time, I lost my dad to the pirate of death? I had fulfilled his dream of having a degree and a title behind my name. I felt so much closer to my dad now than I did when he was alive. I spoke to him, thanked him, and went to visit his grave to tell him everything that was happening at home. We all missed him so much.

Tropicana interview (May, 1988)

Villanova University graduation (May 22, 1988)

With Dr. Shupack and friends

Taking a Breather

I got my official diploma by completing the physics class as I had promised Dean Ellis. While I began settling in with my job, Duc decided to transition from his stockroom job at Bobman Chemicals to studying electronics at a technical school at night. Once he finished his electronics degree at the technical school, he accepted a position at Mars Electronics International, a manufacturing company for coin acceptors and changers for vending machines, located in West Chester, Pennsylvania. (This is the same Mars family that brings us Mars candy and M&M's.) He was the supervisor in the maintenance department, and oversaw the production floor on the third shift. It was hard for me to sync with his schedule even on the weekends. We didn't mind much. At least he was making decent money.

We both worked very hard to save every penny we could for our wedding the following year. I took graduate chemistry courses after work to keep myself busy living away from my family. I love learning, and did not want to waste any education opportunity that was offered free as a benefit to employees. The classes were paid for by the company if I got at least a "B." I took several classes, including Advanced Chemistry at Princeton University, but I began to discover that my heart wasn't totally in it. I started having doubts about my chosen career field.

Duc and I were busy with wedding plans and began looking for a place to rent after we were married. We found a nice one-bedroom apartment in Levittown, which was halfway between my work and his work. He would have an hour's drive to work in West Chester, while I would commute to Monmouth Junction. Our American dream was coming true. My dad had begun the quest many years before, and now it was manifesting. I still choked up when I thought of my dad and how much he would have loved to have been a part of this.

I never said *no* to an opportunity to earn more money. I inherited Dad's vision of working full-time in the corporate world, and I got Mom's constant drive to monetize any and every skill. I was always looking for a way to get busier, striving to add to my income. I was no longer helping my parents make ends meet or working my way through college, but I obsessed about work. In addition to my full-time employment, I always had a part-time job. Then I would find odd jobs to occupy any hours I had between jobs. I worked here and there when the department stores needed people during the holiday season, or I would work processing checks for banks in the late evenings. I joined the multi-level marketing business Amway as a makeup artist representative. If I was awake, I felt like I should be at work. After all, I had a wedding and honeymoon to save up for.

19

A New Beginning

Marry Out of Love, Not Obligation

We set our wedding date for July of the following year, 1989. We had a goal of a debt-free wedding, but then Mom gave me her guest list. I almost fell off my chair.

"Two hundred people? Mom, how could you have that many friends?"

I had 35 friends I wanted to invite, Duc had about 35 family members and a few friends, yet the wedding list totaled 280 people. I was a little uptight, but didn't know how to protest. After all that Mom had been through, I didn't want to deprive her of the pride and joy of being the Mother of the Bride at her first-born's big (BIG) day. It really was her day, as well.

In some ways, ours was a typical American wedding. The couple scrimps and saves and plans for an entire year, only to blow it all in one day. But in many other ways, our wedding was unique. The events of the day began at 7:00 a.m. and went non-stop until midnight. It was a ceremony of two religions and three languages, with guests and family from near and far.

Soijek and his wife came from Germany, cousin Thang Gia came with his wife and two girls from Belgium, and cousin Cao and his wife came from California. We hadn't seen most of them in a decade, except for Soijek who came when Dad passed away. There was so much to catch up on and to talk about. It was by far the biggest family reunion since we left Vietnam.

A traditional Chinese Buddhist ritual of offering incense to the ancestral shrines began at 9:00 a.m. Following that was a tea ceremony in which the bride and the groom offered tea to both sides of the family. This was also when we collected gifts, mostly jewelry or red envelopes with money inside. This is especially wonderful when you have a large number of aunts, uncles, or older cousins, but that wasn't the case for us. For the long-distance guests who did come, we felt the right thing to do was to entertain them as best as we could, since their travel had been so costly. I was praying that by the end of the day Duc and I would have enough money left over for our honeymoon in St. Lucia.

We had a catered lunch at Mom's home for all the close friends and immediate family. Hundreds of pictures were taken with everyone. Then we headed to church for a 2:00 p.m. mass at Mother of Divine Providence, a Catholic church in King of Prussia. This was the venue for the marriage ceremony. I was grateful to have Soijek walk me down the aisle. He was the closest brother Dad ever loved. I knew I was being married under God's blessing, even though I was not a Christian. I was sure Dad would have no objection to my wedding in a church.

After the ceremony, the wedding party and family rushed to Buck County (an hour away) for outdoor pictures. We then rushed back to Philadelphia to the popular Joy Tsin Lau restaurant in Chinatown to receive guests at 6:30 p.m. There were many attendees whose identity was a complete mystery to me. I had no idea who they were. I had to study the videotape later to see who I was saying thank you to. Mom must have invited the entire Chinatown community.

People kept pouring in and more and more tables were added. The problem with Asian weddings is that people do not RSVP, then they show up with their entire family, and of course we politely accommodate with grace. Western culture's courtesy of replying to an invitation is better. We had estimated 200 guests, but we hosted nearly 300.

However, we didn't let that bother us. I had been frugal, of course, saving money in many ways. I did my own makeup and a college friend helped me style my hair. Another college friend helped to arrange all my flower bouquets and decorations. We paid high fees for the photographer, the videographer, and the DJ, but we asked friends and family to help us handle many details ourselves to save money.

And finally, after all these years, I was able to reconnect with Q, the friend who came along with my family when we boarded the boat. She came from Buffalo City and agreed to emcee the introductions for both families, and the toasts in four languages: two Chinese dialects (Cantonese and Teochew), Vietnamese and English. The reception featured a 12-course dinner followed by dancing. At one point, I looked around and saw almost everyone was out of their seats, either dancing or laughing with others, all different ages having a good time.

Chinese custom dictates that for the reception the bride should change out of her wedding gown into a Qipao, a traditional Chinese high-neck long dress. I was very proud to have made a beautiful Qipao myself, saving hundreds of dollars.

The bride and groom go around to each table for toasts and to say thank you to the guests. That took almost two hours for a lot of well wishes, gifts, and, of course, the clinking of glasses demanding that the couple kiss, kiss, kiss.

For the final part of the reception, I changed my outfit once again into an evening gown for the dancing party. I had creatively converted a dress I'd found on sale into my outfit for this part of the evening. I was crazily happy to be marrying the man who had stood by my side throughout all the ups and downs in my family's ordeals. Together, we cut the cake and danced. By the end of the night, I was blissfully exhausted. All day long, I had not been able to eat. I only swallowed a spoonful of soup and a single shrimp that someone fed me. But I wasn't hungry. I was too busy talking, laughing, and smiling for the cameras. I knew Dad was with me and happy for me. I missed him so much. I could hear his loud laughter and see his beautiful smile in my mind.

I talked with so many strangers at my wedding, but one piece of advice stood out and resonated with me. It came from a friend of Mom's and I will never forget what he said: "Happiness is when you are content with your present." I have remembered that wise phrase many times in my life, especially when I catch myself thinking that I need more things to be happy.

The music wound down and the guests gradually left. We settled the bill with the restaurant and the DJ. It was almost midnight before we left the venue. We arranged to have Q go home with us so she could drive us to the airport the next day for our honeymoon departure. Since Q and I only had limited time during the day to catch up with each other, we were talking non-stop the entire drive back to the apartment. It was surreal to me that she was really here and that she had been able to help make this day even more special. Noticing how Q and I were reconnecting, Duc suggested that he stay out on the couch and Q and I could talk to our hearts' content in my bedroom. That was how Duc spent our wedding night, by sleeping on the couch!

Duc truly is a saint and has such a generous spirit. He is so giving to me and my family, and even to my friends. He shows his love for me by caring about everything that is important to me. He has continued to do that throughout our time together in our marriage. He was the first person to ever make me feel unconditionally loved. That was true back then and it remains just as true today. And I vowed that he would never sleep on the sofa again in our marriage, for any reason.

Tea ceremony at the bride's home—a Chinese tradition (July 8, 1989)

My wedding dress was bought at the bridal shop which belonged to the sweatshop owner whom I used to work for in Chinatown. It cost me $700.

Family from near and far

Soijek walked me down the aisle.

I saved money by making my own veil and head piece.

269

I made the two gowns for the flower girls.
Duc's sister arranged the flower girls' baskets.

Q emceeing our wedding reception

The first time I made a Qi Pao
(Chinese gown)

Turning a discount dress
into an evening gown

Fulfilling Dreams

Because I am 14 years older than Nam, he was always like my baby, and now he had Duc's attention as well. When we first dated, Duc used to give Nam piggyback rides. We both loved Nam more like parents than siblings. When I booked our honeymoon trip to St. Lucia, Duc asked me if we could take Nam along. I love my little brother and would do anything for him, but I had to put my foot down on that one.

"This is our honeymoon. I am not sharing you with anyone. Not even my sweet baby brother!" Duc wanted to compensate for the suffering Nam had to endure by losing Dad at such a young age of ten, but I don't think I was selfish for wanting to have a honeymoon alone with my husband. I gave him an ultimatum: "Either go on your honeymoon with Nam or with me. Your pick!" Deep down, I knew I was truly blessed with a selfless husband. *He will make the greatest father of my children someday!*

Now that we were married, Duc and I instantly became a DINK (Double Income No Kids) household. We were eager to provide fun experiences for the family. The first thing we did was take my entire family to Disney World for a vacation in Florida. This was a road trip that Dad almost took the family on, but missed the chance. We were eager for the family to have their first experience of a cross-country vacation now that we were tax-paying, up-standing American citizens.

Mom and I rolled up our sleeves, busily cooking and packing the ice cooler with Chinese dishes like sticky rice, *Banh mi* (Vietnamese style sandwiches), and various pasta dishes that I learned from the cookbook. Vacationing frugally meant bringing seven course meals with us to eat at the rest stops on I-95 rather than stopping at restaurants. Duc drove straight for 20 hours from Philly to Kissimmee in Dad's brown Buick station wagon. It was like having Dad with us everywhere we went.

We stayed at cheap motels and packed food for the road, but four days of Disney park tickets for six people, plus other necessary expenses, added up to a hefty price tag for us. Mom never had to spend a dime. She expected that it was our obligation to cover all the expenses. Dad had supported her parents in Vietnam, and now she expected us to do the same for her. She believed it was her right. But Duc never complained about all the cost of treating my family. We were more than happy to do it. Had he been more Americanized, this could have been a major culture clash. When he married me, he willingly embraced my entire family. I thanked God for my generous husband who always catered to my mom's ongoing expectations.

At home, the girls were busy in their final years of high school and Nam was excelling in middle school. They were all studious, working hard to do well in their education. Nam was everyone's favorite. Just like me, he rarely sought confrontation and was eager to please. They were my world. Every weekend, Duc and I would include them in our recreational activities. We took the family on picnics, shopping, and would buy them whatever they needed if we could afford it.

We also made it a point to be there for Mom. For the first time in her life, Mom experienced a freedom she had never had before. Viet had completed his boot camp training in the Navy and was doing great. He was then stationed in South Carolina and I was glad to hear he had surrounded himself with many faith-based friends. He challenged me to look into my own faith and examine my beliefs. We talked often on the phone and continued our conversations when he came home for visits. He freely shared with me his experience of being baptized in the Catholic Church and told me he was even assisting a chaplain in the Navy. I did not take the challenge at a time, but a seed of faith was sewed. I saw a difference in my young brother now that he had anchored his life in Christ and inspiring mentors. I was happy that he found a higher power to cling on to. I continued to pray to Grandma Trinh and Dad to protect him every step of the way.

Achieving the American Dream of Homeownership

The old Upper Darby house increasingly became a financial liability. There was always a long list of maintenance projects that needed fixing. First, the water heater, then the flooded basement, followed by an expensive plumbing repair. Duc had maintained the lawn and the garden when he lived there, but now that we had our own place, it became difficult fitting all the upkeep into our long-distance weekend visits. Clearly, Mom was not independent enough to run that household without our help. So, Duc and I began saving earnestly for a home so the whole family could gather under our roof.

My parents taught me to never live beyond our means and to strive not to have debt. Some debt is necessary: big items like a car, a home or a college education. Duc and I budgeted very carefully to pay off the balance of our credit cards every month. We learned how to stretch a dollar. We would always pack lunch rather than eat out. We infrequently spent money on entertainment. We lived a very thrifty life, paying off the wedding and the honeymoon, and now saving every dollar we could for a down payment for our future home to rescue Mom from the rundown house in Upper Darby.

When the lease in Levittown ended, we found a cute, single-family, split-level home in West Chester, two miles from Duc's company. The 40-year-old Cape Cod house looked small from the outside but had four bedrooms, two and a half baths, and five split levels when you counted the half-finished basement and the super-hot attic.

It needed a ton of work, but all we saw was endless potential for a nurturing, loving home for our continued life's journey. The house number, 1126, added up to 10, which in Chinese superstition is not a good thing, but Duc and I gave that no regard because we loved the house.

The house was pretty much as the original owners had built it. The plaster walls had three layers of wallpaper, one on top of the other. The carpet was worn out and the small windows were drafty. The family room at the lower level was finished with dark wood paneling. It was a perfect project for both Duc and me to completely get wild with our creativity.

This was before YouTube and the internet era, so we borrowed lots of DIY books from the libraries. After much trial and error, we got ourselves a beautiful love nest. Our motto was: "If there is a will, there is a way!" We found many ways to make it our perfect home!

We knocked out walls to create an open concept, and installed skylights in our bedroom to get more natural light. This seemed like a mistake on weekend mornings when we wanted to sleep late, or during a thunder and lightning storm at night, but we loved it. I learned to make my own drapes which was quite different from making clothing.

We covered the worn-out hardwood floor and stairs with carpet remnants and replaced the kitchen cabinets and counters with new appliances. We built a deck and landscaped the front and back yard where we hosted many volleyball games and picnics for both sides of the family. All of the renovations were done on weeknights and weekends while we both were working full time. It was a massive renovation project and it ate up all our savings, even though we did all the labor ourselves. We paced ourselves, but the thought of having Mom and my siblings move in with us energized me. I was eager to deliver the promise I made to

Dad: "Take care of Mom and make sure my younger siblings follow the path to a higher education."

The "American Dream." America is the only country I know of which has a "Dream" to embrace, work toward with determination, and achieve in your own way and time. I inherited the dream from my parents, and I made it come true. The day we moved into our new home in West Chester was an extraordinary and proud moment for us. We knew we were "living the Dream."

Our home became the central hub for the girls to come home to from college. Mom had a permanent room of her own, and we became Nam's legal guardians so he could start a brand-new chapter of high school in West Chester. Mom was now free to travel. She went to Europe to visit her sister and was one of many who traveled back to visit Vietnam when President Clinton lifted the embargo on Vietnam in 1992.

Our first Cape Cod home in West Chester (1990)

Duc ripped out the entire old kitchen and replaced everything

Viet and Nam help with our deck project (1992)

Mission Accomplished!

Because the commute to work was so long, I carpooled with a few PhDs who lived and used to work in West Chester, but now had to work for the Wyeth facility in Monmouth Junction. Some days when I was late, I would drive the long stretch of the congested I-95 by myself, and think about what my family has gone through.

It felt like I was watching an old, black and white movie of my grandparents' and parents' life in exile. My grandparents on both sides fled China in hopes of building a prosperous life for themselves and for their children. Establishing roots on a foreign soil was never easy. My parents had to make do with the circumstances that were given to them, and then faced the same ruthless fate as their parents decades later.

But then the script changed. Now that I was writing my own story, I've walked into this movie with a full range of colors. I was given a chance to do what I wanted to do, not what I was supposed to do. I had broken the first barrier of my family's history of repeating the same things over and over again. I have acquired the necessary tools to build my own boat to get me to a much better place. I am in total control of my destiny. The thoughts made me feel powerful, and reminded me I didn't have to settle for poverty.

What I liked about being a medicinal chemist was that I was able to put the drug discovery research into action, synthesizing drug-like compounds for in-vitro and animal testing. I needed to broaden this medical knowledge to prevent mishaps in the future from happening to anyone else in my family. In my opinion, it also meant I had a better chance of making an impact on human's lives, more than I would have if I became the pharmacist my grandma wanted me to be.

I was able to get my hands on the front end of research development in the early stages, and watch how the compounds blossomed into different phases. If I was lucky, a compound under my project could turn into a drug to treat any disease or illness, the dream of a lifetime for many scientists. I was told it took thousands of compounds, decades of research and development, and millions of dollars to have a drug candidate to the market. It was not an easy goal. But once it did, that drug could be the blockbuster that generated income for the company for years.

At Wyeth Ayrest Laboratory, I reported to Dr. Joseph. We were working on the Osteoporosis project. Being a rookie, I learned everything from my supervisor. He was a very smart scientist, but not very tidy in the lab. Be that as it may, I was now his colleague: a scientist, a chemist, a professional.

Unlike the chemistry lab at school, I now had my own space where I could creatively concocted wonderful experiments that could potentially improve the quality of human lives. Much of the work was performed inside the fume hood for safety purposes. In college, our lab work was once a week, and a simple setup. But now, the experiments were every day, and much more elaborate.

For the majority of the time, I was in the lab setting reactions and experiments with different compounds. I didn't mind standing in front of the hood all day to monitor, extract and purify, and then collect data for all the reactions. When I wasn't in the lab, I was calculating formulas, writing observations, lab reports, and doing paperwork in the office. There was not a dull moment for the work I did.

While I liked the creative side of science, there were many moments of frustration. For a petite person, I had many physical challenges maneuvering the space. The setups of the labs were mostly designed for six-foot-tall men. I'm a foot shorter, so it was never fun to set up the apparatus and the equipment properly in my assigned fume hood. If I had to change lab locations, I would have to set everything up all over again to accommodate my vertical challenge.

One of my least favorite things was setting up the Schlenk lines. It was a real struggle to put together. The Schlenk lines were needed to provide the reactions with a controlled environment. It had a dual manifold with four or five outlets of tubing that were clamped to the top of the monkey bars, all the way in the back inside the hood (see photo). This was hooked up to a vacuum line and an inert gas line, such as argon or nitrogen. Inside the hood, there were also lab jacks, hot plates, oil baths, round-bottom flasks, tubes, and a whole lot of other equipment clamped in front of the monkey bars.

Often I had to stick my entire body inside the hood to leverage my strength to set up a reaction. A lot of manual and physical strength were needed to properly set up the system. Besides the toxic chemicals, we used carcinogens and neurotoxin solvents like benzene, toluene, and chloroform every day. There was always a chance of breathing in vapors or spilling chemicals when working. It was essential to be protected as best as possible. It was a dangerous career I signed up for, as I had witnessed a few accidents from my colleagues and came close a few times myself.

The loud noise from the exhaust system was deafening. It was on 24/7 because it was necessary to suck out the odor of hazardous chemicals, dust, and toxic gases. There were times I swear I couldn't hear myself think. I am partially deaf due to being constantly exposed to the high frequency noise for so many years.

Nevertheless, I took pride in my profession. I marveled when the reactions worked, and I saw white crystals forming in the flask after the compound was purified and identified. Other times I had to figure out the mystery of the unknown byproducts or the decomposition of the reaction. And the amazing thing was, every compound could be a potential remedy for an illness.

For many of my peers, the white lab coat and safety goggles were just the basic safety gears, but to me they symbolized status, education, and the pride of my dad's dream for his children. This was everything he traded his life for so I could safely grip this chance.

The age gaps began to bother me less as I was surrounded by people who were older than me. Instead of horsing around (according to the zodiac of my false age), the tiger in me was beginning to out shadow the kitty cat I used to be. I was becoming more courageous. I befriended a small group of junior chemists who were in good company with each other. It was the first time I had a circle of professional friends that I felt I belonged to. Life was looking up both financially and socially. I was validated and accepted in the prestigious white lab coat circle, instead of being pegged as a refugee.

I imagined telling Dad "Pa, look! I am now an American scientist! I am no longer a blind ox!"

My dad had done his job, and now it was up to me to write a new chapter for the next generation in my family. In one short decade, my life had transformed from broken pieces of glass into a beautiful mosaic. Although I still had many long nights of flashbacks from PTSD of the harrowing boat journey, and from the not-so-perfect family that I was raised in, slowly but surely, I changed. My attitudes evolved. Besides the scientific journals, I read more self-help books. I discovered the power of self-belief. I was determined to get off the refugee boat that carried the helpless adolescent girl who I used to be. I was ready to stand strong at the helm of my life. After all, I am the new captain of this ship.

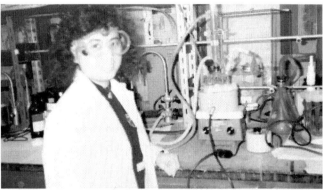

Lab setup at school

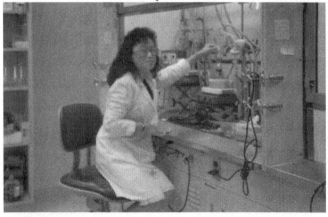

Lab setup at Wyeth. It was a quick pose at break.
I would not have checked the reaction without wearing my gloves.

Epilogue

An Accrued Wisdom and Self-Discovery

Writing my memoir, *I Did Not Miss the Boat*, has been a difficult, but exceedingly rewarding journey. It challenged me to embrace both the trauma, as well as the triumph of my family's exodus from Vietnam as part of the "Boat People". I was told by one of the writers in my writing group that "Forty years is a magic number for PTSD victims who have been through a trauma to reveal their stories." My parents are my heroes, they faced many challenges and adversities that shaped the way they saw life. They had no idea that they, themselves were walking examples of PTSD, which was passed on to them from generations of poverty in migration.

Dad genuinely believed using force was an important tool to discipline and strengthen his family, but he would never have done what he did if, as a young boy, he had been nurtured in a loving, affectionate environment and in a stable society and family.

Mom lacked self-acceptance. Nothing could make her happy because she wasn't content with herself. My love for her was saved when I began to understand this. She is skillful, hardworking, and likes to impress others with her abilities, but because of her low self-esteem, she was always craving acknowledgement. In her childhood, she was taught to suppress her voice, and to depend on others. In order to get the attention from her parents, husband and children, she turned to self-pitying and guilt. It was a habit she could not shake off, and one she unknowingly instilled in us.

My parents' union was built on their commitment to their family. Through their hard work, they showed us how to endure hardship, and how to create hope for a better future. However, through their parenting, they also instilled a lot of damaging beliefs, and had high expectations for who we would become. They taught us that we should put the family before our individual needs, that our submissiveness and **filial piety** were more important than our priorities.

We come from a culture that believes that if you are reaching for a goal to satisfy yourself instead of your family, you are being selfish. This often leads to a lifetime of regrets and resentment when children find themselves unhappy with the direction and the choices they obediently took from their parents.

In Vietnam, when people praised you, you were never taught to say "thank you". Instead, you would say, "Not really, I have so much more to learn." That may sound humble and good, but subconsciously, we were just repeating to ourselves that we are never good enough. It is hard to love yourself when you are constantly telling yourself that you are not enough.

We were blessed that we did not miss the boat that gave us the freedom to live our own lives. Thanks to my parents' selflessness and sacrifices, I was able to have a higher education, and have the opportunity and privilege to re-examine our past and see the good that has come from it. I am breaking the cycle of trauma they inherited, and rising above the traditional limitations that bound so many of us in grudges, shame, and resentment. We all make mistakes, but our mistakes don't need to make us. By exploring where they came from, who they were, and the motivations that guided their lives, I was able to forgive, and my love and appreciation for my past grew deeper.

They say "Expectations are premeditated resentments."

There is no denying that my parents' love for each other and for us was insurmountable, but so were their expectations. Duc said his mom taught him to love by giving fully, without a shred of expectation. By following his mom's example, I learned the ultimate lesson from my selfless, devoted husband: Love does not need expectations. This keeps our 30-year relationship going strong. I am who I am today because of the unwavering support, belief and unconditional love my husband has given and continues to give me.

I am grateful to say all my siblings are happily married to life partners of their choice, and not out of obligation. All my in-law siblings are kind, dedicated, devoted spouses and parents. I believe we are a generation of refugees/immigrants caught in the middle of two very different worlds; two very different generations and cultures. The generation before us is expecting us to be traditional and the generation that follows us is expecting us to be contemporary.

I am sure my siblings have their own battles to fight and their own agonies to confront. Although we experienced the same family history, we each saw the struggles through a different lens.

This memoir is a declaration of victory for me. This was a journey of self-discovery, written for my parents and for countless refugees/immigrants who remain silent.

The ending of this memoir is the beginning of a new adventure in my life. After so many years of letting my parents steer the ship, I finally took control of the sails.

I have created a family of my own, built several successful careers, and am living a passionate, purposeful, spiritual life. The wisdom learned and adventures in the next phase of my life will have to be shared in the next memoir.

If you have a story to tell, I hope you will break your silence and share it.

This is my dad's world...

The Viet-Nam of his life!

Like siblings in most families, our relationships have their ups and downs. However, I always treasure the sentiments, letters, poems, and words of encouragement that my brothers and sisters expressed to me as an adult. They gave me strength and they kept me going when we were experiencing the rough times with each other.

Viet wrote something very special to me in 1994. It was the nicest tribute I received even though I never thought I deserved it. I cried for days reading this poem.

SIS.. ON BEHALF OF AMY, NAM, LORI, AND MYSELF.. WE WOULD LIKE TO DEDICATE THIS POEM TO YOU.

MORNING STAR
(by v. ong)

POWER
MY DEAR SISTER
IS YOUR FIGHTING HAND
THE ROOTS THAT SINK INTO THE EARTH
UPROOTED BY NO GOD OR MAN

STRENGTH
MY DEAR SISTER
IS YOUR INNER FAITH
FAITH THAT CARRY THE SKY
AND HOLD THE SUN IN PLACE

LOVE
MY DEAR SISTER
IS YOUR GENTLE TOUCH, YOUR SOOTHING WORDS
ALL THE MINUTE DETAILS
THE NUANCES YOU BRING
THE BRIGHTNESS OF YOUR SMILE
THE STORY BEHIND YOUR RING

FRIENDSHIP
MY DEAR SISTER
IS UTMOST IMPORTANT TO ME
TO TRUST, AND TO BELIEVE
THAT YOU WILL BE THERE FOR ME
AND BE MY GIVING TREE

SILENCE
MY DEAR SISTER
IS THE PLANE WE QUICKLY REACHED
COMFORTED IN ONE
THE ENERGY OF TWO BEINGS
DEFINING THE INFINITE SUN

YOU
MY DEAR SISTER
ARE THE MORNING STAR
THE WHITENESS OF LA LUNA
AND ALL THINGS THAT ARE

THANK YOU
MY DEAR SISTER
IS MY GRATITUDE
YOUR WORDS, OUR CONVERSATIONS
SERVES AS SPRITUAL FOODS
SO THANK YOU TO THE UTMOST
WITH SMILES AND PRAYERS
THANK YOU MY GOOD, GOOD SISTER
AND MAY YOUR HOLIDAY BE BLESSED

I also love the poem that Phan wrote to me in 2003. She has no idea how much I am proud of her and admire her for the mother she is to her three wonderful children.

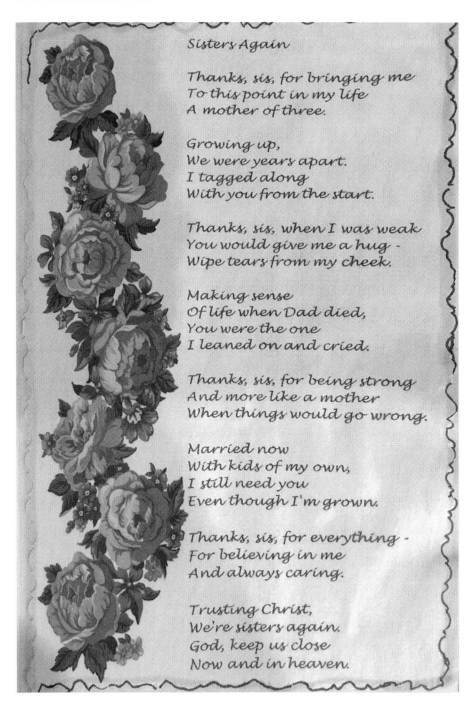

Sisters Again

Thanks, sis, for bringing me
To this point in my life
A mother of three.

Growing up,
We were years apart.
I tagged along
With you from the start.

Thanks, sis, when I was weak
You would give me a hug -
Wipe tears from my cheek.

Making sense
Of life when Dad died,
You were the one
I leaned on and cried.

Thanks, sis, for being strong
And more like a mother
When things would go wrong.

Married now
With kids of my own,
I still need you
Even though I'm grown.

Thanks, sis, for everything -
For believing in me
And always caring.

Trusting Christ,
We're sisters again.
God, keep us close
Now and in heaven.

Comments on this Memoir from My Youngest Brother

In a time where there are hundreds of YouTube videos of one-time water bottle flips and backyard ninja obstacle courses, there seems to be an endless supply of "extraordinary" events these days. But just one generation prior, before the internet, the story of our family's journey to the United States never felt extraordinary…because it happened to us. It was our story and nothing that happens to us ever really feels extraordinary, right?

As the youngest member of our family, the people and events that occurred while in Vietnam, and the entire journey to America, were always unconnected puzzle pieces that emerged through repeated stories told by various family members. For me, *I Did Not Miss the Boat* filled in many of the missing pieces to the puzzle that is my family's history. I am grateful for this book because I truly believe that a better understanding of where I came from strengthens the foundation on which I can build a future.

Told through the perspective of my sister, I am able to re-live some of the events that I *do* remember but from her vantage point and with her context. Like new scenes revealed through a director's cut edition of an old familiar movie, reflecting back through this book gives me a better understanding of not only my past but of my sister. Always inspiring and continuously giving, writing this book is just another example of how she has courageously led our family and pushed us to do better for ourselves and our community.

—*Nam Ong*

I am so appreciative that Nam read my manuscript and took time to share his thoughts. These are the rewards that I treasure knowing I have made a difference and have fulfilled the promise I made to Dad. A mission accomplished!

I also shared my manuscript with Tim and Nancy Rauk, my first American friends, two people who played a significant and pivotal role for me and my entire family. I am thrilled to include herein their contribution to my memoir, our story from their unique perspective.

The Honor Was Ours

Reflections on Lea Tran's book, *I Did Not Miss the Boat*
by Pastor Tim and Nancy Rauk

Dear Lea,

As the pastor of one of the sponsoring churches in Onamia, Minnesota, that welcomed your family to the United States 40 years ago, I am delighted and honored to have had a small part in the telling of your family's story through your memoir, *I Did Not Miss the Boat*. You recount the journey of your family in such an inspirational and moving way. And since it was the War in Vietnam that brought us together 40 years ago, and your chronicling of your story that has reconnected us in 2020, I found myself recounting what was going on in my life as your family journeyed from Vietnam to their new country here in the United States.

1975 was a pivotal year, both in the United States and in Vietnam. After three decades of war, nearly 10 years of French involvement and two decades of American involvement, the North Vietnamese army invaded South Vietnam uniting the country in 1975 to become the Socialist Republic of Vietnam. For some, this was a huge victory: the evil imperialistic United States has been expelled from southeast Asia. For others, this was a huge defeat: the evil communists of North Vietnam imposed their rule on the whole country, subjugating the freedoms of the people of South Vietnam. And the Ong family was caught in the middle. For people in the United States, there were many mixed feelings which included relief that the seemingly endless war was finally over. Lea, the story you share in your memoir, *I Did Not Miss the Boat*, so effectively and vividly invites the reader into your life in South Vietnam and how the communist tyranny drove your family to risk their very lives in an epic journey to freedom as part of the *boat people* migration. You offer the reader an important glimpse into a story that helps us better understand the impact of the War in Vietnam.

Like most Americans, my knowledge about the country of Vietnam was minimal to say the least. The word "Vietnam" was only a flashpoint for political contention and debate, invoked by politicians making statements about American patriotism and national pride. Most people didn't know anything about this little country on the other side of the world: its people, its history or the war. Most people couldn't locate it on a map. I was in high school in 1965 when the news from Vietnam began to intensify. Every night the evening news would report the number of American soldiers who died in Vietnam, and suddenly those numbers began rising exponentially. During my sophomore year in high school (1965) less than 2,000 American soldiers died in Vietnam. By my senior years (1967), the number had risen to over 11,000. In my first year of college the number reached its peak of 16,899. And when the names of young men I had known in high school began to appear as casualties in the Vietnam War, suddenly it became very real to me. And rarely was there acknowledgement of the much larger loss of human life being experienced by the people who called Vietnam their home.

My years in college saw the greatest number of American and Vietnamese casualties. I witnessed firsthand the growing discontent among college students who challenged our government, questioning the wisdom and morality of the war. I remember driving along the Mississippi River in Minneapolis on my way to college, hearing a news report of potential progress in the peace talks and feeling great hope that maybe the war would finally be coming to an end. But nothing came of it.

People were noticing that the responsibility for fighting the war was falling largely on the poor and those who didn't have political connections to avoid being drafted into the United States Army. In 1969, in an effort to bring more fairness to the responsibility for military service, a random lottery was held, assigning a draft number to every man born between 1944 and 1950 based on the date of their birth. The smaller your number, the more likely it would be that you would be drafted into the service. I eagerly checked the newspaper the morning after the lottery to see what number was assigned to my birth date. It was 352. This meant that my likelihood of being drafted was very, very small.

I entered the seminary after graduating from college in 1971 and got married in 1973. All this time the war continued. A national fatigue replaced hope that a peaceful solution to end the war was possible. For many people, the issue of the war was overshadowed by the dramatic intrigue of the

Watergate scandal which led to President Nixon's eventual resignation. By then, casualties of U.S. servicemen had dropped significantly and there was again hope for a peace agreement that would allow South Vietnam and North Vietnam to coexist, the way North Korea and South Korea had found a contentious but relatively peaceful coexistence.

In 1975 I graduated from the seminary and looked forward to my first call as an assistant pastor at a church in Litchfield, Minnesota. Then came the news of the fall of Saigon. Most people didn't really know what that meant for the people living in South Vietnam, except that it appeared that the war was over, the casualty counts would end, and finally, the troops would be coming home. The chaos of the long, drawn out Vietnam War had taken a toll on the psyche of the American people. But now we began to hear stories of the crisis that awaited those on the losing end of the war and the people of the former South Vietnam. The first stories were of South Vietnamese leaders and soldiers fleeing the country as the North Vietnamese army took control of Saigon.

In the United States, the call went out, largely to the faith community, to help settle refugees from Vietnam who had fled the country as the war effort collapsed. Many churches across the country responded to the need. There was a feeling of optimism, that after years of a seemingly never-ending war, we, here in the United States, could do something to help support those people from South Vietnam who were forced to flee the country after the fall of Saigon. Almost immediately groups around the country, such as Lutheran Social Services (LSS), began encouraging local church communities to sponsor refugees displaced by the Vietnam War.

I served a church, First Lutheran in Litchfield, Minnesota that was one of the churches that responded to this call to sponsor a refugee family who had been among the first to leave Vietnam. We remember going to the airport to meet a family of four: father, mother, and their two sons. It was apparent that this was a family of means. He had been a high-ranking officer in the South Vietnamese Navy. What a dramatic change it was for them to find themselves in a rural community in the middle of Minnesota. The home was old and small, and while they were grateful, we could tell that they were accustomed to a more affluent life in Vietnam. The church community welcomed them and helped them get started with their new life in the United States.

In 1977 we accepted a call to Bethany Lutheran Church in Onamia, Minnesota. The stories now from Vietnam were of refugees known as *boat people* who were fleeing Vietnam on boats that were often barely sea worthy. This migration reached its peak in 1978 and 1979. The call continued to go out from Lutheran Social Services for church communities to sponsor and welcome people who were suffering the ongoing effects of the turmoil in Vietnam.

I don't remember how the conversation in Onamia started, but I remember visiting with Father Jim Hentges, the priest at Holy Cross Catholic Church, about the possibility of our two churches joining together to sponsor a refugee family in Onamia. The Methodist Church in town also joined in the effort and many people from Onamia offered their support and ideas. A small, modest home was rented as part of the effort to offer a refugee family from Vietnam a new home and the opportunity to start a new life.

We knew nothing about the family being sent to us. Only that it was a family of 7: dad, mom, and 5 children. We remember meeting your family at the airport: how your mom and dad, with limited English skills, were able to radiate their appreciation for the opportunity to start a new life in a safe home. It must have been so overwhelming for all of you. I can't imagine the uncertainty that you all felt as you drove from the airport, leaving the city of Minneapolis and traveling a couple of hours into rural Minnesota to the unknown small town of Onamia. What a shock it must have been for your family to leave the warm climate of Vietnam and have to acclimate to the very strange and harsh climate of a Minnesota winter. We couldn't imagine what it must have been like to leave a culture where you could easily communicate with the people in your community and suddenly find yourselves living among people who were all strangers, speaking English; a language that sounded as strange to you as your language sounded strange to us. Yet it was always clear that your mother and father were making this move because they cared deeply for the well-being of their family.

Soon after arriving it was discovered that all you children had contracted scabies at the refugee camp. Kay Mickus and Nancy were prepared to help in the process of treating the children in the family but it was your mom who insisted on taking charge. She was going to make sure her children were properly cared for and she meticulously saw to it that every family member received the proper treatment to eradicate the scabies.

It was winter when you arrived in Onamia and there was an immediate need for the whole family to be outfitted with winter clothing. A collection of winter coats, hats, mittens and boots had been gathered and brought to your new home. Each of you began trying on winter clothing to find the combination that would best fit you. Your mom and dad, too, looked through several coats in search of the one that would keep them warm during the impending Minnesota winter. Well, I had taken off my own winter coat and hung it over a chair. I turned around to find your dad trying on my coat, not knowing that it wasn't one of the intended choices. He seemed to like it so much that I didn't have the heart to try to explain to him that it was my coat. And in fact, throughout the winter I enjoyed seeing him wearing that coat. It didn't really fit him very well. I'm six feet, one inches tall and your dad couldn't have been over five and a half feet tall, but he wore it with pride. And I needed a new coat anyway.

Lea, we noticed immediately that much of the responsibility for communication landed on you, the oldest daughter, to bridge the language barrier. You took on this responsibility with amazing grace, maturity and patience. But I suspect it was far more stressful than anyone knew. It appeared that the stress had taken a toll on your health. Nancy remembers being with you during a visit to the doctor that revealed that you had developed an ulcer; something that the doctor said is very unusual for a young person your age. Given all the changes that you were compelled to navigate as a family, and the added responsibilities that you took on as translator for the family, it was understandable that there would be negative side effects.

Lots of different people stepped in where they thought they could be of special help. Your dad got a job at the hospital in town. The hospital administrator, Gene Helle, was on the committee that worked to help in the settlement effort for your family. He was instrumental in making the job available. And Gene's wife, Karen, led the effort to teach "English As A Second Language." I also know the teaching staff at the Onamia Public Schools made a special effort to address the unique needs of you and your siblings.

Something I remember very clearly is sitting in a waiting room at the hospital, arranging checkups and health care for the family. Your dad had a small Casio calculator/clock that he was looking at to pass the time waiting for the doctor. It was programmed to play simple tunes, with a built-in clock, calendar and alarm. I showed interest in the calculator as a way of encouraging communication. Your dad then took the calculator, and handed it to me, indicating that he wanted to give it to me as a gift. I tried to refuse this generous gesture. Your whole family had come to America with nothing to your name. I had a comfortable life and far more than you. Yet your dad wanted me to have this clock/calculator. I reluctantly accepted his gesture of appreciation, but had always felt a bit guilty about it. I still own that clock/calculator.

It was immediately apparent to those who worked with your mom, that she was a gifted cook. The idea was developed to hold a dinner at church that would feature food from Vietnam. This would be a way to further introduce your family to the community and maybe raise some funds for your family's settlement needs. Nancy remembers working side by side in the kitchen (with our second son, Adam, in a backpack) with your mom and dad. Your mom was the head chef, and your dad a capable assistant overseeing all the food preparation and the training of people from the community who helped in the preparation and serving. Clearly, this was your mom and dad's dinner, planned, prepared and implemented with great care and culinary expertise. The dinner was a huge success. Tickets had been sold in advance and many people turned out for the dinner. After the dinner was over, as a crew of volunteers cleaned up and washed dishes, the monetary proceeds from the dinner were presented to your mom and dad. They seemed surprised. They had put on the dinner as a way of showing their gratitude to the community. They didn't expect that their efforts were for their family's monetary profit. The dinner was a wonderful gift from your family to the Onamia community.

The whole town of Onamia most truly felt blessed to have your family as part of the Onamia community. We all knew that it must have been a very lonely time for all of you, not being able to visit with people in the language that was familiar and comfortable for you. So, when you had the opportunity to move to Philadelphia where there would be people who shared your experience, culture and language, the people of Onamia fully understood. We didn't understand the pain and horror you and your family had gone through to be driven from the community that was home to you in Vietnam, ending up in our little community in rural Minnesota, but we were deeply impressed and inspired by the resilience we observed in your family. Seeing the commitment and bond of love that was at the core of your family life was something everyone in Onamia could empathize with and understand, because it was the same love and commitment that we all bring to our own families. Onamia was deeply enriched because of the time you and your family spent making Onamia your home.

And now, 40 years after your family arrived in the United States, our lives once again come together around the telling of your story. What an honor it has been to hear the many details in your memoir that you were not equipped to share 40 years ago. Anyone who reads your memoir will find themselves intimately invited into the Ong family's epic journey. You fearlessly open your heart to the struggle that must have felt hopeless at times, but you reveal the determination, the tenacity and the resoluteness that epitomizes the spirit of the refugee *boat people. I Did Not Miss the Boat* is an inspiring retelling of the narrative that exemplifies the American spirit which offers hope and a chance for a new beginning to all people yearning to breathe free.

Acknowledgements

The writing of this book would not be possible without mentioning the love and support of friends, family and colleagues who sowed a seed in my brain many years ago to share my story.

After 40 years apart, it was serendipity that I reconnected with Tim Rauk, the lead pastor of the Lutheran church who sponsored my family's move to Minnesota in January of 1980. I owe an enormous amount of gratitude to Tim, not only for his generous heart and humanity, but also for making this memoir journey a full circle reflection of a successful refugee story.

I reached out to Tim in the fall of 2019 and asked if he could help confirming some questions I had about Onamia. He ended up becoming the chief editor of this memoir. I am indebted to Tim for translating many of my random thoughts into coherent sentence structures.

I want to thank my niece, Emily Liu, for her journalism ability in challenging my thought process in many chapters of this book. My appreciation also goes to many friends who nudged me, inspiring me to write this memoir–Debbie Perlow, Vanessa Grey, Jennifer Robinson, Edna Valentino, Laura Walton, Shannon Myers… just to name a few.

Last but not least, I am grateful to Barbara Dee of Suncoast Publishing Company for her guidance, her words of encouragement and for making this journey so pleasant.

Connect with Lea Tran

Speaking

Book Lea for keynote speaking at your event—companies, Non-profits, Associations, community groups. Lea has both virtual and in-person presentations ready to inspire.

Workshops

"BYOB" – Build Your Own Boat means learning the mindset and skills to feel confident and ready to meet any challenge and leverage your opportunities.

Mastermind Group

Lea coaches successful women in a powerful, difference-making format.

TEDx Talk

Enjoy Lea's TEDx talk, "I Did Not Miss the Boat." Lea also coaches those who aspire to give a TED talk.

FB Community

Join Lea's private Facebook group, "Don't Miss Your Boat." Facebook.com/groups/DontMissYourBoat

Lea regularly interacts with members, answers questions, and gives FB live talks, all designed to inspire and empower her community.

Events and Free Resources

Lea Tran's next book is in the works! Please sign up at www.LeaTran.com to be notified when the release date is announced. Also, her web site is frequently updated with free resources you'll enjoy.

About the Author

Lea Tran is a dynamic Keynote speaker, human connector, and community builder. Lea uses her knowledge, experience, and time to compassionately promote social development to inspire her audience not to miss the opportunity to live fully to their potential.

A graduate of Villanova University in Pennsylvania in 1988, Lea began her career as an organic chemist at Wyeth and Merck Pharmaceutical companies for 17 years, where she holds patents on various drug discoveries. Prior to moving to Florida with her husband in 2015, Lea owned and operated a successful high-end window drapery business for ten years.

Lea's mission is to inspire people to transform themselves, to step out of the shadow of fear or obligation and live with freedom, passion, and purpose.

www.LeaTran.com

https://www.facebook.com/groups/DontMissYourBoat/

https://www.linkedin.com/in/distinctivelea/

Made in the USA
Columbia, SC
21 February 2025

54149398R00170